Anthropology and the Bushman

Anthropology and the Bushman

Alan Barnard

Oxford • New York

First published in 2007 by
Berg
Editorial offices:
1st Floor, Angel Court, 81 St Clements Street, Oxford, OX4 1AW, UK
175 Fifth Avenue, New York, NY 10010, USA

Berg is the imprint of Oxford International Publishers Ltd.

Library of Congress Cataloging-in-Publication Data
Library of Congress Cataloging-in-Publication Data

Barnard, Alan (Alan J.)
    Anthropology and the bushman / Alan Barnard.
        p. cm.
    Includes bibliographical references and index.
    ISBN-13: 978-1-84520-428-0 (cloth)
    ISBN-10: 1-84520-428-X (cloth)
    ISBN-13: 978-1-84520-429-7 (pbk.)
    ISBN-10: 1-84520-429-8 (pbk.)
    1. San (African people)—Kalahari Desert—Social life and
customs. 2. Ethnology—Kalahari Desert—Field work. 3.
Anthropology in popular culture—Kalahari Desert. 4. Kalahari
Desert—Social life and customs. I. Title.

    DT1058.S36B35 2007
    305.896'1—dc22   2006101698

British Library Cataloguing-in-Publication Data
A catalogue record for this book is available from the British Library.

ISBN 978 1 84520 428 0 (Cloth)
ISBN 978 1 84520 429 7 (Paper)

Typeset by Avocet Typeset, Chilton, Aylesbury, Bucks
Printed in the United Kingdom by the MPG Books Group Ltd

www.bergpublishers.com

Contents

Figures and Tables

Figures

Tables

Preface

'The Bushman' is an image that remains in anthropological consciousness, although transformed through history, especially in recent decades. This book is a social and intellectual history of that image as handed down to anthropology from earlier anthropologists and archaeologists, social theorists and travellers, and Bushmen and Khoekhoe themselves. It is also an exploration of the diversity of that image, for its appearance changes in space as well as time. 'The Bushman' in contemporary South Africa can be quite different from 'the Bushman' as understood in Japanese or American writings.

One disclaimer: although it has quite a lot of references and covers a long period, this is not intended to be 'the great big book of Bushman studies'. That would take many volumes, each (going backwards in time) probably of interest to fewer and fewer readers. My hope instead is to provide something more readable. My focus is on anthropologists and anthropology, but what is said here should, I hope, be of interest to a much wider public. It may be of interest especially to development practitioners, to scholars in related disciplines such as archaeology and history, and to those of Khoisan descent who simply want to know more about anthropology's involvement in their heritage.

Unless clearly essential for my sense, I shall dispense with quotation marks on words like 'Bushman' throughout. The word is certainly not without its problems. Indeed the same can be said for the currently more politically correct term 'San', which historically and in the Khoekhoe dialects in which it is found has carried connotations of poverty, low status, thievery and scavenging, as well as purposeful food-gathering (that being perhaps its most literal translation). 'Khoisan' today is a word that includes both the 'San' hunter-gatherers and the 'Khoikhoi' or 'Khoekhoe' herder-hunter-gatherers. Most of this book concerns the former and those anthropologists who have worked with them, although throughout much of the history of these studies, especially in early times, the place of the 'herders' has been integral to the definition of the 'hunters'. In general, Khoisan names are given in the preferred form of the individuals themselves or, where appropriate, in a simplified Khoisan form rather than a European one – for example, /Han≠kass'o rather than Klein Jantje (the various click symbols are explained in Chapter 1). I should add that there are many Japanese anthropologists among today's Bushman experts, and their names are given in Western form, with given name first and family name last.

The book is based on three things: (a) my immersion in Khoisan studies for nearly thirty-five years (with ethnographic and linguistic fieldwork in Botswana, Namibia and South Africa, and the odd bit of archaeological and archival work), (b) specific library and Internet research devoted to the book, and (c) conversations with colleagues both recent and through the years. A great many people have helped to define my interest and refine my arguments. I have benefited especially from discussions of the history of anthropological thought with scholars in Khoisan studies and hunter-gatherer studies, as well as from more formal interviews with some of them. It would be invidious to name some of those here and not others, so I will simply acknowledge the suggestions of the publisher's anonymous reader. He or she pointed out a number of omissions in the first draft, and although this is not 'the great big book of Bushman studies' it is now a slightly bigger and, I hope, rather more balanced account.

I am also grateful to my close colleagues at the University of Edinburgh, and to the members of Khoisan groups and people of Khoisan descent who have guided me in my own studies, and, as always, to my wife and best critic Joy. I acknowledge too the British Academy, the Economic and Social Research Council, the James A. Swan Fund, the Japan Society for the Promotion of Science, the National Science Foundation, the Nuffield Foundation and the University of Edinburgh, for grants to support for my Khoisan research and my research on the history of Khoisan studies.

This book is dedicated to southern Africa's foraging peoples, for the many insights they have given anthropology, and in the hope for a future for them with land, liberty and individual self-determination.

Alan Barnard

−1−

Introduction

'Studying the Bushman?' When in the early 1970s I first did fieldwork in the Kalahari, that was a pretty standard question from non-Bushmen of all sorts. The idea of 'studying the Bushman' was very well known throughout southern Africa, and it seemed quite unproblematic in the sense that the exercise was so obviously important. Most black and white people I met in Botswana seemed to have a pretty clear notion of which red people (as many of Botswana's former hunter-gatherers call themselves) were the 'true Bushmen', and therefore worthy of study, and which were not.

Of course I always answered 'yes', but in a very real sense I was not studying Bushmen, much less 'the Bushman', at all. Anthropologists do not study people; we study either societies or cultures in the abstract or, more likely, aspects or 'systems' of society or culture (like economics, politics, kinship or religion). Our method of presentation may be either through the more traditional approach with generalized data or through the more recent style of individual narratives. Some anthropologists study a community's biological make-up or their relation to the environment. These studies too are at least a step or two away from the literal 'study of people'. It is fair to say that anthropologists work with people, in this case those known variously as 'Bushmen', 'San' or 'Basarwa', but exactly what anthropologists actually study is somewhat harder to define. It is also very difficult to pin down exactly why 'the Bushman' ever was, and remains, so plainly important to anthropology and to what outsiders think anthropology is all about.

This book is not primarily a summary of ethnographic findings. I have already written a somewhat technical book on that topic (Barnard 1992). Rather, my concern here is more with anthropology in interplay with Bushman or San people and with the idea of 'the San' or 'the Bushman'. We anthropologists constantly change our images of these people in diverse ways. These reflect our time, our national traditions and our shifting and often complex theoretical positions. I hope it will be enlightening to anthropologists, of course, but I hope too that it will help explain what anthropologists do and have done among the San. The book covers a number of different themes, two crucial ones being (a) the history of ethnographic representations of peoples known as 'Bushmen' or 'San', and (b) the influence of these representations on anthropological thought (theory, method and message to the world beyond anthropology). A related theme (c) is the nature of the models anthropologists carry with them in the field and employ in their writings: scientific, humanistic, and so on. A fourth theme, (d) the political and social history of southern Africa – forever in the background in Bushman studies – is touched on too. Bushmen or San themselves seem forever in the background within southern Africa's history, often even as if part of the landscape, 'nature' rather than 'culture', victims rather than actors, part of the world that once was, rather than the world being made by 'history' or indeed by 'contemporary politics'. San are important for anthropology, in part, because their presence can be so easily manipulated. To some anthropologists, they are environmentally aware. To others, they are politically naive. Some admire their scientific knowledge, others their supposed mysticism or artistic abilities. Their portrayals as well as their actual fortunes have gone up and down through history, although themes like spiritual awareness and art appear and reappear through the decades.

There is an old Russian proverb: 'He who looks to the past is blind in one eye; he who forgets the past is blind in both eyes.' History is about both the past and the present. More specifically, my approach in my dabblings in 'history' is both 'pastist' in that I try to describe characters and events in the spirit of their times, and 'presentist' in that I like to keep one eye on current issues and debates. While for some of the greatest of the historians of anthropology, notably George Stocking (e.g. 1968 [1965]: 1–12), 'presentism' is regarded as an affliction, for the practitioner-historian like me it can provide a second point of focus and aid in the creation of a more reflective historiography. It also enables a more collective reflexivity for anthropology, whose disciplinary awareness often loses out when practitioners engage only in individualistic reflexive activity. I therefore present this book as a contribution both to the anthropological understanding of the hunter-gatherer societies of southern Africa and to the history and historical consciousness of anthropological ideas.

'Bushmen' and the West: a Literary Context

The image of 'the Bushman' in the Western imagination is a product of centuries of contact. It is a changing image, because both San society and Western thought have undergone great changes in this period. The transformation of that image is interesting and important both for what it shows of San society and for what it shows of Western cultural values. While the basic image has changed, essentially from negative to positive, the centuries-old stereotypes of Bushmen as 'primitive' and 'natural' have remained.

While this book is not a history of Khoisan hunter-gatherers as such, I hope their story comes through as well. One of my literary inspirations for it is such a history, *The Bushmen of Southern Africa*, by the former television journalist Sandy Gall (2001). Gall describes with passion the tragedies that have befallen southern

Africa's hunter-gatherers from the times of early contact with Portuguese explorers and Dutch settlers at the Cape to the loss of Bushman lands in present-day Botswana. Gall's concern is with the Bushmen themselves, while here I focus on them as seen through the eyes of their ethnographers, through the sepia ink of the great and not-so-great theorists of human society, and to some extent too through their portrayals in popular literature and film.

Other literary influences are worth a mention. One is Basil Davidson's (1994) *The Search for Africa*, a provocative collection of that author's essays, some mainly descriptive, some partly autobiographical, and some taking issue with accepted ideas of the 'ownership' of Africa's immaterial heritage. Another is Adam Kuper's (1988) *The Invention of Primitive Society*, which reveals the history of anthropology as one of an illusion of the 'primitive', transformed each generation but nevertheless ever-present. Kuper has recently published a second edition which in a new final chapter (Kuper 2005a: 203–18) makes explicit the relation between anthropology's primitivism and the image of 'the Bushman' within the indigenous peoples movement. I do not share all his conclusions, but I share his concern with anthropology's misconceptions. Important too is L.R. Hiatt's (1996) *Arguments about Aborigines*, on the use of Australia's hunter-gatherers in the academic and (to a lesser extent) practical controversies that have engaged scholars since the nineteenth century.

What I try to do in this book is capture something of the flavour of those others and apply it to the interpretation of the multiple images of the San. My book may be read either in light of such works or without reference to them at all. Accordingly, I expect different readers will gain different things from it. I assume no prior knowledge on the part of my readers, either in such works or in the numerous works that have appeared through the centuries on Bushmen and their neighbours.

Of course, it is not only in the West that Bushmen are anthropologically important. One of the most interesting developments in Bushman studies over the last few decades has been the advance of Japanese anthropology, through theoretical concerns with cultural ecology, with really intensive work on the social behaviour of Kalahari foragers, and through comparisons between these human foragers and the non-human primates that were the original concern of the first Japanese ethnographers of the San. Often the style of Japanese writings is quite different from that of Western ones, and comparisons between Western and Japanese styles can be very revealing. This too is touched on, in the hope that such diverse traditions of anthropology can shed light both on their subject matter and on each other's cultural suppositions.

Actually, rather few anthropologists are familiar with all the nuances of ethnic and linguistic boundaries among Bushman groups. For the benefit of those who are not, as well as for my wider audience, let me say a bit about the classification of Bushman and Khoisan peoples and the pronunciation of some of their ethnic group names.

San and Khoisan

Who are the San?

The San, Bushmen or Basarwa are the original modern human inhabitants of southern Africa. For some fifty years, scholars have argued a cultural continuity between African peoples living thirty or forty thousand years ago and the San of today. But it is worth emphasizing that the San today are, of course, thoroughly modern. I do not mean this purely in the sense that some of them speak English and know how to drive or fix cars. I mean it in the sense that they have as much cultural sophistication as anyone, and have 'cultures' much more complex in many ways. For example, there are San who retain a traditional knowledge of plants and animals that is at least as good as that of many a Western biologist. They can identify and know the names (in their own languages) of several hundreds of different species of plant, as well as their seasonal locations, their ecological associations with other species, and how to prepare them as foods or medicines. They may know more than a hundred species of animal as well, their migration patterns, their social behaviours and psychologies, their anatomy and physiology, their life cycles, and so on.

Equally, Bushman 'culture' is sophisticated, and also diverse, in language, in aesthetics and even in social organization. For example, some Bushman languages are phonologically complex and others syntactically complex. A language called !Xoõ has 126 consonant sounds (Traill 1994: 13). My own fieldwork language, Nharo or Naro, has some seventy or more pronouns (or person-gender-number markers), depending on how one counts them. A chart by the leading linguist on the language in fact shows positions (with some duplicates) for 188 of them (Visser 2001: 238). Why should people who live in groups of a couple of dozen have 70 or 188 pronouns? (Actually, this is one of the few questions to have occurred to anthropologists that we seem not to have tried very hard to answer.)

Many Bushmen are skilled artists and musicians, wise interpreters of human (and animal) thought, and consummate natural theologians. Different groups even have different musical modes, different artistic designs, and quite different styles in utilitarian objects such as projectile points. At least in the last case, we know from archaeological evidence that they have long had such diversity (Wiessner 1984). They also have very complicated kinship systems and rules of etiquette, and the great variations in things like kinship among the different groups add to the overall complexity. Socially, each group has different rules about how people are classified and which relatives one may sit close to, joke with or marry. Among some groups, genealogical distance is important: as in, say, England, one does not marry a brother, a sister or a cousin. Among others it is abstract category: one does not marry a father's brother's or mother's sister's daughter, but may marry a father's sister's or mother's brother's daughter (Barnard 1992: 265–81).

Bushmen are part of a larger constellation of ethnic groups known since the late 1920s as the 'Khoisan' peoples. Bushmen are not the most numerous of the Khoisan peoples, but they are the most geographically dispersed and linguistically diverse. As we shall see in more detail in a later chapter (Chapter 4), the word Khoisan is a European concoction, originally for individuals of a supposed physical type, but now much more commonly used as a term of cultural or linguistic description. In southern Africa today, most people who claim Khoisan descent speak either Afrikaans or a Bantu language as their first tongue. Even so, a few hundred thousand can speak a Khoisan language; and tens of thousands, including many who speak Tswana or some other language as their main one, are by any reasonable self-definition Bushmen or San.

Khoe and San: Meanings and Changing Fashions

Khoisan is made up of two words: Khoi and San. As a linguistic label, Khoi or Khoe refers to those who use this word in their own languages to mean 'person'. These include the cattle and sheep-herding Khoekhoe or 'People of People', who were once called 'Hottentots', the latter term now regarded as offensive and therefore no longer in use in polite circles within southern Africa. The term Khoe can also include the hunter-gatherers known as the Central Bushmen or Khoe Bushmen, in other words those who speak languages related to Khoekhoe.

San means Bushmen, hunter-gatherers, or foragers, not in any Bushman or San language at all, but in some of the Khoekhoe dialects. It can carry negative connotations too, related to the fact that foragers in general are low-status people. Accusations of thievery, for example, have for centuries been levelled at cattle-less San, or more accurately *saan* (in Cape Khoekhoe) or *sān* (in Nama), meaning those Khoekhoe who fell on hard times and lived by scavenging and robbing their richer kinsfolk. The term 'San' or 'Saan' (common gender plural) or the term 'Sonqua' or Soaqua' (masculine plural) has been used in Dutch and English writings off and on since the seventeenth century, either as a word for impoverished Khoekhoe or as an ethnic label proper. In the earliest writings it was even more common than 'Bushman'. Dutch 'Bosjesman' only replaced the earlier 'Sonqua' in government documents about 1770 (Wilson 1986: 256).

'San' came back into fashion in academic circles in the 1970s, and it has remained the usual term (instead of 'Bushmen') particularly in archaeology and historical studies, and especially in Japan and within southern Africa itself. Social anthropologists who in the 1970s were using 'San' began to drift back to 'Bushmen' in the 1980s and 1990s, but anthropology in the last decade or so has once again become more favourably inclined towards 'San'. The reasons are largely political. 'San' in the 1970s struck some as both artificial and paternalistic (since it was an imposed, 'politically correct' term not in use by any group of

Bushmen). An example recorded by Megan Biesele (1993: vi) shows us the problem. In her book *Women Like Meat*, she chose to use 'Bushmen' in preference to 'San' as the generic term and defended her usage on the grounds of a hope that the term might eventually be 'ennobled'. She notes too that one Ju/'hoan leader made the same argument at a community meeting in 1991, the year after Namibia's independence, while his brother at the same meeting said he 'never wanted to hear the term used again in post-apartheid Namibia'. Many at the meeting had never heard the word 'San', and no one present argued in favour of its use.

However, by the late 1990s 'San' was the usual term among social planners, government officials and NGOs in both Namibia and the newly democratic South Africa, and was finally catching on among the relatively small numbers of for-mally educated and politically active San themselves. In this book I use terms as I feel appropriate for the context, since in my view there cannot be a true correct term in any absolute sense. 'The San' is just as much an image or collection of images as 'the Bushman', and each term has both positive and negative connota-tions.

There are objectors to nearly every generic term in use, and there are disagree-ments about which term best refers to whom – as, for example, 'Khoekhoe' nowa-days includes Damara as well as Nama, but once, among Nama themselves and in academic usage alike, did not. Moreover, the fit between lifestyle and language is not a precise one, since the Central San speak Khoe languages, and only Northern and Southern San speak what we might call 'San languages'. Since linguistic rela-tionship is perhaps the strongest indicator of ancient historical relatedness, there are good grounds for thinking of language first, with subsistence second. Indeed, throughout the recorded history of southern Africa there are numerous cases of hunters becoming herders and vice versa. Some of these are detailed in the next chapter.

The following list shows the basic classification of Khoisan peoples by lan-guage: Figure 1.1 illustrates the approximate migration routes of Khoe-speaking peoples, from a location somewhere northeast of their present locations, some 3000 years ago.

Khoe-speaking peoples
Khoekhoe or 'Hottentot' cattle and sheep-herders (Cape Khoekhoe, Korana, Nama, Damara, etc., who live in Namibia and western parts of South Africa)
Khoekhoe-speaking Bushmen or San (Hai//om, who live today in a small area in northern Namibia)
Central Bushmen or San (Nharo or Naro, G/wi, G//ana, Bugakhoe, Kxoe, etc., a diversity of groups who live mainly in central Botswana and the Okavango swamp)

Non-khoe-speaking Bushmen or San
  Northern Bushmen or San, also known as !Kung (!Xũ and Ju/'hoansi; who
  live in north-western Botswana, north-eastern Namibia and southern Angola)
  Southern Bushmen or Southern San (/Xam, ≠Khomani, !Xoõ, etc., a diversity of groups who once inhabited much of South Africa but today include
  mainly groups in southern Botswana)

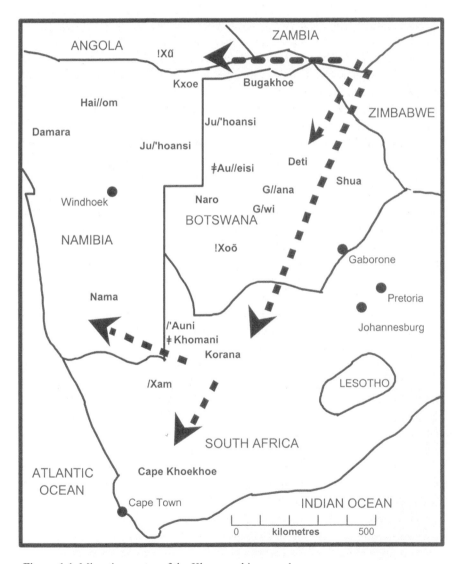

Figure 1.1 Migration routes of the Khoe-speaking peoples

Writing Group Names and Words with Clicks

As the names of some of the Khoisan groups suggest, there are 'click' sounds in these languages. These sounds are usually written with symbols found on typewriters and computers, though not among the letters of the Latin alphabet. In order to pronounce the names of ethnic groups accurately, a basic knowledge of clicks is required. However, the names can be rendered in English either by ignoring the click altogether, or by substituting a 'k', or alternatively a 'p', 't' or 'k' – whichever is the closest to the click sound in point of articulation. There are five basic clicks, which I shall describe, as is customary in linguistics, beginning in the front of the mouth and moving towards the back of the mouth.

The first is the bilabial or 'kiss' click, produced on the lips, just like an audible kiss, and represented by a circle with a dot in the middle: ⊙. This click is found only in Southern Bushman languages. The second is the dental click, with the tongue placed on and then drawn away from the teeth, as in the sound of annoyance (if said twice): 'tisk tisk'. It is represented by a slanted or vertical line: / or |. The third is the alveolar click, similar to the dental but with the tongue just behind the teeth and drawn very sharply away with a loud thud. It is written with a 'not-equal-to' sign or a double dagger: ≠ or ǂ. The fourth is the lateral click, with the tongue pulled from the side of the mouth in the sound that (said twice) makes horses go. It is written with a double slanted or vertical line: // or ||. Finally, there is the palatal click, with the tongue pulled sharply from the roof of the mouth and sounding a bit like a cork popping from a wine bottle. It is written with an exclamation mark: !.

At one time, there were actually twenty-eight different systems in use for writing clicks (detailed in W.H.I. Bleek 1858: 6). Happily, only two basic systems, with some variants, survive (Table 1.1). The one described above is the one used in this book to write Khoisan words and ethnic group names, and by nearly all anthropologists, archaeologists and linguists who have a need to write in Khoisan languages. The other one is also useful for many readers to know, not least because it is the one employed in Southern Bantu or isiNtu languages, such as Xhosa and Zulu, whose speakers borrowed some of the click sounds from the Khoisan many centuries ago. In these Bantu languages, the dental click, /, is written 'c'. The lateral click, //, is written 'x'. And the palatal click, !, is written 'q'. There is no symbol for the bilabial, ⊙; but, when on occasion this system is employed to write Khoisan languages, the alveolar click, ≠, is generally represented by 'tc'. This is the case, for example, in the new orthography of the language known to anthropologists as Nharo, or, in its new orthography, as Naro.

The Khoisan system originated in the writings of German Egypologist Karl Richard Lepsius and dates from 1854, while the Bantu system originated through the work of Scottish missionaries among the Xhosa around 1823 (see also Barnard 1992: xviii–xxii). As is standard practice, in this book ethnic group names and

Table 1.1 Click sounds in the two most common systems

	Khoisan system			Bantu system
Bilabial click	⊙			(no symbol)
Dental click	/	or	|	c
Alveolar click	≠	or	ǂ	('tc' can be used)
Lateral click	//	or	||	x
Palatal click	!			q

other words in African languages are generally written according to the orthography of the given language unless there is good reason to depart from this practice (such as to reflect historical context). The vertical click symbols are employed especially by linguists in writing Khoisan words, and are also used more generally by any literate people in writing Khoekhoe words (as in 'Nama' translations of the Bible or in official Namibian Khoekhoe orthography). The slanted ones are much more common among anthropologists, and therefore in this book the slanted symbols will be used.

Each of the clicks may be accompanied by a consonant or a cluster of consonants, and especially in Khoisan languages there are additional symbols to represent such complex sounds. Here too, there are different systems, though fortunately only slightly so. For some linguists in Germany, for example, a tilde above a click symbol indicates nasalization of the click, while a squiggly line below indicates voicing. In this book, I use the more common system of writing consonant symbols before or after the click symbol, in this case 'n' for nasalization or 'g' for voicing. For instance the ethnic group name G//ana or //Gana is pronounced with the lateral click and voicing – roughly the simultaneous pronouncing of the click and a 'g'. Click consonant clusters include 'releases' on various consonants, such as a glottal stop (usually written with an apostrophe), 'h' or 'x' (the 'x' pronounced in this, Khoisan, orthography, like the 'ch' in Scots *loch*, meaning 'lake', or the 'g' in Afrikaans *gras*, meaning 'grass').

There is a tiny caveat on writing clicks, which could be important for some readers if safely ignored by most. For various historical and linguistic reasons, there is one widely spoken Khoisan language that does not play by these rules, but has its own, slightly different, formula. In Khoekhoe (Nama-Damara), a 'g' after a click symbol means the lack of a glottal stop in speech – since there is no phonemic distinction in this language between voiced and voiceless consonants. Therefore, the lack of a 'g' in writing in Khoekhoe means that there is a glottal stop. For example, the click in /gā (to take shelter from) is released directly on to the vowel, while that of /ā (to squeeze) is followed by an unwritten glottal stop. Likewise, the ethnic group name Hai//om (the Khoekhoe-speaking San of northern Namibia) contains a glottal stop after the click, a sound not shown orthographically here because the word is customarily written in the Khoekhoe style.

For the sake of completeness, let me just add that in Khoekhoe the letters 'p', 't' and 'k', where there is no click, are employed next to high-tone vowels, while 'b', 'd' and 'g' are the respective low-tone equivalents. The orthography makers did this because the language distinguishes tone but not voicing. For example, *pā.i* (porridge) has initial high tone, and *bā.i* (vegetable dye) is pronounced much the same but with initial low tone. The practice is not followed in writing other languages, however. Its general importance comes into play when comparing words in Khoekhoe and related dialects, and of course for anyone wanting to know how to pronounce a particular Khoekhoe word.

That really is pretty much everything most readers will ever need or want to know about the diversity of Khoisan groups and their ethnic group names. The remainder of this book is devoted to the San and those who have worked with them.

–2–

From Early Encounters to Early Anthropology

The exact origin of anthropology is a matter of debate, mainly on what we mean by 'anthropology'. However, in spite of titles like *Readings in Early Anthropology* (Slotkin 1965) or *Early Anthropology in the Sixteenth and Seventeenth Centuries* (Hodgen 1964), there can be little doubt that anthropology as we know it was not in existence until after the exploration of coastal southern Africa and the 'discovery' of Khoisan peoples. What is less known, perhaps, is the fact that 'the Bushman' was not immediately obvious to sixteenth- and seventeenth-century writers on the Khoisan. The Bushman is a concept that emerged slowly through the centuries.

First Reports

> The inhabitants of this country are tawny-coloured [*baço*]. Their food is confined to the flesh of seals, whales, and gazelles, and the roots of herbs. They are dressed in skins, and wear sheaths over their virile members. They are armed with poles of olive wood to which a horn, browned in the fire, is attached. Their numerous dogs resemble those of Portugal, and bark like them. (Da Gama 1947 [1497]: 5)

So begins perhaps the first objective European description of the Khoisan – on what is now the Berg River at St Helena Bay on the west coast of South Africa. That was on Wednesday, 8 November 1497. One of Vasco da Gama's men, Fernão Veloso, 'expressed a great desire to be permitted to accompany the natives to their houses, so that he might find out how they lived and what they ate' (Da Gama 1947: 6). They caught a seal and shared the meat and some roots with Veloso. Soon some unrecorded altercation occurred, and these people, who had appeared 'as men of little spirit, quite incapable of violence', turned hostile and chased Veloso and the other Portuguese who had landed back to their boat. The Khoisan apparently wounded several Portuguese.

Although Da Gama's translator speculates that these are 'Hottentots', I think they were San, and other specialists agree (e.g. Boonzaier, Malherbe, Berens and Smith 1996: 54–5). In this area, the distinction between Khoekhoe and San was historically not as significant as one might imagine. The mouth of the Berg in the seventeenth century was the northern boundary of a transhumant Khoekhoe group called the Cochoqua, but it had for many centuries before also been home to hunter-gatherers. It is well established, especially in the Western Cape, that herders who lost their livestock easily reverted to a hunter-gatherer existence (see Marks 1972; A.B. Smith 1986).

The Portuguese never settled in Bushman areas, but made their colonies instead in Angola and Mozambique. The Dutch settled at Cape Town or Kaapstad in 1652. Yet, before that, Dutch and English ships traded extensively with Khoekhoe and utilized the services of those who might reasonably be considered 'Bushmen', particularly those called Watermen or Strandlopers (Dutch for 'Beach-rangers'). These were probably impoverished coastal Khoekhoe who lived by hunting, gathering and fishing. The most famous was a 'chief' called Autshumato, later known as 'Herry' or 'Harry the Strandloper'. Around 1631 or 1632, he was taken by a British ship all the way to Java, in order to be taught English en route. He and twenty followers were settled on Robben Island, where they kept watch for ships and reported their movements to the British as they passed (see, for example, Elphick 1985 [1975]: 82–6).

Dutch Settlement and Early Accounts

The Dutch encountered both Khoekhoe and San, whom they called sometimes Bosjesmans (Bushmen) and sometimes Saoqua or Sanqua, which is the masculine plural form of 'San' ('San' is common gender plural). The word Bosjesmans has been dated to 1682, with the various forms of San occurring slightly earlier. The earliest venture to the interior noting cattle-less San was apparently that of Jan Wintervogogel in 1655. He encountered 'a certain tribe, very low in stature, and very lean, entirely savage, without any huts, cattle, or anything in the world, clad in little skins' about fifty seventeenth-century Dutch miles, or 370 kilometres, north of Cape Town (quoted in Willcox 1978a: 76). These San were entirely peaceful, and subsequent tales alternated between such descriptions and tales of warlike groups, no doubt caught up in the battles among Khoekhoe, San and Dutch. The Dutch seem to have had no idea that the land might belong in some sense to these people, and fighting broke out, with major Khoekhoe–Dutch wars beginning in 1656, 1673 and 1701 and raiding and counter-attacks on San and Khoekhoe continuing through much of the eighteen century (see, for example, Gall 2001: 49–61). The second war indeed involved San, apparently in the service of the Cochoqua, whose loss of several thousand head of sheep and cattle must have reduced them to the status of *saan* (impoverished food-gatherers) themselves.

Peter Kolb and the Earliest Travellers

The two greatest ethnographic accounts in the world in the eighteenth century were Joseph-François Lafitau's (1724) of the Iroquois of North America, and Peter Kolb's of the 'Hottentots'. Lafitau was a priest and missionary, and, although the French Enlightenment ignored him, his writings were widely influential on Scots like Adam Smith, Adam Ferguson and William Robertson. Kolb, Kolbe or Kolben (as his name is variously given) had been sent to South Africa as an astronomer and meteorologist, but when funds dried up he worked as a magistrate's secretary. His legacy is his *Caput Bonae Spei Hodiernum*, which was first published in German in 1719, then in Dutch in 1727, in English in 1731 and in French in 1741. The full title describes its contents rather well: *The Present State of the Cape of Good Hope: Or, A Particular Account of the Several Nations of the Hottentots: Their Religion, Government, Laws, Customs, Ceremonies, and Opinions; Their Art of Wars, Professions, Language, Genius, &c., Together with A Short Account of the Dutch Settlement at the Cape* (Kolb 1968 [1719]: i).

Kolb has little concern for what in the seventeenth century had been seen as an economic divide (hunters versus herders) or what would later become a major ethnic divide (San versus Khoekhoe). For Kolb, the Sonquas (San) were neither merely impoverished Khoekhoe nor a different ethnic group entirely, but rather a specific 'nation' or branch of the Khoekhoe, albeit a group with its own customs and geographical association. He writes:

> Bordering on the *Koopmans*, Eastward, lie the *Sonquas*, a lively, daring People, very dexterous in the Management of their Arms. And this martial Genius and Proficiency they owe to their Country, which is mountainous, rocky, and the poorest in all the Region about the Cape ... This Poverty of their Country brings them likewise to be dextrous at the Chace [*sic*]. They pursue all the Game they discover, and 'tis rarely it escapes 'em. And this is one great Reason why so little is seen among 'em. (Kolb 1968 [1719]: 76)

He notes that the Sonquas also gathered honey, which they traded with the Europeans for knives and other implements, as well as for brandy, tobacco and pipes (1968: 76–7). He also reports that, although they had been described as cave-dwellers, in fact they live in huts like other Khoekhoe (1968: 218).

In spite of Kolb's account, Bushmen were still not that well known in the eighteenth century even among the educated European public. I have argued elsewhere that the very concept 'hunting-and-gathering society' was possibly invented by Adam Smith around 1748 (Barnard 2004a: 37). This is all the more remarkable because, though very well read in many respects, Smith himself, in his most famous work, seems to have been entirely ignorant that any hunter-gatherers existed anywhere on the African continent:

The most barbarous nations either of Africa or of the East Indies were shepherds; even the Hottentots were so. But the natives of every part of America, except Mexico and Peru, were only hunters; and the difference is very great between the number of shepherds and that of hunters whom the same extent of equally fertile territory can maintain. (Smith 2003 [1776]: 805)

Smith's notion of 'hunters' was of the lowest level of society, both earlier and more primitive than that of 'shepherds', of 'farmers', or of those of 'the age of commerce'. The simple fact is that, along with others of his age, the ethnographic distinction between Hottentot and Bushman had yet to come to fruition. If 'hunting-and-gathering society' was invented, at the earliest, in the 1740s – possibly by Turgot and possibly by Smith (Barnard 2004a: 33–7) – then 'the Bushman' came later, as we shall see, with François Le Vaillant (1790) and other explorers of the southern African interior. Smith's younger colleague at Glasgow and successor in four-stage theory, John Millar (1806: 36), mentions only 'Hottentots', and relied exclusively on Kolb for his southern African material, in spite of the availability of other sources. And so it was with the French *philosophes* as well, with Paris-based writers of the eighteenth and early nineteenth centuries expressing variously admiration or repugnance at the 'Hottentot' (Cohen 1980: *passim*), and with no explicit mention of the Bushman.

Historian Richard Elphick (1985 [1975]: 41) has commented on the absence of a clear distinction between Khoe and San in the seventeenth and eighteenth centuries, and has noted that even Khoekhoe themselves made no systematic distinction between these categories. The term 'San' (or, more accurately, *saan* or *sonqua* – or *soaqua*) was applied both to hunter-gatherers and to small-scale pastoralists, and apparently to non-Khoekhoe-speaking aboriginal inhabitants of southern Africa and poorer segments of the Khoekhoe population. In the decade of the 1700s Johannes Starrenburgh reports on Khoekhoe who had once owned cattle and lived under chiefs then having 'mostly all become Bushmen, hunters and robbers' (quoted in Elphick 1985: 39–40), and of August Frederik Beutler on the Eastern Frontier telling of 'Hottentots' who 'live like Bushmen from stealing, hunting and eating anything eatable which they find in the field or along the shore' (quoted in Elphick 1985: 40).

Confusion could reign in the opposite direction too, as in Andreas Sparrman's sympathetic account from the 1770s of people calling themselves 'good Bushmen' who raised cattle, Robert Jacob Gordon's tale from the same decade of cattle-keeping 'Bosjesmans' giving milk to his men, and Hendrik Jacob Wikar's report of 'Bushmen' who traded sheep and cattle and even a group called the 'Samgomomkoa' (Elphick 1985: 26–7). Wikar lived for years with Khoekhoe beyond the frontier and spoke Khoekhoe well. His term Samgomomkoa means roughly 'San with cattle people', and he reported a number of such ambiguities in ethnic classification (see also Wikar 1935 [1779]: 28–33).

By the 1790s the Dutch East India Company was in financial trouble, and Holland itself fell to French forces. British troops were landed near Cape Town in 1795 and quickly took the Cape Colony. The British established Lord Macartney as governor in 1797, and this marked the formal transfer of authority. Apart from a brief interlude of Dutch control between 1803 and 1806, the Cape was now British. The immediate significance of all this for the study of Bushmen lay in Macartney's private secretary, John Barrow (later Sir John Barrow, naval administrator, sponsor of Arctic exploration and founder of the Royal Geographical Society). Macartney had been ambassador to China, and when there Barrow had written an important account of his travels. He would now do the same in the Cape, and on the frontier. The first volume of his account (Barrow 1801) was widely read in English and translated into French, Dutch, German, Swedish and Norwegian. He describes encounters with Xhosa, Khoekhoe and Bushmen – the latter being numerous in mountain areas, and apparently aggressive and warlike, though without chiefs (1801: 274). Barrow's account is relatively objective, but it does reflect too the tense relations among groups in that especially difficult time of raiding and warfare, and of changing allegiances and identities (see Szalay 1995; Newton-King 1999).

The first utterly clear distinction between Bushmen and 'Hottentots' came just a few years later, with Henry Lichtenstein, a young German doctor who accompanied the new Dutch governor and wrote his own account of travels in the interior. Although not generally portraying them in a very good light, he nevertheless writes clearly on his views.

> Equally untrue is the assertion that the nation of the Bosjesmans is composed of fugitive slaves and Hottentots. They are, and ever have been, a distinct people, having their own peculiar language, and their own peculiar customs, if the terms *language* and *customs* can be applied to people upon the very lowest step in the order of civilization … A wild, shy, suspicious eye, and crafty expression of countenance, forms, above all things, a striking contrast in the Bosjesman with the frank, open physiognomy of the Hottentot. (Lichtenstein 1928 [1812]: 143, 145)

The Strange Case of the 'Strandlopers'

If Khoekhoe and San were often not distinguished in the earliest records, sometimes Strandlopers were. What is more, the term has come and gone through the centuries. The seventeenth-century 'Strandlopers' of Table Bay were a group who called themselves Goringhaicona. M.L. Wilson (1993) argues that the proper use of the term 'Strandloper' is only for these people, but the name came to be widely employed, and its designants were even distinguished as a 'race' quite apart from Khoekhoe or San. Wilson's detailed research on this concept reveals that the term seems to refer in early writings variously to Cape Khoekhoe who had left their cattle behind and camped on the shore, to Nama farther north on the west coast, to pure hunter-gatherers who traded with Nama for copper, to outcasts from various Khoekhoe communities, and possibly to clients and mixed groups.

The term was certainly used in early accounts for the people met by Da Gama at St Helena Bay in 1497, for Harry the Strandloper's folk, and so on. Sometimes they were called Watermen, and sometimes Vismans, Vishman or Vischman ('Fish[er]men'). Wilson (1993: 307) remarks that the use of such words for subsistence activities in the late seventeenth century resembled later distinctions between 'Hottentots' (Khoisan with cattle) and 'Bushmen' (Khoisan without cattle). 'Strandloper' was last used in official records in 1681 (Wilson 1993: 309). There is no mention of the term in Kolb's account of indigenous populations in his *The Present State of the Cape of Good Hope* (1968 [1719]), although Valentyn (1973 [1726]: 309) makes passing reference to 'Strandlopers'. Kolb was at the Cape from 1708 to 1713, and Valentyn in brief periods from 1685 to 1714.

It is not unlikely that the Gorinhaicona disappeared as a distinct group by the time of the smallpox epidemic which hit Cape Town in 1713, but the 'Strandlopers' were to be resurrected, not only by later historians and historian-archaeologists like Wilson, but also by explorers of the late eighteenth century, craniologists of the nineteenth and archaeologists of the twentieth (summarized in Wilson 1993: 313–35). Explorers such as William Paterson and Robert Jacob Gordon in the 1770s report on not just mussel-eaters, but whale-eating inhabitants of the Namib desert north of the Orange. Nineteenth-century craniologist Shrubsall (e.g. 1898) included 'Strandlopers' as a distinct analytical category in his surveys of 'Bush races', while noting nevertheless that the category contains variously 'purer' or more 'mixed' specimens. Twentieth-century anthropologist Schapera (1930: 29) urged simply dropping the term because of its lack of meaning in terms of race. His contemporary, archaeologist Goodwin (Goodwin and Van Riet Lowe 1929: 265), suggested abandoning the proper noun 'Strandloper' and using instead a verbal form: 'a strandloping type of subsistence'. Later archaeologists, including Goodwin himself, eventually allowed 'Strandloper' to return in their writings, though they gradually came to prefer speaking of Wilton, Smithfield and Albany tool traditions. In an interesting twist, archaeologist Parkington later (1984: 164) resurrected the Cape Khoekhoe word *soaqua* 'not as denoting a tribe but rather, in lower-case letters, as denoting a behavioural complex'.

Images of Sociocultural Characteristics and Their Persistence

Mathias Guenther (1980) has commented on one particular important change in image through the centuries: that of Bushman as 'brutal savage', mainly in the eighteenth and nineteenth centuries, to the one of Bushman as 'harmless person', mainly in the twentieth century. He argues that these images represent not only transformations of Western ideas or of Bushman society as a whole, but also differing encounters with Bushmen during this period. For example, part of the 'brutal savage' image stressed the notion of Bushmen as cunning warriors with violent attitudes towards strangers. Such images represent a partial truth – not the truth about Bushman society in any general sense, but rather the truth of violent confrontation that took place on the frontier of white settlement in the southern Africa of the seventeenth, eighteenth and nineteenth centuries. The brutality that existed was, of course, at least as much the making of whites as it was of Bushmen. Whites killed Bushmen for sport, chased them into mountainous areas of the interior, or enslaved them. Whites spread diseases, including smallpox, measles and syphilis. They came in large numbers, heavily armed, and took lands that had for millennia been utilized for hunting and gathering by the Bushmen. For these reasons Bushmen retaliated, and the negative, violent image that grew up around them reflected these actions, especially in the Karoo and mountain areas of South Africa and Lesotho.

Positive images of Bushmen, as much as negative ones, are often associated with their status as 'primitive' people. Bushmen are seen as timeless, without history, as exhibiting characteristics of 'natural' humankind untainted by the evils of Western or other 'high' civilizations. The truth in this image comes in two guises. The first is represented by Western civilizations' self-critiques, for example in eighteenth-century notions of 'the noble savage', or specifically what Rousseau (1971 [1755]) referred to as *l'homme naturel* or *l'homme sauvage*. It is also represented through twentieth-century disillusionment with the over-technological, over-industrialized and war-torn societies of the West. The second is the recognition of features in Bushman society, or hunter-gatherer society generally, which the West can regard as of merit, often as a result of anthropological research. Such features include egalitarianism, politics by consensus, an ethos of sharing, and living in a way perceived as close to nature.

Among the first to present a romantic image of the Bushmen was the French traveller and illustrator, François Le Vaillant, who painted and described Bushmen as well as the Nama and Xhosa peoples, and the animals and plants he encountered in his South African travels. His watercolours present an idyllic image of the Bushman life that captivated audiences throughout Europe, and his books were rapidly translated into English, German, Dutch, Russian, Swedish, Danish and Italian. Le Vaillant distinguished two kinds of 'Bushmen': first, those who comprised the marauding bands of runaway slaves, escaped criminals (often of mixed ancestry) and other malefactors; and, secondly, the 'true Bushmen', whom he called, after a Khoekhoe name for them, *Housouanas* (e.g. Le Vaillant 1790: II, 341–2; see also Shaw 1973: 127, 144–7). His watercolours of the latter show attractive faces, with intelligent and reflective expressions. His subjects were bedecked with beautiful metal necklaces, earrings and hair ornaments. Even his paintings of their weapons are idealized: bows, arrows and quivers are perfectly proportioned and without flaw.

Le Vaillant's romantic image was later challenged, as particularly in the nineteenth century Europeans came to see themselves as superior to all other peoples, not simply through more advanced technology or more enlightened institutions of government, but biologically too (Cohen 1980: 91–2). Biological differences between peoples were played upon. In the Bushman and Khoekhoe cases, this meant that short stature, 'peppercorn hair' and steatopygia (fat on the buttocks) were denigrated as characteristics of 'inferior' branches of the human race. Beginning with the Khoekhoe woman Sara Baartman, such people were exhibited in Europe as 'freaks', and, more specifically, as 'freaks' supposedly representative of their peoples. Sara Baartman, known also as 'Saatjie' (Little Sara) or the 'Hottentot Venus', was exhibited in London from around 1810 and later that decade in Paris, where she died and where her body was to remain as part of a museum collection until 2002 (see also Fauvelle-Aymar 2002: 305–59).

Typically, even in the best early travellers' reports, Bushmen are portrayed either as guides or as ignorant and fearful folk. The further into the interior travellers ventured, the more peaceable they found the Bushmen. The first great explorer to venture into what is now Namibia was James Edward Alexander, in the 1830s. This Scottish soldier had served in India, Burma and Portugal, travelled overland through Persia, the Near East and the Balkans, visited North and South America and the West Indies, and later explored North America and fought at Sebastopol and in New Zealand. His account of Bushmen, Nama and Damara is among the most sympathetic and complimentary of any. His tale of Bushman encounters with whites is revealing:

> The Boschmans here saw three new things, white men, horses, and a waggon ... the waggon they believed at first was alive, and afterwards, that it was one of the strange white things (ships) which had come out of the sea, and was now travelling over the land.
>
> The Boschmans in the neighbourhood of the Great River even, used lately to be very much afraid of waggons: thus, Mr. Schmelen's [the missionary's] people once caught a Boschman, and he told them that the first time he and his people saw the missionary's waggon they ran away from it for a whole night, thinking it was some terrible monster, and that they always jumped over its spoor, and would not touch the wheel tracks on any account. (Alexander 1838: II, 20–1)

I suspect this kind of story is not uncommon in later ethnographers' notebooks either. There are hints of such 'Coke bottle from the sky' stories around, among Bushmen and anthropologists alike. A G/wi man from the Central Kalahari Game Reserve, for example, in 1974 told me of the time he and his people first saw a fence, and sat down to debate over what it might be and what to do about it. The difference between the nineteenth and late twentieth centuries is that travellers of the earlier period were happier to relate such stories than ethnographers of the later period. Bushmen might have been afraid of wagons or ignorant of fences, but in general they are not afraid to admit to it. Published accounts would not again convey this cultural modesty until gradually. in the late twentieth century, a few ethnographers like Marjorie Shostak, Megan Biesele and James Suzman took steps to put the people in. It would take Bushmen themselves to put the modesty there as the virtue (see Le Roux and White 2004). The sad fact is that for self-deprecating stories of ignorance to be relayed by ethnographers would have only confirmed the prejudices of white and black societies.

Images of Physical Characteristics and Their Persistence

There is no doubt that anthropological or ethnological ideas were brewing in eighteenth-century Paris, Edinburgh, Göttingen and St Petersburg, but Native Americans still held more fascination for Europeans than did Africans. While the 'Hottentot' was well known, the 'Bushman' was an idea slow to catch on, even in Scotland where the notion of an 'age of hunters' (or hunting-and-gathering society) was commonplace among moral philosophers. Late eighteenth-century intellectuals in Europe knew of Kolb, but Le Vaillant and Barrow came too late, and the likes of Wikar and Sparrman were either two obscure or too little known to make a difference in yielding examples for Enlightenment texts.

The early decades of the nineteenth century were lean years for the proto-discipline; and race came to dominate discussions, where it had not before that at least among those interested in topics like the origin of language or the progress and stages of society. A racial stereotype of the Bushman, along with other stereotypes, was beginning to crystallize, although protagonists in discussion of 'race' differed radically on the causes and implications even of agreed features of 'racial' difference (Banton 1987: 22–4, 54–60). In England and France, a battle was raging between the polygenists (those who believed that humankind had multiple origins) and the monogenists (those who believed in a single origin). The latter, like Thomas Hodgkin and James Cowles Prichard, were mainly religious Nonconformists and social reformers. Both of them were students of Dugald Stewart, who in turn was a follower of Adam Smith.

Perhaps surprisingly, given their significance to later generations, Bushmen still figured not at all in the first edition of Prichard's (1813) *Researches into the Physical History of Man*, the most important book of the monogenist camp. By the posthumous fifth edition, though, we do find that 'Writers on the history of mankind seem to be nearly agreed in considering the Bushmen or Bosjesmen of South Africa as the most degraded and miserable of all nations, the lowest in the scale of humanity' (Prichard 1851: 177).

The polygenists came to see the Bushman and 'Hottentot' as specimens of a race very different from and quite inferior to the European. Yet even here, information was lacking and ethnographic examples thin on the ground. The main polygenist text was Robert Knox's (1850) *The Races of Men*. Knox mentions but briefly and intermittently the 'yellow race' that includes 'Bosjemen' (*sic*) and 'Quaiquae whom we call Hottenttots' (1850: 548), and a lithograph depicting people in a rock shelter is captioned 'The savage Bosjemen; – Troglodytes; who built no house or hut; children of the desert' (1850: 221). Most revealingly, Knox states: 'Accordingly, no attempt that I know of has ever been made to ascertain the extent of the Hottentot and Bosjeman race towards the north, that is, into the interior of Africa; a problem surely worthy a solution [*sic*], for no more singular race of men exist on earth than the Hottentot race' (1850: 272).

The physical peculiarities of the 'yellow race' would grow in interest over the next century, until in the 1950s modern ethnographic studies came to be made. German travellers and anthropologists of the late nineteenth and early twentieth centuries, such as Gustav Fritsch (1872: 396–410) and Leonhard Schultze (1928), made detailed records of heights, as well as comments on the supposed peculiarities of genitalia, breasts and buttocks. Light skin colour and peppercorn hair were noted as differing from the skin and hair of neighbouring Bantu-speaking peoples, and Bushmen and 'Hottentots' came to acquire a status among African peoples that set them apart. How much this contributed to modern anthropological perceptions is difficult to assess, but it is noteworthy that in *The Khoisan Peoples of South Africa* Isaac Schapera (1930: 51–72) devotes fourteen pages to summarizing the literature on physical characteristics and eight pages to summarizing that on dress, decoration and bodily mutilations. In the late twentieth century popular writers, notably Sir Laurens van der Post (e.g. 1958: 13–15), would continue the emphasis with descriptions of the semi-erect penis, steatopygia and the elongated labia minora that had been the mainstay of the anthropology of a long past era, but seemed to remain in the background as modern ethnographers took off for the field. Such characteristics as small stature (though certainly not all Bushmen are small) and Bushman facial characteristics have even been suggested as genetically adaptive to the Kalahari environment (e.g. Tobias 1978a: 25–7), which they may be. Nevertheless, the propensity for descriptions of this kind to remain for so long in the anthropological and the popular literature must surely contribute to the image of Bushmen as unique specimens of some kind, in the collective anthropological mind.

Of course, nowhere was this truer than in South Africa (Dubow 1995: 32–65. Anatomical and more recently genetic studies were geared towards testing whether Khoisan were unique, or similar to other African peoples. Since the 1960s the tendency has been in the latter direction (e.g. Jenkins 1968), but before that the Bushman and 'Hottentot' were too often perceived as the ultimate 'other', childlike in appearance and childish in behaviour. Even the private papers of the celebrated anatomist Raymond Dart reveal this tendency, notably in an unpublished paper from the 1930s:

> This is exactly the sort of form which the European child's head has at birth and it is this retention of child-like characters in adult physique, that characterises the whole frame work of the Bushmen. In scientific terminology we express this by calling their structure Pedomorphic (literally child-form). The face is flat like that of a child; the small body with its delicate limb-bones, the diminutive hands and feet, the tiny ears, their simple needs, their incessant playing and dancing in which old and young participate alike, their love of mimicry and story-telling – whatever the avenue of study – we draw in the Bushman, as it were from the eternal fountain of youth. (R. Dart, Kalahari Expedition File, 1936/7, quoted in Dubow 1995: 32)

Conclusion

The European public was exposed to diverse images, both pictorial and literary, as well as physical. Until late in the eighteenth century, the Bushman was undistinguishable from the 'Hottentot', or seen as a branch of the Khoekhoe nation. Literary images by Enlightenment figures began to focus on Bushmen as hunter-gatherers once they built their theories of society on an economic foundation (see Barnard 2004a).

Also by the end of the eighteenth century, ethnography, ethnology and (physical) anthropology were emerging in various countries, especially among scholars writing in German (Vermeulen 1995). Yet these new sciences were still more concerned with 'Hottentots' than with Bushmen, and ethnographers tended to work in northern climes. Africa was the preserve of geographers. In spite of the popularity of writings of geographer-adventurers like Sir John Barrow, the idea of 'the Bushman' was slow to catch on. Little that we would recognize as ethnography was yet available, and only gradually in the early decades of the nineteenth century did the Bushman fully come to be an object of European fascination. Yet he, and she, would remain so into our own time and no doubt beyond.

Victorian Visions of the Bushman

By the early nineteenth century travellers had invented the hunting-and-gathering 'Bushman', though his invention was very slow to be discovered by the literati. Gradually, through published artists' impressions, reports in South African publications, and the greater separation of the 'Bushman' from his cattle-herding cousins, the image we recognize today emerged.

In this chapter we shall see the effects of those events, and the influence of the remarkable family whose records dominated Bushman studies in the late nineteenth century and much of the twentieth. Renewed interest in this, the Bleek family, has since the institution of South African democracy in the 1990s seen growing significance and even greater fame, especially among the South African public. It is an interesting comment on what anthropologists perceive as well-known late twentieth-century ethnography that simple searches of South African websites will find far more references to the Bushman studies of Wilhelm Bleek than to Richard Lee or Lorna Marshall.

The Beginnings of Anthropology as We Know It

Anthropology as we know it really began around 1870 or 1871, at the height of Queen Victoria's long reign and of the growing influence of the British Empire in Africa and the world. These years mark many other significant events too. In 1870 the Kimberley diamond rush began. In 1871 at Ujiji in present-day Tanzania, Henry Morton Stanley 'found' David Livingstone; and further south, deep in the southern African interior, Karl Mauch 'discovered' the ruins of Great Zimbabwe. In Berlin, Germany was united under Bismarck; in London, anthropologist Sir John Lubbock got his Bank Holidays Act through parliament (thereby inventing public holidays); and, in Edinburgh, the world's first rugby international was played, with a victory for Scotland over England.

Also in 1871, two rival anthropological societies, the mainly polygenist Anthropological Society of London and mainly monogenist Ethnological Society of London merged to form the Anthropological Institute (later Royal Anthropological Institute). This both unified institutional anthropology in Britain and marked the acceptance of a single paradigm: the monogenist idea that humankind is one, and with it the evolutionist notion that all humankind passes through the same stages of social evolution (albeit with Englishmen at the 'latest' stage and Bushmen at a much 'earlier' one). Edward Burnett Tylor, Lewis Henry Morgan and Charles Darwin all published their significant human-evolutionary books in 1871, and Lubbock published his just a year earlier (see Barnard 2000: 29–31). It was also in 1870 that Bushman studies began in earnest, with the entry into the field by Wilhelm Heinrich Immanuel Bleek (pronounced like 'Blake').

Wilhelm Bleek and Lucy Lloyd

W.H.I. Bleek's biography is very well known to Bushmanists, but not so much to other anthropologists. Among the best short biographical accounts are the introduction to David Lewis-Williams' *Stories that Float from Afar* (Lewis-Williams 2000a) and Etaine Eberhard's (1996) 'Wilhelm Bleek and the Founding of Bushman Research'. A fuller treatment can be found in Otto Spohr's (1962) bio-bibliographical sketch. Pippa Skotnes's (1996b) *Miscast* gives a brilliant portrayal of the Bleek family and their informants in the context of nineteenth- and twentieth-century Bushman imagery and Bushman research. I draw on these and many other sources here (see also Bank 2006).

Bleek was born in Berlin 1827. He completed his Ph.D. on grammatical gender in African languages at the University of Bonn in 1851. Like F. Max Müller, he was well connected to the British establishment. He knew Sir Charles Lyell, Charles Darwin and Thomas Huxley, and in 1855 he accompanied the exceptionally liberal and controversial Anglican bishop, J.W. Colenso, to Natal to compile for him a grammatical description of Zulu. A few years later he was fortunate to secure the appointment as librarian to the bibliophilic governor of the Cape Colony, Sir George Grey. It is perhaps worthy of note that Grey himself was no ordinary book collector, nor was he even an ordinary colonial governor. Grey explored, met Aborigines and did rock art tracings in Australia in the late 1830s before his appointment, in 1840, as governor of South Australia. Grey collected Maori myths and legends in New Zealand in the 1840s and early 1850s while governor of New Zealand, and continued his interest in Maori culture upon his return there in 1861. Although Grey's time in the Cape Colony, 1854 to 1861, was short-lived, it was significant for the Colony and for Khoisan studies. Grey encouraged Bleek in his studies of Bushman languages and folklore, and the library was to serve too both as the source of employment and as the academic base of both Bleek and his eventual successor as librarian, Theophilus Hahn, ethnographer of the Nama. Grey gave the library to Cape Town in 1862 and started a new library in Auckland. Both libraries are still intact.

Bleek's position enabled him, in 1870, to make an unusual request of Sir Philip Wodehouse, the new governor. Bleek asked for and was granted the privilege of taking home to his house in Mowbray, a suburb of Cape Town, some of those /Xam imprisoned at the Breakwater Prison near Cape Town Harbour. Bleek described his initial encounters with the prisoners in his 'Report Concerning Bushman Researches' (appendix to Bleek and Lloyd 1911: 441–8):

> On the recommendation of the Rev. G. Fisk, the best-behaved Bushman boy was selected, and in August of that year, he was placed with me for this purpose by Her Majesty's Colonial Government. This experiment was found to answer; but it was taken into consideration that one young Bushman alone, would soon lose a good deal of accuracy in speaking his mother-tongue, and, further, that the boy in question could relate hardly any of the numerous tales and fables which are met with in the traditionary literature of this nation. On these grounds His Excellency Sir Henry Barkly was pleased to direct that one of the most intelligent of the old Bushmen should join the other. Both are still with me. (Bleek and Lloyd 1911: 443)

Fisk was the prison chaplain, and Barkly was Wodehouse's successor as Governor of the Cape. The young /Xam was /A!kunta, and the older one //Kabbo. In fact their period of penal servitude had ended in 1871, and they and others remained by choice in the Bleek household. The prisoners had been brought to Cape Town in the first place to build a breakwater, whose remnants today lie clearly visible just off the present breakwater north-west of the modern shopping complex known as the Victoria and Alfred Waterfront. Those released into Bleek's custody were to work for him and his sister-in-law Lucy Lloyd as informants on the /Xam language, as well as on /Xam folklore and related customs, in some cases for many years. After Bleek's untimely death in 1875, Lloyd carried on his work until her retirement in 1884.

Wilhelm Bleek himself collected some 3,600 pages of notes, in eighty-four bound volumes. It is interesting that in his own time doubt was cast on the genuineness of his informants' tales, though one orientalist (Bertin 1886: 78), arguing against Bleek's critics, pointed out that the difficulties in pronouncing the clicks associated with the animal characters in the stories does imply a Bushman origin for the stories. Otherwise, he says, the /Xam would have had to have added these sounds to stories belonging to some other group, and this seemed unlikely. Bleek had worked on Khoekhoe in his youth. He had long had an interest in Bushman languages too and had believed that all African languages were related, but this notion was quickly disproved once he began to learn /Xam. The relative uniqueness of Bushman languages, Bushman folklore, Bushman religious beliefs, and so on, are today taken for granted, but in many such ways the idea of the 'Bushman' that has come down to us is a product of Bleek's work. According to Bleek's biographer (Spohr 1962: 50–1), Bleek himself took primary responsibility for linguistic work, while even in his lifetime Lucy Lloyd spent more time than Bleek on folklore and ethnographic concerns.

Lloyd was born in England in 1834, and in 1849 she and her four sisters (including Jemima, later Wilhelm Bleek's wife) accompanied their father and stepmother to Natal (S. Schmidt 1996). After Wilhelm and Jemima's marriage in 1862, when Bleek moved to Cape Town as librarian, Lucy shared their Mowbray home, eventually with their four surviving daughters as well as her /Xam informants. Among the daughters was Dorothea, who in 1910 and 1911 became the first member of the family actually to visit /Xam country, in search of descendants of her father's and aunt's informants. Lucy herself may never have ventured into Bushman country, but does have the distinction of being among the first ethnographers of the people later known as !Kung. Between 1879 and 1884, the household included four *!kun* boys (as Lloyd called them), who made arrows for her, drew pictures and told narratives that were intriguingly comparable to those of the /Xam (see Bleek and Lloyd 1911: 403–33; Deacon 1996a). Lloyd collected some 8,400 pages of /Xam material and 1,200 pages of !Kung texts. She died in 1914, and Dorothea took her place as premier Bushman researcher in the world. Dorothea was later to do ethnographic and linguistic research among Bushmen in areas now part of South Africa, Namibia and Angola, as well as pioneering work with the Hadza in what is today Tanzania.

Wilhelm Bleek intended to apply for funding to support further research and the publication of his material. Sadly he died just as the effort was about to be made, and it was left to Lloyd to ask for funding. Her requests were unsuccessful, as were, for some time, her later attempts to find a publisher for what is now the great classic of Bushman studies, Bleek and Lloyd's (1911) *Specimens of Bushman Folklore*. Lloyd eventually completed this monumental work with the help of two of Bleek's daughters, Edith and 'Doris' (Dorothea). It consists of /Xam texts with full diacritics on even-numbered pages, and English translations on odd-numbered pages. Lloyd divided the material into two parts, the first covering 'Mythology, Fables, Legends, and Poetry', and the second 'History (Natural and Personal)'. The former ranks with the best of nineteenth-century folkloristic material. The latter contains, among other things, the first personal histories of Bushmen, such as //Kabbo's two accounts of his capture and journey to Cape Town. The translations in *Specimens* are literal and therefore extraordinarily rich in /Xam idiom, if perhaps at the expense of English style. From one of //Kabbo's accounts we read, for example:

> We went to put our legs into the stocks; another white man laid another (piece of) wood upon our legs ... We slept, while our legs were in the stocks. The day broke, while our legs were in the stocks. We early took out our legs from the stocks, we ate meat; we again put our legs into the stocks; we sat, while our legs were in the stocks ... We lay down, we slept, while our legs were inside the stocks. We arose, we smoked, while our legs were inside the stocks. The people boiled sheep's flesh, while our legs were in the stocks. (//Kabbo, in Bleek and Lloyd 1911: 297)

In South African museums, photographs and paintings of /Xam informants //Kabbo, Dia!kwain and /Han≠kass'o and other nineteenth-century /Xam stand alongside those of Bleek and Lloyd wherever rock art is displayed. Bleek and Lloyd have become elevated almost to cult status, and it is perhaps a sad fact that, just as Bleek is better known in South Africa today than any modern Bushman ethnographer, so too //Kabbo, Dia!kwain and /Han≠kass'o are far better known than any living Mosarwa or San (see also Deacon 1996b, c). In *Specimens*, their names are given after the title of each tale, as indeed they are in recent collections like those of Lewis-Williams (2000b) and Jeremy Hollmann (2004). The ethnicizing tendency of modern ethnography is not in the tradition of either Wilhelm Bleek or his academic followers today, who ironically, as in these two cases, are often archaeologists by training rather than folklorists or social anthropologists. As we shall see later, South Africa's new motto, *!Ke e: /xarra //ke* (officially, 'Diverse people unite') is a product of the speech and minds of /Han≠kass'o, Lloyd, Dorothea Bleek and the premier interpreter of symbolism in rock art, David Lewis-Williams.

Theophilus Hahn and the Sān

For some five years after Bleek's death, Lloyd was in charge of Sir George Grey's library. She was twice given notice to quit in 1880. Upon recommendation by Max Müller and others, Theophilus Hahn was appointed to take over – on grounds that he was a trained philologist, with a recently earned Ph.D., and Lloyd was not. Hahn himself made no mean contribution to Khoisan studies, but he was a very unpopular fellow. Two of the Grey Trustees brought a suit against the Library Committee to keep Lloyd and prevent Hahn's appointment. Lloyd tried, without success, to persuade the Library Committee not to hand over the key to him; and the case went, without resolution, to the Supreme Court (Lewin Robinson 1954: 45–7). Thus, in February 1881, Hahn took up his appointment as Colonial Philologist and Custodian of the Grey Collection.

Hahn wrote on wine-making, the Cape Dutch language (which he detested) and other sundry topics, but his main intellectual interest was the Nama language and religion. He had grown up among Nama, as his father had been a missionary with them; and he spoke Nama perfectly. His most important work was undoubtedly *Tsuni-//Goam*, a brilliant proto-structuralist treatise on Nama mythology, custom and etymology. This was written hurriedly in August–September 1879, apparently from memory and in stream of consciousness mode – or at least that was my impression when I came across the manuscript some years ago. Hahn was a great follower of Max Müller and believed fervently in both comparative mythological studies and the psychical identity of the human mind.

Of special relevance here, though, are his comments in that book on the relationship of Bushmen to Khoekhoe and the use of the term *sān* for 'Bushmen' in *Tsuni-//Goam*:

> The old Dutch also did not know that their so-called Hottentots formed only one branch of a wide-spread race, of which the other branch divided into ever so many tribes, differing from each other totally in language ... While the so-called Hottentots called themselves Khoikhoi (men of men, *i.e.*, men *par excellence*), they called those other tribes Sā, the Sonqua of the Cape Records ... We should apply the term *Hottentot* to the whole race, and call the two families each by the native name, that is the one, the *Khoikhoi*, the so-called *Hottentot proper*; the other the *sān (Sā) or Bushmen*. (Hahn 1881: 2–3)

He adds that the root *sā* (from which we get the ethnic designation 'San') means 'to inhabit, to be located, to dwell, to be settled, to be quiet'. It therefore implies 'Aborigines or Settlers proper' (1881: 2). However:

> The word Sā(b) has also acquired a low meaning, and is not considered to be very complimentary. The Khoikhoi often speak of *!Uri-sān* (white Bushmen) and mean the low white vagabonds and runaway sailors who visit their country as traders. One also often hears, '*Khoikhoi tamab, Sab ke*,' he is no Khoikhoi, he is a Sā, which means to say, '*he is no gentleman, he is of low extraction, or he is a rascal.*' (1881: 2)

In other words, *sān* or (as it is now written by anthropologists) *San* is the Khoekhoe word for 'Bushmen' or 'rascals' (masculine singular being *sāb*, and feminine singular *sās*), while *Hottentots* was Hahn's generic term for what those anthropologists later called 'Khoisan'.

The Bushman and Anthropology

Such concerns as Hahn's were a luxury of the few writers of ethnographic commentary who had experience of 'other cultures' and the fewer still who had insight into cultures through indigenous languages. The main problem for early anthropologists was that they lacked field experience. Morgan, among the Iroquois, and Tylor, among Mexicans and London schoolchildren, had such experience, but the majority of anthropologists relied on the accounts of travellers and settlers. Lubbock's (1874: 6–7) quandary about what to do with descriptions of Bushmen and others is not untypical. He quotes Lichtenstein's *Travels* at length in its description of a Bushman who (in Lichtenstein's words) 'had the true physiognomy of the small blue ape of Caffraria'. Lichtenstein had followed that remark by an account of what happened when the man was given a piece of meat, and again compared him, this time in his actions, to an ape. What was Lubbock to do with such a description, which it transpires is at odds with tales of the features and actions of other 'savages'? Lubbock (1874: 7) says: 'Under these circumstances it cannot be wondered that we have most contradictory accounts as to the character and mental condition of savages.' Yet he goes on to find similarities among travellers' accounts on the various continents and attempts to build a picture of living 'savages' with which to explore the understanding of the prehistoric.

In Lubbock's works and those of his contemporaries, diverse accounts were to be compared and weighed, both across the continents with reference to a general category like 'savages' and for a specific people: 'As to the Bushmen, we have rather different accounts. It has been stated by some that they have no idea of perspective nor how a curved surface can possibly be represented on a flat surface of paper; while, on the contrary, other travellers assert that they readily recognise drawings of animals or flowers' (Lubbock 1874: 30). For accurate description, anthropology was at the mercy of travellers. Its task was to compile, interpret and generalize, with the ultimate goal being the understanding of the various stages of human development and the mechanism of human social evolution.

Lubbock was one of the few major figures of nineteenth-century ethnology or social anthropology to mention Bushmen. There is no mention in the major comparative-evolutionist works of Sir Henry Maine, J.J. Bachofen, J.F. McLennan or L.H. Morgan, all published in the 1860s and 1870s. Theodor Waitz (1863: 334), in his *Introduction to Anthropology*, simply reports that along with the inhabitants of Tierra del Fuego, the Australian Aborigines and some South-East Asian peoples, the Bushmen (Bosjesmans) 'occupy the lowest scale in civilization', although rather more references to Bushmen and Bushman custom appear in his six-volume *Anthropologie der Naturvölker* (Waitz 1859–72). In *Primitive Culture*, E.B. Tylor (1871: I, 344–5) says only that the word *Bosjesman* is the Dutch equivalent of '*Bushman*, "man of the woods or bush"', although his later *Anthropology* (1881) makes passing reference to Bushman racial characteristics and the 'clicks' in Bushman languages. By the end of the century, there was greater interest, especially, it seems, among the diffusionists. Friedrich Ratzel (1897: 262–79) in *The History of Mankind* includes much on Bushmen of the Cape, if not the Kalahari. Most of his concern is directed towards material culture and the dwellings of Cape Bushmen, though he also considers their capacity for music, their crude individualism, their accurate observation of the heavens and their mythology.

Physical anthropologists perhaps had an easier time than early social anthropologists in finding material on Bushman to include in their comparative studies. Writing in the *Journal of the Anthropological Institute*, F.C. Shrubsall (1898: 273) confidently asserted that 'Bush crania' were typically 'sub-dolichocephalic, metriocephalic, orthognatic, mesomeme, platyrhine, leptostaphylinic, cryptozygous, and microcephalic'. But it was not only in that field that such a degree of generalization was maintained. Even in historical studies we find examples like:

Bushmen: frame dwarfish, colour yellowish brown, face fox-like in outline, eyes small and deeply sunk, head dotted over with little knots of twisted hair not much larger than pepper-corns, ears without lobes, stomach protuberant, back exceedingly hollow, limbs slender; weapons bow and poisoned arrow; pursuits those of a hunter; government none but parental; habitations caverns or mats spread over branches of trees; domestic animal the dog; demeanour that of perfect independence; language abounding in clicks and in deep guttural sounds. (Theal 1902: 8)

Theal goes on to note a few exceptions and to give an ethnographic description, but it is not a very flattering one. Worse still, this great historian does not credit the Bushman even with the capability of social evolution. Theal (1902: 18–19) doubts missionary reports of Bushmen having become civilized and Christian, and credits only those part-Bushmen of 'mixed blood' with the capability of advancement to pastoralism, employment and European habits.

The Bushman and Africa

Travelogues

Anthropologists and anthropology students of the twenty-first century tend to think of Bushmen as hunter-gatherers. In the nineteenth century they were quintessentially African, more primitive than Zulus and less well known. By the end of the century, Europe was rapidly being made aware of this 'new' continent, but not yet through ethnography. The main sources were in two other genres, related to each other and in due course to ethnography, but both much more popular: travelogue and romance.

The history of African exploration is replete with accounts of adventures through the Kalahari, certainly from the 1840s onwards, but it would be a mistake to imagine that European readers were given sufficient detail to understand Kalahari Bushmen in the way that they were at that time able to understand, for example, Native North Americans. David Livingstone had been a missionary among the Tswana, and he was much more familiar with Bantu-speaking groups than with Khoisan. His first descriptions of Bushmen in *Missionary Travels* are those during his first journey to Lake Ngami, in 1849, where he reports on them hunting rodents and notes their aboriginality, their love of liberty and their distinctness in language, habits and appearance. Intriguingly, he suggests that 'The specimens [of Bushmen] brought to Europe have been selected, like costermongers' dogs, on account of their extreme ugliness' (Livingstone 1912 [1857]: 38). Whatever the truth of this, the images of Bushmen and life in the Kalahari available in Europe at the time were quite inadequate, and the snippets in travelogues were not enough to bring the Bushman into the forefront of the anthropological imagination.

A great many followed Livingstone to Lake Ngami, and more explored the area to the west in what is now north-western Botswana (Ngamiland) and north-eastern

Namibia. One historian has recorded biographical details of no fewer than 333 'pioneers' of the region (Tabler 1973). Their adventures and their records of encounters with Bushmen became important more than a century later, when in the 1980s and 1990s anthropologists and historians argued over the degree and nature of contact such Bushmen had with outsiders. Two of particular interest were Francis Galton and Charles John Andersson, who explored the region together between 1850 and 1852. Andersson, illegitimate son of an English gentleman and a Swedish servant, had intended to make a life of hunting and exploration in Iceland when, en route, he met Galton in London. Galton persuaded the young naturalist to travel with him to Africa instead. Andersson was easily the most important explorer of south-western Africa. Beginning with *Lake Ngami* (Andersson 1856), he wrote several narratives which were popular in England and the United States as well as diaries and letters which have been published in recent decades by the Windhoek Archives (National Archives of Namibia). He stayed on in Africa after Galton returned to England, and explored, traded, mined copper, and instigated a war between Herero and Nama forces, in which he fought on the Herero side. He died of diphtheria in his fortieth year, in 1867.

Sir Francis Galton, Darwin's cousin, became famous as a psychologist, geneticist and the founder of the eugenics movement. His African fame rests on his *Narrative of an Explorer in Tropical South Africa* (Galton 1853). Both Galton's narrative and Andersson's tell of numerous short encounters with groups of Bushmen, including people we now know as the Ju/'hoansi or !Kung, made famous in ethnography through the efforts of Lorna Marhsall, Richard Lee and others since the 1950s. The difference between these early accounts and those of Marshall or Lee is that the early ones so frequently mention Bushmen not as if in isolation, but in the context of meetings between members of different ethnic groups, of conflict, of servitude, and of travel and trade. Galton, Andersson and their fellow adventurers did not always treat Bushmen well themselves, sometimes shooting them, sometimes holding them hostage. They did help to make Bushmen better known, and to build the myth of Kalahari adventure that ethnographers later took up. Their influence on the 'Kalahari revisionists' like Edwin Wilmsen, in the 1980s and since, was considerable. It was also significant in building up a wider regional understanding important for the development of modern ethnography. Schapera too, for example, found travelogues of profound importance, and when I was about to return to southern Africa for my first major fieldwork in 1973 he advised me to read, not ethnography, but the early travellers.

Romances

It must not be forgotten that, if African travelogues were popular, African romances were even more so, and most certainly had an impact on anthropological thought among the public. African romance was a genre invented and made popular by H. Rider Haggard. He had arrived at the age of nineteen in Durban in 1875, the year Bleek died in Cape Town. Haggard travelled widely in southern Africa in government service, and began his literary career in England in 1881. *King Solomon's Mines* (Haggard 1885), *She* (1887) and subsequent African romances were spectacular successes, far more so than either his serious non-fiction writings on topics like British–Zulu relations or his novels. The categories are important. The 'novels' are realistic tales in settings familiar to readers, while both editors of the time and later literary critics would distinguish 'romances' as more fanciful, sometimes mystical, and related to the later developments of 'science fiction' and 'sword and sorcery'. This is the milieu from which many overseas gained their knowledge of Africa and its peoples, including no doubt overseas anthropologists (see Barnard 1989, 1994).

Haggard's African romances take the characters across the edge of the Kalahari. Bushmen do not really figure, though in *He*, which is a parody of *She*, Haggard's close friend, Scottish folklorist and anthropologist Andrew Lang, introduces Ustani the 'Boshman' chief. This strange character is 'a member of the nearly extinct Boshman tribe of Kokoatinaland'. He was short and tattooed, and his 'long silky hair, originally black, had been blanched to a permanent and snowy white by failures in the attempt to matriculate at Balliol' ('He' 1887: 8–9). One wonders what impression this conveyed, published as it was many years before Lang's serious commentaries on Bushman mythology (Lang 1913: I, 169–71, II, 34–40).

Of course, not all representations in literature were funny. In his study of 'the savage in literaure', anthropologist and literary critic Brian Street (1975) gives several examples of negative stereotypes of the Bushman in nineteenth- and early twentieth-century English fiction. He relates these to the tendency in European non-fiction of the time to concentrate on people's place in a scale of evolution and on comparisons between 'superior' European and 'inferior' savage institutions. Comparisons to apes and monkeys were also rife, and for writers such as John Buchan and Bertford Mitford the Bushman offered a literary tool with which to enhance the glories of European culture and even European art. For example, from one of Buchan's more serious works we read of the Bushman as 'one of the lowest of created types', a 'troglodyte, small, emaciated, with protruding chest and spindle legs', and who 'had no social organisation and whose only skill is fol-lowing spoor and a rudimentary cave art' (quoted in Street 1975: 86). And from Mitford, the Bushman is 'no more than half ape', a 'descendant of the baboons', and the Bushman's cave art is 'repulsive, grotesque, obscene, the handiwork in bygone ages of the most primitive race in the world, now nearly extinct, the wild Bushman' (also quoted in Street 1975: 86).

Art and Ethnography

The Bushman in Western Art and Photography

Khoisan peoples, and especially the San, were probably for the first few centuries of contact better depicted through artwork than through written words. Among relatively recent collections of such early Cape art are *The Khoikhoi at the Cape of Good Hope* (Smith and Pheiffer 1993) and *Vanished Lifestyles* (Steyn 1990). The former, according to the author of its text, contains the drawings of a single anonymous artist, possibly Jan Victors, a student of Rembrandt. The drawings, in pencil, pen and wash, are mainly of everyday life among the Khoekhoe, and at least one appears to show Bushmen. The caption reads (in Dutch): 'Because the Hottentots live scattered about, here and there, ... therefore they are called Bushmen by those who live in the kraals, that is, in a crowd together.' It continues in a new paragraph: 'According to Colbe [Kolb], the Bushmen are like robbers, and they keep themselves hidden like them amongst the mountains where they cannot get caught' (Smith and Pheiffer 1993: 56).

Vanished Lifestyles includes many more paintings and drawings, from a variety of later artists. Among the artists who stand out are Samuel Daniell and C.D. Bell. Daniell spent some months with Bushmen in 1802, and his paintings present an image of decorative beauty in a savage landscape. Steyn's commentary is on the Bushmen rather than on the art, but elsewhere critics have sought to explain what Daniell saw in his subjects, and more importantly what his viewers might have seen. In the words of Pieter Jolly (a rock art specialist), Daniell's painting *Bushmen Hottentots Armed for an Expedition* [*sic*] depicts Bushmen 'in stylised, classical pose high above the surrounding countryside – primitive but proud lords surveying a wild domain' (Jolly 1996: 199). Jolly and others have seen 'noble savage' imagery in Daniell's work, and such a vision of Bushmen was undoubtedly appropriate for the age of empire that was to come. The Scottish immigrant Bell, Cape Surveyor General until 1872, became famous for his idealized painting of *The Landing of Jan van Riebeeck*. In his portrayals of Bushmen, he captures well the sense of life, work and play in San society, and, as with F. Le Vaillant, W.J. Burchell and many others, gives a sympathetic treatment.

Not so with photography, of course. The contrast is striking between nineteenth-century paintings and, for example, the photographs included by Namibian–American anthropologist Rob Gordon (1997) in his account of the 1925 Denver African Expedition. Equally, the photographs of Bleek and Lloyd's informants and contemporary paintings of the same individuals tell quite different stories (see Godby 1996). The worst photographs from the 1870s, described by Michael Godby, show //Kabbo and others naked and miserable, hunched over and being measured. The best, and the paintings from the period, illustrate elegantly dressed and smiling individuals, sometimes even with coat and tie, ring and earring, hat and European-style walking stick. The Denver Expedition photos, as well as those chosen by Schapera for his *Khoisan Peoples of South Africa* (1930), show that not much had changed by the 1920s. Indeed, things seem to have got worse. The film of the Denver Expedition was advertised as '"*The Bushman*": An Epic of Wild Beasts and Wilder Men, Greatest Film Ever Brought Out of Africa!' (Gordon 1997: 88). In his accompanying talk, the film-maker intoned: 'Making the acquaintance of the pure breed of bushman was like gaining the confidence of a wild thing. We baited them like we would bait an animal' (quoted in Gordon 1997: 91).

Bushman Art and Western Ethnography

The beginnings of the study of South African rock art are usually dated to the late 1860s, when geologist and trader George William Stow began copying paintings he found in the mountains. He acknowledged the relation between recording the paintings and working out the past history of Bushmen in a letter in 1870. Stow had been 'making pilgrimages to the various old Bushman caves among the mountains', and copying the paintings, he says, 'gave rise to the idea in my mind of collecting material enough to compile a history of the manners and customs of the Bushmen, as depicted by themselves' (quoted in Lewis-Williams 1981: 15). Stow died in 1882, and both his superb compilation of Bushman ethnography (Stow 1905: 1–231) and reproductions of his watercolour copies of Bushman paintings (Stow and Bleek 1930) were published long after his death. Lucy Lloyd purchased the manuscript of the former from Stow's widow, and it was edited by the great historian George McCall Theal, while Dorothea Bleek added the text to the latter.

Stow's Bushman ethnography is not much read these days, but it does stand within the grand amateur tradition. Indeed, at least in their finished state (as edited by Theal and checked for accuracy by Lloyd), Stow's chapters on the Bushmen might well count as the first true Bushman ethnography – as opposed to travelogues with ethnographic description. Its production was outstanding for the time. Twenty-two illustrations are included in Stow's *Native Races of South Africa*, and eleven of these deal with Bushmen – Stow's copies of rock art, watercolours of implements, and photographs. The text is based on Stow's first-hand observations, including anecdotes from his meetings with Bushmen. It appears that Stow also used local magistrate J.M. Orpen's unpublished notes. Where he differs from other writers of that time is in his skilful blend of generalization and example, and in his constant citation of comparative material from earlier travellers such as Le Vaillant, Sparrman and Barrow, and scholars such as Bleek and Lloyd. He even cites Max Müller on comparative mythology. For reasons of space, Theal deleted many of Stow's extracts from the works of other writers, but the text of the book as printed still numbers over 600 pages.

From an early twenty-first-century point of view, the oddest thing about Stow's account is that it is written almost entirely in the past tense. There is no assumption of an ethnographic present, and Stow consciously combines history with his ethnography. From his arrival in the Cape in 1843, Stow had taken up residence in the frontier zones and beyond. He signed the preface to his book at Bloemfontein, in 1880. He mentions locales, reserves several chapters for specific Bushman groups, and describes events and changes as often as 'Bushmen in their undisturbed state'. It is clear too that he had much respect for individual Bushmen and for this undisturbed state, including their music and dance (Stow 1905: 102–24) as well as their art. There is no doubt that some Bushmen were still painting in Stow's time. Theophilus Hahn and others reported the existence of living artists in South Africa and the German territory of South-West Africa (modern Namibia) in the nineteenth century, and the existence of rock paintings of ox wagons undoubtedly confirms their elusive presence. Stow's second-hand account is famous:

> The last-known Bushman artist of the Malutis was shot in the Witteberg Native Reserve, where he had been on a marauding expedition, and had captured some horses. He was evidently a man of considerable repute among his race. He had ten small horn pots hanging from a belt, each of which contained a different coloured paint. The informant of the writer told him that he saw the belt, that there were no two colours alike, and that each had a marked difference from the rest ... Thus perished the last of the painter tribes of Bushmen! (Stow 1905: 230)

Stow's best copies of Eastern Cape and Orange Free State rock art were published in 1930, having passed from Mrs Stow to Lucy Lloyd, and upon Lloyd's death to Dorothea Bleek. Dorothea felt it her duty to publish them and to set them in the context of a disappearing art form, mirroring disappearing folklore and, worse, a disappearing people. In her introduction to the published collection, she notes that Stow himself had heard tell of the last artist in the region where he worked. That was about the time of the 'Basuto war of 1866', whereas in Barrow's time they had still been painting in earnest (Stow and Bleek 1930: xvi-xviii). Dorothea compares this to the situation with the folklore, specifically noting that in 1910 'children and nephews' of her father's and aunt's informants had preserved no knowledge at all of the stories recorded between 1870 and 1880.

There is no doubt that Stow's art is wonderfully executed and beautiful, to the Western mind, in composition – although occasionally later experts came to doubt the accuracy and sometimes even the genuineness of his copies. All the reproductions are rectangular, in 'landscape' (as opposed to 'portrait') mode, and in effect many are fragments, or only partial copies, of larger painting-covered rock areas. Seventy-four appear in the book, mainly in rich dark reds, browns and grey-blacks. The folio reproductions are typically about half the size of Stow's paintings and the originals from which they are copied. Dorothea found sixty of the original

Bushman rock paintings reproduced in the book, but a number had deteriorated even then, in the 1920s.

Although at times on the wane, the close relation between mythology and rock art has existed almost since the beginning of South African rock art studies. If not recognized by Stow, it was picked up by his contemporary, J.M. Orpen. Orpen copied paintings in the Maluti Mountains of present-day Lesotho. More importantly, he tried to explain them in the context of myths told to him by his guide, a Bushman named Qing who had 'never seen a white man but in fighting' (Orpen 1874: 2). Orpen's account in the *Cape Monthly Magazine* was widely read, and it enabled Wilhelm Bleek both to compare Maluti to /Xam mythology and to comment:

> This fact [of the existence of Bushman paintings] can hardly be valued sufficiently. It gives at once to Bushman art a higher character, and teaches us to look upon its products not as the mere daubing of figures for idle pastime, but as an attempt, however, imperfect, at a truly artistic conception of the ideas which most deeply moved the Bushman mind, and filled it with religious feelings. (W.H.I. Bleek 1874: 13)

One of those to read Orpen's account was Andrew Lang, who later fostered its republication in the *Journal of Folklore*. Lang did not regard Bushman mythology very highly, but repeatedly claimed 'their religion is on a far higher level than their mythology' (Lang 1913: II, 34). Lang cites both Bleek and Orpen, but there is no doubt that Orpen's record is not to the high standard of Bleek, and it was collected via interpreters from one main informant and under more difficult conditions.

Conclusion

In the late nineteenth century, anthropology as we know it was emerging. Until very late in the century it was not yet taught in universities and was still the practice of amateurs, who wrote for an educated public as well as for specialists. Anthropological theory grew to prominence before ethnography became commonplace. Thus ethnographic description, particularly of Bushmen, is as often to be found in travelogues as in anything else. And it is from travelogues that theorists first took their ethnographic understanding, and perhaps from the genre of romance their image.

The classic notion of the myth-telling, rock-painting Bushman is a product of the Victorian era, and it owes much too to the pioneering research of George Stow and the Bleek family. Bleek's research marks the beginning of the academic tradition of Bushman studies, which began in the summer of 1870, just a year before many of the most important publications in nineteenth-century anthropology and the founding of the Anthropological Institute. Yet only in 1911 was *Specimens of Bushman Folklore* finally published, with subsequent facsimile reprints in 1968 and 2001. Further Bleek and Lloyd material was published through Dorothea Bleek's efforts in the 1930s, but it was in the 2000s that Bleek's plan to publish extensively from his notes was fully revived, through the efforts of artist and Bleek scholar Pippa Skotnes. The Bleek Collection is now on UNESCO's 'Memory of the World' Register for Documentary Heritage, and all the notebooks of Bleek and Lloyd are available to scholars via the website of the J.W. Jagger Library of the University of Cape Town.

–4–

Beckoning of the Kalahari

Many twentieth-century anthropologists would come to see the Bushman through the eyes of Isaac Schapera. His *Khoisan Peoples of South Africa* (Schapera 1930) summarized all that was then known of Khoisan peoples and brought to the attention of English-speaking readers a wealth of German-language material collected from the 1860s onwards. In German-language anthropology, Bushmen provided one of several models of the ultimate and primal ancient culture, the *Urkultur* that in that tradition was long believed to underlie all subsequent cultural spheres spread by migration and diffusion across the earth.

In anglophone anthropology, the concern with Bushmen was not that great except within South Africa itself, where ethnographic, linguistic, archaeological, rock art, historical and biological interests combined to give quite a different picture. From the 1920s, South Africa became one of the first countries to see the emergence of professional social anthropology, and studies by a number of writers, not least Schapera and Dorothea Bleek, contributed to new images of the Bushman in anthropology. Meanwhile, the public face of the Bushman was changing too, and cultural-historical anthropology competed with structural-functionalist for professional and public perceptions of the Bushman 'race'. And developing alongside social anthropology was a South African archaeological tradition that was to parallel social anthropology and take the lead in Bushman studies until the dawn of the modern era of Kalahari ethnography in the 1950s.

Stone Age Archaeology in South Africa

Janette Deacon's (1990) 'Weaving the Fabric ...' gives a splendid review of the history of Stone Age archaeology in South Africa. She begins her story in the 1850s, with butterfly collector turned artefact gatherer Colonel J.H. Bowker and his brother Thomas Holden Bowker. Which one made the first discoveries, and whether it was in 1855 or 1858, is a matter of very long debate (albeit a not-very-important debate). What is important is, first, that they accumulated stone tools not long after similar collections were being made in Europe and, secondly, that they and their contemporaries collected with a view towards comparison. Encouraged by these European discoveries, T.H. Bowker sent part of his collection to England.

Soon others followed suit, and before long luminaries such as Sir John Lubbock (e.g. 1870) published comparative commentaries on the artefacts uncovered in the Cape.

From 1881, again following developments in Europe, classification schemes began to appear. Scholars at first used European terms, such as 'Palaeolithic' and 'Neolithic', though Cambridge anthropologist A.C. Haddon, on a visit to South Africa in 1905, argued that South African archaeology must develop its own understandings of its 'Stone Age', especially in its geological contexts. Leading archaeologists of the following decade such as Louis Péringuey (1911) used a mixture of local and European terminology. Péringuey was Director of the South African Museum and Volume 8 of the museum's journal (really more an occasional paper series) was given over to the subject. Actually an entomologist by trade (and a specialist on beetles), this amateur archaeologist seems to have been the first scholar to use the word 'San' in preference to the word 'Bushman'. He (correctly) recognized San workmanship in the artefacts of South Africa's 'Stone Ages', and even speculated (incorrectly) on the influence of shipwrecked mariners and wandering adventurers on the tool-making practices of the San. Péringuey was also important for his work in establishing the antiquity of humanity in Africa at a time when many European scholars believed that *Homo* emerged in Europe and evolved to its 'high' European form *in situ*. Indeed, his discoveries included stone tools now believed to be at least 500,000 years old, known in his day as 'Stellenbosch Culture' (from their discovery in Stellenbosch in 1899), although they were later to be classified as Acheulian (by analogy with similar finds from St Acheul in France).

The professionalization of archaeology in South Africa began with A.J.H. Goodwin. He graduated from Cambridge in 1922 with a degree in archaeology, and with Haddon as one of his mentors. He became research assistant in ethnology at Cape Town in 1923, and there did library research under A.R. Radcliffe-Brown. After Péringuey's death in 1924, Goodwin was given the opportunity to sift through the collections at the South African Museum, and in so doing came to see the necessity of working within a local rather than a European framework – grouping tools first by type and then by site.

Goodwin's field research and comparative work soon led to the classification of the Stone Age into two broad periods: Early (typified by Stellenbosch Culture) and Late (including the Eastern, Smithfield and Pygmy industries, said to be similar to the European Middle and Upper Palaeolithic and Mesolithic). This scheme, which Goodwin first presented in 1925, was supplemented just two years later by the introduction of the Middle Stone Age, which included the Eastern or Stillbay culture of the 1925 scheme, while the term Pygmy was replaced by Wilton. Smithfield culture came to be divided into Smithfield A, B, and C. By the end of the decade the classification was well established (published as Goodwin and Van Riet Lowe 1929), and indeed was soon in use in other parts of Africa and India too.

Goodwin's collaborator, Clarence 'Peter' Van Riet Lowe, became director of the Bureau of Archaeology in Johannesburg in 1925, while Goodwin himself made his base at the University of Cape Town. He taught ethnology and archaeology there for several decades. After Van Riet Lowe's death in 1956 and Goodwin's in 1959, there was an influx of foreign scholars, with Ray Inskeep (from Cambridge) taking over Goodwin's position at Cape Town. Despite his importance in the history of South African archaeology, Goodwin had only supervised one Ph.D. student – Revil Mason, later Director of the Archaeological Research Unit at the University of the Witwatersrand (Wits). Meanwhile, the Cambridge connection maintained its importance, for example, through the field research of J.D. Clark in what was then Northern Rhodesia and in his works of synthesis (e.g. Clark 1959); and subsequently through Cambridge graduate John Parkington. We shall meet up with Parkington again later.

Social Anthropology in South Africa

Queen Victoria died in 1901, and Victorian values no longer seemed to represent the height of civilization. Diffusionist thinking had already supplanted evolutionist in German and Austrian anthropology, and would soon take hold in the United Kingdom too. It was as if Ancient Egypt had succeeded England as England's own model of the greatest achievement of humankind. The great pioneer of ethnographic fieldwork, W.H.R. Rivers, announced his conversion from evolutionism to diffusionism in 1911. It was no coincidence that this was just after a trip to Egypt, which he undertook with diffusionist Egyptologist and anatomist G. Elliot Smith. In 1922, Howard Carter, working under Lord Carnarvon, discovered the tomb of Tutankhamun in Egypt's Valley of the Kings. Rivers died that same year, among the last of the old guard in British anthropology.

The year 1922 was in fact the key date for the transformation of anthropology in the British Empire and Commonwealth. The new generation was led by Bronislaw Malinowski and Rivers's student A.R. Radcliffe-Brown. Radcliffe-Brown moved from the Pacific Island of Tonga to South Africa in 1920, and took up his first chair, at the University of Cape Town, in 1921. There he joined the new School of African Life and Languages (see Hammond-Tooke 1997: 15–38). Malinowski began the most significant phase of his career in 1922, with the founding of social anthropology at the London School of Economics, and both Radcliffe-Brown and Malinowski published their major ethnographies in 1922.

Their new kind of anthropology was functionalism, sometimes divided into two forms: functionalism proper and structural-functionalism. The former was the product of the thinking of Malinowski, a Polish-born anthropologist who migrated to Britain, to Australia, back to Britain and finally to the United States. His formal theory (Malinowski 1944) emphasized biological needs and their cultural responses, but his students took from him instead his more general approach, which was the emphasis on studying what is apparent in the present and not speculating on how things came to be. Malinowski's most significant fieldwork was in the Trobriand Islands of today's Papua New Guinea, and he wrote up his key Trobriand ethnography in the Canary Islands. He visited South Africa in 1934 and showed some sympathy towards the new-found nationalism of King Subuza II (Sobhuza II) of the Swazi (Kuper 2005b: 190–1), whereas the general trend of anglophone anthropology, both analytically and politically, was towards a model of society that incorporated 'natives' and Europeans alike.

Structural-functionalism was represented by the Englishman Radcliffe-Brown and his many students around the world (e.g. Radcliffe-Brown 1952). Radcliffe-Brown did not like to be labelled a functionalist or structural-functionalist, but considered himself simply a scientist who studied the structure and function of society, rather as a biologist would study the structure and function of parts of a plant or animal. He travelled the world widely, holding teaching positions in several South African universities as well as in England, Australia, the United States, China, Brazil and Egypt. Although it was short-lived and he had few students, his time at Cape Town was significant for anthropology and especially, of course, for South African anthropology. He would return to Australia, where he had been before the First World War, to take the foundation chair at Sydney in 1926.

While Radcliffe-Brown introduced anthropology to Cape Town, Winifred Tucker Hoernlé did the same at the University of the Witwatersrand in Johannesburg. Her husband, R.F. Alfred Hoernlé, was professor of philosophy there, and although Winifred never gained a chair she had great influence through the many students she taught at Wits between 1923 and 1938. One of them, Max Gluckman, called her the 'mother of South African anthropology'. Winifred Hoernlé had had a similar training to Radcliffe-Brown, having studied anthropology and psychology at Cambridge under A.C. Haddon and W.H.R. Rivers from 1908 to 1910. Her theoretical ideas were similar to those of Radcliffe-Brown. She was a Khoisan specialist herself, and did fieldwork among the Nama of Little and Great Namaqualand in 1912 and in the 1920s (see, for example, Hoernlé 1985). She eventually resigned her lectureship in order to forge a career in race relations.

Meanwhile in the Afrikaans-speaking universities, anthropology was beginning in quite a different mould – with influences from German-language diffusionism and from American cultural anthropology, which ultimately had the same roots. Indeed, this tradition was also to influence government policy on southern Africa's hunter-gatherers, notably in South West Africa (now Namibia) in the 1920s and 1930s (Gordon 1992: 147–54). Ethnographic accounts of Bushmen were few, but Stellenbosch professor P.J. Schoeman (1957) wrote of his travels with an elderly Hai//om man and of the effects of the incursion of Bantu-speakers on the ability of Hai//om and !Xũ to maintain a hunting lifestyle. Schoeman, among others, sought protection for Bushmen under apartheid, and from 1949 to 1953 he had served as chairman of the Commission for the Preservation of the Bushmen (Gordon 1992: 160–7). In 1964, the infamous Odendaal Commission finally established the boundaries of apartheid Bushmanland along with those of similar 'homelands' for other peoples, and the effects are still felt across Namibia to this day.

The most important intellectual figure in the Afrikaans tradition was W.W.M. Eiselen, who began teaching anthropology at Stellenbosch in 1926 (under the name *etnografie*, subsequently *etnologie* and later *volkekunde*). A year later he was joined by Khoisan-language expert J.A. Engelbrecht, who did ethnographic fieldwork with the Khoekhoe-speaking Korana (!Orana) of the Northern Cape. The second-year course material included a discussion of Bushman culture and comparisons with other *natuurvolke* ('nature peoples'), and the third-year material a more theoretical treatment of the culture history of Africa. In contrast, the Cape Town curriculum dealt with such things as the origins and development of law, the social functions of ritual and totemism, and broadly 'primitive sociology' (Hammond-Tooke 1997: 60–1, 199). It was in the latter curriculum under Radcliffe-Brown, and the Wits equivalent under Hoernlé, that the 'British' tradition of South African anthropology came to be.

Among Radcliffe-Brown's Cape Town students was Isaac Schapera, an enthusiast young scholar from Little Namaqualand, who had grown up, the son of a Jewish immigrant and shopkeeper, amidst Nama-speaking people there. 'Sakkie' or 'Schap' as he became known to his friends and colleagues, was in fact the only Cape Town student to see through an undergraduate training with Radcliffe-Brown. Radcliffe-Brown suggested in 1926 that he should go on for his Ph.D. either to Berkeley to work under Robert Lowie, or to London to work under Malinowski. He chose London, but worked more under the Africanist C.G. Seligman than under Malinowski (Kuper 2005b: 181–4). Like Malinowski himself and several London School of Economics students of the time, he chose a library topic for his thesis: 'The Tribal System in South Africa: a Study of the Bushmen and the Hottentots' (Schapera 1929). A revised version, using the new collective term for 'the Bushmen and the Hottentots', was published a year later: *The Khoisan Peoples of South Africa: Bushmen and Hottentots* (Schapera 1930). Schapera was later to hold Radcliffe-Brown's old chair at Cape Town, and to return as professor to the London School of Economics. He made his name as an ethnographer with his postdoctoral research on Tswana tribes of the Bechuanaland Protectorate (modern Botswana), but his *Khoisan Peoples* is still held in the highest regard both within Bushman studies and outside.

In spite of the generic term 'Khoisan', Schapera sought clearly to differentiate 'Khoi' (herders) from 'San' (hunter-gatherers). His usage is borrowed from German biological anthropologist Leonhard Schultze (1928: 211), who had invented it only a couple of years before. From Schultze (1907, 1928) also he took eleven of the photographs included in the book, and both Schultze's term and most of his photos had been intended to show biological affinities. Schapera describes such 'physical characters', along with geography, history and dress, in Part I of his book, while Part II deals with 'Culture of the Bushmen', Part III with 'Culture of the Hottentots', and Part IV (the shortest) with Khoisan languages. His overwhelming concern was with what he termed 'culture', including social organization, economic life, religion and magic, art and knowledge, and so on. Yet his criteria for inclusion of people in the category Khoisan was primarily biological. Schapera (1930: 3) classifies the 'native inhabitants' of southern Africa as 'the Bushmen, the Hottentots, the Bergdama [Damara], and the Bantu', and he notes that the Damara 'are racially a true negro people, differing in appearance from both the Bushmen and the Hottentots'. Yet he adds that Damara speak the same language as the Nama, and like Bushmen live in small nomadic groups and hunt and gather.

Schapera died at the age of ninety-eight in 2003, and although I never asked him about this directly it has always seemed clear to me that his exclusion of Damara from Khoisan was based on the mistaken priority given to race over culture in the 1920s. I think he would have agreed, and his style of ethnography from the 1930s onwards would come to emphasize social action and social structure, and history too, both over race and over an abstract notion of culture. As Gluckman (1975: 24) put it, 'Schapera's achievement was to bring into anthropology the view that district commissioner and chief, missionary and magician, were persons within a single social system, composed of groups of different culture, and that their relationships to one another and to others should be studied in the same way.'

The content of *The Khoisan Peoples*, however, reflects the dependence Schapera had on library sources. Unlike his later writings on Tswana, in which the wider social system with DC and chief or missionary and magician came alive, *The Khoisan Peoples* concerns simply the accumulated detail of 'traditional' life recorded by amateurs like missionary S.S. Dornan in the 1910s or medical officer to the South West Africa Administration Louis Fourie in the 1920s. Fourie himself had attempted an overiew of Bushman life in South West Africa (Namibia) just two years before (Fourie 1928), although the result was heavily weighted towards the ethnography of the Hai//om, the group Fourie knew best. Schapera sought to generalize, not so much for Bushmen as a whole, but in terms of regional similarities: Northern Bushmen (Hai//om, !Xũ, 'Auen', etc.), Central (Naron or Naro, etc.) and Southern (especially /Xam). He also brought to light for his English-speaking audience the nineteenth- and early twentieth-century German writings of Gustav Fritsch, Siegfried Passarge and many others. He aimed for balance, for packing as much fact as possible within a small space and for ethnographic accuracy. In this he succeeded, and implicit in his monograph is, on occasion, his adjudication between conflicting sources. However, he stayed away from the explication of debates, notably the very important one between Fritsch and Passarge, the importance of which would only come to light in anglophone Bushman studies in the revisionist era of the 1980s and 1990s (Wilmsen 1997: 13–37). We shall explore this squabble, along with its more recent counterpart, in Chapter 8.

Amateurs and Antiquarians: Dornan, 'Doris' and the Abbé

The professionals had their jobs to do, but, once Schapera left the field to work instead with Tswana, Bushman studies was left in the hands of committed amateurs and enthusiasts of various sorts. Much the same is true of Khoekhoe studies too: for example, L.F. Maingard, the great expert on Korana language and culture, was actually the professor of French at Wits and an immigrant from Mauritius. For him, Khoisan languages, customs and even prehistory were a hobby, although he did make it to the central Kalahari and even wrote a few comparative papers, using his own work and that of Dornan and Dorothea Bleek (e.g. Maingard 1963). This, I think, added an excitement to the scholarly routine, an excitement not characterized generally in anthropology in the studies of other peoples at that time.

The Rev. S.S. Dornan

Samuel Shaw Dornan was one of the major ethnographers of the lean years prior to the First World War. He was born in County Down in Ireland in 1871. He migrated to South Africa and served in the Anglo-Boer War of 1899 to 1902, subsequently joining the Paris Evangelical Mission in Basutoland (modern Lesotho). He also worked as a government surveyor in that territory before moving to Southern Rhodesia (Zimbabwe), where he worked in the Native Presbyterian Mission and conducted ethnographic fieldwork on the border with the Bechuanaland Protectorate (Botswana). He published a major monograph (Dornan 1925) and a number of shorter works, the most important being his essay on 'the Tati Bushmen' (1917).

The main title of his monograph, *Pygmies and Bushmen of the Kalahari*, is perhaps misleading, as the text deals with Bushmen and not much with those we think of as Pygmies. However, he does consider the Kalahari Bushmen and Ituri Forest Pygmies to be related peoples, the latter possibly 'a mixed northern remnant of the Bushmen' (Dornan 1925: 46). He also compares what he saw as the division of the Bushmen into two 'strains' to the situation among Central African Pygmies: each group having a 'light strain' and a 'dark' one (1925: 71–2). He considered the 'Hottentots' a 'mixed race', and the last third of his monograph is devoted to 'Hottentots', Damara, Herero, Kgalagari, Tswana and other neighbours of the Bushmen. Because of his concern with race and racial history it is easy to write off Dornan simply as a racist, but his ethnographic record speaks to me as much of his concern to document details and make comparisons among Bushman groups, often with examples from experience, sometimes from his reading. Still, there is a tension in his writing which reflects, I think, an equal tension in his own mind between his preconceived ideas of race and mental capacity on the one hand, and his observations on the other. This passage shows those tensions:

> The Bushmen were low in the scale of mentality. They had an extensive knowledge of the outdoor world, especially of the habits of wild animals, and the means of capturing and killing them. They were wonderful hunters and trackers, and knew all that could be known of the country in which they dwelt, but when taken out of their own district had no special ability for finding their way about. Their reflective faculties were poorly developed. (Dornan 1925: 53)

Because of its length, the subtitle of his monograph is rarely ever used in bibliographical citations. Yet it explains his interest well: *An Account of the Hunting Tribes Inhabiting the Great Arid Plateau of the Kalahari, Their Precarious Manner of Living, Their Habits, Customs & Beliefs, with Some Reference to Bushman Art, Both Early & of Recent Date, & to the Neighbouring African Tribes.* He follows the passage quoted above with the line 'The most wonderful thing about the Bushmen was their artistic talent' (1925: 53), and it is clear that he wanted to document all that he could, good or bad, about the peoples of the Kalahari and surrounding areas, and to explain what he saw in both historical and regional-comparative perspectives. The latter is Dornan at his best, and his monograph is exemplary of the strange amateur tradition prevalent in that era and which marks a real transition between the nineteenth- and twentieth-century styles of ethnographic reporting, as well as between nineteenth- and twentieth-century theoretical concerns in anthropology.

D.F. Bleek

Dorothea Frances Bleek has many names. She was known as Doris within her family, as Missis to her informants, as Miss Bleek, D.F. Bleek or Dorothea Bleek in the literature, and often simply as Dorothea among Khoisan specialists in academia today. In 1913 her aunt Lucy had been South Africa's first female recipient of an honorary doctorate, granted by the University of the Cape of Good Hope (later the University of Cape Town). Yet in 1936 Dorothea turned down an honorary doctorate at the University of the Witwatersrand on the grounds that 'There could only ever be one Dr Bleek.'

Dorothea Bleek's importance in Bushman studies rests on no fewer than three great contributions: continuing to publish material from the collections of her father and her aunt (linguistic, folkloristic and ethnographic); real fieldwork with /Xam, /'Auni and other groups in South Africa, with Naron, Auen (≠Au//eisi) and other groups in Namibia, and with !O !Kung (!Xũ) in Angola; and the publication of her *Comparative Vocabularies of Bushman Languages* (D.F. Bleek 1929) and her posthumous *Bushman Dictionary* (1956). The *Bushman Dictionary* is truly a monumental work, including 773 pages of material from twenty-eight Bushman languages and dialects, including her Hadza material from Tanzania. She worked on it for many years, along with pulling out ethnographic bits and pieces from what had been collected by her father and aunt. This was published mainly in the journal *Bantu Studies* (now known as *African Studies*) between 1931 and 1936 and has recently been republished with an excellent commentary by Jeremy Hollmann (2004). Through the 1930s and 1940s she gradually gave her collection of Bleek family Bushman notebooks to the J.W. Jagger Library of the University of Cape Town, and these would eventually form what we know today as the Bleek Collection.

Dorothea's primary stint as a fieldworker was with the Naron (as she knew them), later called Nharo or Naro. This was in 1921 and 1922, after preliminary work in the Windhoek jail in 1920. Dr Fourie had arranged for her to stay at the empty police station at Sandfontein, on the border of South West Africa and the Bechuanaland Protectorate (by the present-day border posts of Buitepos in Namibia and Mamuno in Botswana). The confusion over what ethnic group names to use was looming, for she was working there both with the Central people she called Naron (and Passarge had called Aikwe) and the quite different Northern people she called Auen or //k'au//en (and Passarge had called Aukwe). Dorothea Bleek's *The Naron* (1928) was the first genuine Bushman ethnography, in the sense of an attempt at a 'complete' account of the way of life of one specific group, and nothing else (if we ignore the comparative material on 'Auen' at the end). It numbered only sixty-seven pages, but brings in details of mode of life, times and seasons, marriage, motherhood, medicine, initiation ceremonies, religious beliefs, music, dance, art, games, folklore and grammar, among other things. It was to be influential as a major source for Schapera (1930), even if not itself widely read in the anthropological world beyond southern Africa.

Dorothea was never much of a theoretician, but arguably neither were those who used her work. Schapera himself was interested in the facts of Bushman life, not in the implications for generalization about hunter-gatherers or comparisons with non-hunter-gatherers. Yet of all the works later cited by Marshall Sahlins in his famous essay on the 'original affluent society' (Sahlins 1974: 1–39), few are as exemplary for his viewpoint as this uncited one from Dorothea Bleek:

A race that is satisfied with such a slender outfit leads of necessity a simple life, has little work to do and many idle hours to dispose of. For years I have been studying Bushmen in different parts of the country, some in servitude, others living their natural life, and from what I have seen, as well as from the picture of themselves given in their folk-lore, I am sure they all lived a care-free, idle life, as long as they were unmolested by invaders of their land. Men hunted for a few hours or a few days, then had nothing to do as long as the game lasted. A woman's daily task of gathering roots and wood and fetching water was soon finished except in times of scarcity. Half or more than half of each day was spent in lounging about, watching bird and beast, and talking – always talking. (D.F. Bleek, in Stow and Bleek 1930: xxiii–xxiv)

It is remarkable that anthropology had not noticed, but then Bleek was writing here for rock art enthusiasts, and probably mainly South African ones at that. She was most certainly not writing these words as a contribution to anthropological theory. What she was suggesting went against anthropology's mistaken perceptions of hunter-gatherers, who were supposed to live a difficult and hard-working life, presumably a life without much time for the frivolities of art, music or storytelling. Indeed, the concept of 'work' seems to have a peculiar place in the Bleek family's image of the typical Bushman. In *The Naron* (D.F. Bleek 1928: 42–4), Dorothea comments on both the Bushman's carefree lifestyle and his great capacity for manual labour for the white man. And *Specimens of Bushman Folklore* is enigmatically dedicated 'To all faithful workers' (Bleek and Lloyd 1911: v).

If Dorothea had contributed to anthropological theory, it would perhaps have been more likely for her to have joined the diffusionist camp. I say that not only because of her conscious German heritage, but also because, like Stow, and like the Cape archaeologists of her day, she saw migration and diffusion, especially in art and artefact, of crucial importance for understanding the peoples of southern Africa. Later, in her introduction to Stow's work, she remarks on the similarities between southern, central and North African rock art and the rock art of rock shelters of Spain, and she credits Spain as the source for these traditions (Stow and Bleek 1930: xxv). Elsewhere, she comments on prehistoric painters of the Wilton tool tradition of southern Africa, that they 'must have left Rhodesia before the art there had reached its widest development' (Van der Riet, Van der Riet and Bleek 1940: xix). She adds that they might have come into contact with Smithfield people, the other main Later Stone Age tool tradition, and that their painting 'seems to have deteriorated *en route*, perhaps a natural result of passing regions where painting was difficult, such as the edges of the Kalahari' (1940: xix).

This interest in migration was commonplace in rock art studies of the period, as it had been long before, for Stow. Although writers tended to regard the art as Bushman rather than pre-Bushman in the locales where it was found, they typically saw in it changes due to their travels. For instance, Herbert Kühn (1930: 47), writing on South West African (Namibian) rock art, argued that the Bushman who had painted it had affinities with the painters of Lake Tanganyika and North Africa, and even that 'the representatives of the Bushman art are actually a race allied to the Caspian' (1930: 54). Wherever it came from, Bushman art may have been Bushman, but it was not indigenous.

The Abbé Breuil

The most extreme case of other-origin was the mysterious 'white lady' of the Brandberg. The great rock art pioneer of what later became Namibia, Abbé Henri Breuil, described the painting and its artistic, cultural and geological contexts in his monograph by that title (Breuil 1955). He actually produced a number of other splendid books in folio format and with his own rock art drawings, covering many sites of the Brandberg of east-cental Namibia and the nearby Erongo Mountains. Yet is it is the 'white lady' that captured people's attention.

Breuil tells the story of his own discovery of the painting in the introduction to the book on the 'white lady'. He had been studying French cave paintings. Then during a trip to southern Africa in 1929 he was, in Johannesburg, shown a water-colour copy of the 'white lady' painting that had been done in 1917, not long after its 'discovery'. In 1937, he saw copies of the 'white lady' painting and more paint-ings from the same shelter, in a printed book (Frobenius 1931: plates 78–84). In 1938 he was shown tiny negatives of the painting, but enlargements were not easily come by in those years. Before enlargements could be made, the war intervened. A few years later, he reports:

> My secretary and assistant, Miss Mary E. Boyle, had been working in the Bermudas since February 1941. One morning a young airman came up to her desk and without any preamble said: 'General Smuts would be much obliged if you would fly the Atlantic, go to Lisbon where the Abbé Breuil is working, board a neutral ship with him and travel to Lourenço Marques, a neutral port. For the Abbé's very specialised knowl-edge is needed in South Africa.' He then saluted and left her. (Breuil 1955: 2)

Breuil and Boyle were assigned to the Archaeological Survey of the Union of South Africa in Johannesburg, and there in late 1941 he chanced upon enlarge-ments of the 'white lady' photographs. Breuil and Boyle debated over whether 'she' was Cretan or Greek. Breuil sent a further enlargement of the head to Smuts, with a note reading: 'I send you the portrait of a charming young girl, who has been waiting for us on a rock in the Brandberg range for perhaps three thousand years; do you think it well to keep her waiting much longer?' Smuts replied, 'We are at war ...' Breuil and Boyle left South Africa in 1945 without having seen the 'white lady'. A year later Smuts came to Paris for the peace conference. Over lunch with Breuil he asked 'When are you coming to visit our Lady of the Brandberg?' and Breuil replied, 'Field-Marshall, I await your orders.' Smuts sug-gested he come during the next southern African winter, 1947, and he did (Breuil 1955: 3).

The 'white lady' is, of course, no lady at all, but a man, with a penis, holding in his right hand what is apparently a chalice, and in his left a bow and arrows.

The Kalahari Beckons

The idea that the Bushmen were not sophisticated enough to have done great art was not uncommon in a world view still dominated by diffusionist thinking. It is easy to imagine the impact of both Darwinism and social evolutionism on everyday thinking in the late nineteenth and early twentieth centuries. In fact, though, it was diffusionism as much as evolutionism that had the lasting influence on Western thinking on the place of the Bushman in history. To Fritz Graebner, Father Wilhelm Schmidt and others, Bushmen and other 'primitive' hunter-gatherers were remnant populations of early culture, people still clinging to that culture, in spite of migration and acculturation to the ways of food production of peoples all around them. Schmidt (e.g. 1933: 537–787) especially took an interest in Bushman, both because (unlike Graebner) he believed that Bushman culture was older than Australian Aboriginal and because he saw in it vestiges of a revealed primitive monotheism. He sent Father Martin Gusinde to the Kalahari to do fieldwork, although Gusinde (1966) soon fell into the trap of worrying over whether 'Yellow' Bushmen were purer than 'Black'.

In the nineteenth and early twentieth centuries Africa was not generally seen as the original habitation of humankind. Although Charles Darwin had favoured Africa, more commonly Asia and even Europe were hailed as likely sites of a Garden of Eden, either literal or otherwise. And so the 'early' image that seems to lie deep in today's unconscious understanding of 'the Bushman' was not the norm. Bushmen were primitive, but they were not early. It is no wonder that, when Raymond Dart identified the first australopithecine fossil in South Africa in 1924, British scholars objected that it must be of an ape rather than an early hominid since they believed that humankind had originated in northern Europe – in Sussex to be precise (see, for example, Lewin 1989: 47–84). South Africa's greatest historian of the turn of the century begins his account of early times on the subcontinent with the words: 'In the present condition of geological knowledge it is impossible to determine whether South Africa has been the home of human beings for as long a time as Europe, but it is certain that men have roamed over its surface from an exceedingly remote period' (Theal 1902: 1). Still, the remote origins of Bushmen, both in time and in geography, were assumed: 'They were members of a race that in early ages was spread over the whole continent south of the Sahara, and of which remnants still exist on both sides of the equator' (1902: 9). This was the prevalent image, and in a sense it still stands today: Stone Age hunter-gatherers similar to modern San once occupying the whole of Sub-Saharan Africa, and other peoples, with livestock and techniques of cultivation, coming down from northern places some thousands of years ago.

In 1936 Dart led an expedition to the river Nosop to study some seventy /'Auni and ≠Khomani. The expedition included Dorothea Bleek, linguists C.M. Doke and L.F Maingard and musicologist P.R. Kirby, among others. In all, eight researchers, joined by various domestic assistants and local farmer Donald Bain, made up the team. As Bain would bring the researchers to the Bushmen, he would later bring the Bushmen to the public. A few months after this field trip, he brought a number of /'Auni and ≠Khomani to the Empire Exhibition in Johannesburg, where they entertained audiences with skills such as lighting fires (Hudelson 1995: 6–7). In that same era, Franz Taaibosch, a 'Pygmy African Bushman', the 'only genuine' Bushman in America, became a regular attraction in the Ringling Brothers Barnum and Bailey Circus in North America. Through the 1920s and 1930s, 'Klikko' or 'Clico, wild dancing South African Bushman', as he was advertised as, dressed in oversized leopard skins and heavy boots, danced for generations of spectators who could only have had the flimsiest idea of the culture from which he had come (Lindfors 1999). It seemed that the anthropological study of Bushmen went alongside the display of people as 'Bushmen', both near and far from their homelands.

Bushmen were first similarly exhibited in Europe in 1847, at the Egyptian Hall in London. Both their treatment and their image improved later in the century, but it was always the European or North American entrepreneur who was in charge of the situation. In 1883 Canadian entrepreneur William Hunt, who called himself Guillermo Farini, brought a group to Europe and exhibited them in London's Royal Aquarium as the 'Aq', also described in his publicity material as the 'earthmen', 'pygmies' and 'yellow devils'. The exhibition was called 'Farini's Desert in the Aquarium', and the entrepreneur later claimed to have discovered a lost city in the Kalahari – 'proof' that Western civilization had penetrated deep into the most 'primitive' part of Africa long, long ago. Farini (1886: 356–9) claimed to have uncovered the ruins of a lost city somewhere in the Kalahari, though shifting sands must soon have buried it, along with the hieroglyphic inscriptions he sought. In 1949, the South African Air Force dispatched planes to try to find it, to no avail. Plans for archaeological excavations were reportedly called off after that, although an old-timer called Kalahari Mac claimed to have seen it and a Cape Town businessman in the 1950s spent his holidays trying to find it in his private jet (Bjerre 1960: 31–3).

The lost city has been resurrected in fiction too. South African novelist Wilbur Smith sets his *The Sunbird* (Smith 1972), by my reckoning, somewhere near Nata in eastern Botswana, a known area of Iron Age Great Zimbabwe influence and subsequently an area much studied by revisionist archaeologists interested in the long period of contact between Iron Age and hunter-gatherer peoples. The first half of *The Sunbird* features two fictional archaeologists and their discovery of the Phoenician City of the Moon. The second half of book is a flashback to the last days of the city, and main characters of the modern age have exact counterparts. The Bushman, named Xhai, is the only character to appear under the same name in both halves of the book. And in the flashback Xhai ends his days painting a 'proud god like figure with its white face, red-gold beard and majestic vaunting manhood' (Smith 1972: 537–8) above the devastated city.

Conclusion

At the end of the Second World War, anthropology was on the rise. While archaeology as a discipline has always been more local in its concentration of interest, social and cultural anthropology was based on comparison and centred far away from southern Africa, in Europe and North America. Through Schapera's youthful library research and the gradual worldwide dissemination of other writings on Bushmen, the time was right for a North American or European takeover of Bushman studies. It would be North American, but it would begin in a most unlikely manner and most certainly not within the professional tradition of a Franz Boas or a Radcliffe-Brown.

–5–

Amateurs and Cultural Ecologists

Modern Kalahari ethnography has it origins in a melting chocolate bar and the economic failure of the first microwave oven. At the risk of oversimplifying, let me explain the chain of events.

The Raytheon Corporation, founded in 1922, was active in developing radar during the Second World War. After the war, a Raytheon engineer working with a tabletop radar contraption noticed that his chocolate bar was melting, apparently as a result of microwaves. Laurence Marshall, co-founder and chairman of the corporation, was keen to develop peaceful post-war pursuits for his company. The 'radar cooker', as he called it, seemed to fit the bill. However, he had a good deal of trouble selling the idea to railway companies or any other likely consumers. Fellow directors at Raytheon opted to pursue other ventures instead, and Marshall sold up his shares, retired and took his family off to study the Bushmen, who, he believed, lived a more peaceful existence than the 'civilized' societies of the West (see J. Marshall 1993: 22–6).

The Marshall Family

Lorna Marshall and the Marshall Expeditions

Laurence Marshall was born in 1889 and died in 1980. His wife Lorna was the proud owner of the prototype microwave oven until 1978, when it was moved to a museum. She was born in 1898 and died in 2002. Laurence and Lorna and their children Elizabeth and John each had a role to play in the family's expeditions and in their work among G/wi and especially among so-called !Kung Bushmen (now known as Ju/'hoansi). Laurence took part in all the family's eight expeditions – the Peabody Museum Kalahari Expeditions (1950, 1951 and 1952–3) and the Peabody–Harvard Smithsonian Kalahari Expeditions (1965, 1956, 1957–8, 1959 and 1961) – primarily as organizer and still photographer. For ease of reference, Lorna preferred to call them simply the Marshall Expeditions. She was there for most of them, though not the first or in 1956 and 1957–8. She acted as the main ethnographer, while Elizabeth wrote as well, and John was responsible for filming.

Lorna once told me that her family's original plan had been to study animal behaviour, but friends at Harvard had warned them that a certain degree of expertise was required for that, whereas, they said, with virtually no training at all almost anyone could do ethnography. Be that as it may, none of the Marshalls were 'trained' before they went; Laurence had studied civil engineering, and Lorna English literature. That background seems to have been more than sufficient, because what they eventually produced was some of the finest ethnography of any people, with well-ordered detailed accounts of social organization and religious belief and practice far superior to those of many professional anthropologists.

The Marshall Expeditions included a number of other people, some with relevant specializations, such as botanist Robert Story, musicologist Nicholas England, archaeologist Robert Dyson and physical anthropologist Eric Williams, and others with local knowledge, such as Fritz Metzger. To me, Metzger is the most interesting, especially here in comparison with Lorna. Metzger grew up in the area, and he had himself authored a children's book, *Naro and His Clan*, written originally in German but first published in English in 1950, just a year before he joined the Marshalls. Essentially, it is a biography of a Ju/'hoan man, though it is told with some license. While hardly the most cited book on Bushmen in anthropology, it has seen a number of editions, including a new and better English translation (Metzger 1993). *The Hyena's Laughter*, a subsequent book of Bushman fables 'collected by Fritz Metzger' (Metzger 1995 [1952]), plays with the mythology, rather than retelling it verbatim in Bleek and Lloyd fashion. Both are splendid texts, and the irony is that they are undoubtedly more widely read in Namibia today than the works of amateur ethnographer Lorna Marshall, who, by turning professional in at least one respect, that is, in the audience she sought, left any potential large local audience behind.

Lorna's most important articles were the seven published in the journal *Africa* between 1957 and 1969. Together these comprised almost a full ethnography of the Ju/'hoansi. The four on social organization, together with some added material, for example on subsistence and on play and games, eventually formed the basis of her book *The !Kung of Nyae Nyae* (L. Marshall 1976), and the three on religion provided the central material for her later book *Nyae Nyae !Kung Beliefs and Rites* (L. Marshall 1999). *Nyae Nyae* was Lorna Marshall's spelling for the area variously referred to on maps as Neinei, Nyae-Nyae or Nyainyai, a corruption of Ju/'hoan N//hoan!ai (Dickens's orthography). The Ju/'hoan term designates a somewhat more specific area, but Marshall and others have used it broadly for the !Kung or Ju'/hoan area that lies in north-eastern Namibia along the Botswana border.

Lorna's most interesting work is probably that on religion, but she rightly became famous for two significant ethnographic discoveries: Ju/'hoan kinship terminology (including the naming system) and the mechanisms of sharing. The former (e.g. L. Marshall 1976 [1957]: 201–42) is a complicated system which enables each Ju/'hoan to trace their relationship to every other Ju/'hoan in what I later called a universal system of kin classification (e.g. Barnard 1978). Where genealogy ends (or even before, hence the complications), it works through personal names: a namesake is a grandrelative, and, for example, one's grandrelative's sister is one's 'sister' and one behaves towards her accordingly. Through such systems, hunter-gatherers in the Kalahari and in many other parts of the world maintain social relations. However, where everyone is classified as 'kin', in a sense there are no kin. Mechanisms of sharing thus take over some of the functions of kinship, and Lorna (e.g. L. Marshall 1976 [1961]: 287–312) demonstrated the workings and interrelations of good manners, meat-sharing, gift-giving and social control. The full meaning of all this would have to wait until the fieldwork of Polly Wiessner in the 1970s (e.g. Wiessner 1977), but Lorna's findings were enough to give significant inspiration to Marshall Sahlins in his essays 'The Original Affluent Society' (Sahlins 1974 [1968]: 1–39) and 'On the Sociology of Primitive Exchange' (1974 [1965]: 185–275).

Lorna Marshall's work does not fit precisely into any theoretical niche. In some ways it is more reminiscent of the classic British tradition than the American one, for example in its implied emphasis on the social functions of customs witnessed and in its concerns with social over psychological explanation in ritual. But there was something new as well, at least new for Bushman studies: the recording of details of subsistence activities, including plants utilized, along with material on the relation between environment and social relations. Although not overtly theoretical, then, Lorna's ethnography came to occupy a comfortable position among those interested in unencumbered description (common in American anthropology through much of its history), those who like functional explanation (more common in the British tradition) and those who favoured a more ecological approach. The last was fast gaining favour in North America, especially in hunter-gatherer studies, thanks to the popularity of Julian Steward's *Theory of Culture Change* (1955) and Elman Service's *Primitive Social Organization* (1962).

Elizabeth Marshall Thomas and John Marshall

Elizabeth and John both made their names in time, Elizabeth as a writer and John as a documentary film-maker and activist. As is well known to Kalahari enthusiasts, Elizabeth wrote a popular account of the expeditions called *The Harmless People* (Thomas 1959), but she later also wrote a further travelogue of the family's expedition to Uganda, two works of fiction set in Palaeolithic Siberia, and, in recent years, popular books on dogs and cats. One of Elizabeth's earliest writings (an assignment at Radcliffe College) was an anthropological story that won her a short-story prize, and it is said that it was that experience which led to her taking on a book-length account of the family's travels through the Kalahari. She remains a best-selling author, although unlike her brother she would mainly put the Kalahari behind her and move on in her work to other things – although from time to time she has gone back to her experiences with non-violence among the Ju/'hoansi (e.g. Thomas 1994).

The Harmless People remains Elizabeth's most important book for anthropologists and is her only one on Bushmen. Although clearly a travelogue rather than ethnography, the emphasis is on the daily activities of the people she encountered rather than on the Marshall Expeditions. The details of Bushman life given in it have long been cited by anthropologists, including Sahlins. It is interesting that she chooses to talk about the family's experiences among G/wi or G/uikhoe of what was then Bechuanaland (whom she calls Gikwe) as much as among the Ju/'hoansi of what was South West Africa (whom she calls Kung). She even at times makes comparisons between the two groups, although comparison was certainly not central to her purpose.

John Marshall began his film-making carer in 1950, when his father gave him his first sixteen-millimetre movie camera. He was only seventeen at the time, but he was in the right place: with the !Kung, as they became known, in the northern Kalahari. He claimed he always just filmed 'people', that he was not an 'ethnographic' film-maker but just made documentaries, and he made them all in the same way, with the focus on people, whether he was in the Kalahari or with the police in Pittsburgh – his other major topic of documentary film.

John's spoken version of the first Marshall Expedition, revealed in an interview with Carolyn Anderson and Thomas Benson (1993: 135–6), emphasizes the chance nature of it all. His father Laurence had been to Cape Town the previous year to try to sell a radar system to the harbour authority there and had met a surgeon called E. van Zyl. Van Zyl was a romantic who wanted to find the fabled lost city of the Kalahari. Laurence returned in 1950 with John, after it had been recommended by J.O. Brew of the Harvard University's Peabody Museum that a search for 'wild Bushmen' might be more fruitful than a quest for a mythical Phoenician civilization.

> So we went looking for 'wild Bushmen', with the expedition to find the lost city. We got to a place called Kai Kai and Van Zyl took a final assault in the morning to find the lost city and we all waited at Kai Kai while the doctor and his brother, the senator, went out to find the lost city. And they came back and said the Herero had moved it during the night. So we didn't find the lost city, but Dad met two guys named /Qui !gumsi and a guy named //Ao N//oro. And Dad asked them, if he brought the family back, same time, same place next year, would you be here, would you take us to meet your families, who they explained, lived by hunting and gathering purely. (John Marshall, in Anderson and Benson 1993: 136)

Of course, they returned in the following year, and the rest is history. But what John says about the apparent lack of interest in Bushmen at that time is revealing too about both American anthropology and the unique nature of the Marshall fieldwork.

We tried to find an ethnographer or a graduate student who wanted to go and study daily life of hunter-gatherers on the plains of Africa. We couldn't find one. Isn't that incredible? We went through Harvard, Yale, Princeton, Chicago, and a couple of other places that Dad called up ... Dad said he'd back them for a long time, for an in-depth, long-term study because he thought that would be unique, and nobody responded. (John Marshall, in Anderson and Benson 1993: 136)

One wonders what might have been the response at Harvard or Yale if he had suggested a search for the lost city instead.

In the 1950s John made many excellent, short documentaries on aspects of Ju/'hoan life. Most were released commercially only many years later, for example *A Joking Relationship* (released 1962), *An Argument about a Marriage* (1969), *A Curing Ceremony* (1969), *Bitter Melons* (1971) and *Debe's Tantrum* (1972). However, his most famous film was *The Hunters*, shot in 1952 and 1953 and released in 1957. This depicts four men chasing after a single giraffe over a five-day period. Unlike the short films, this is not quite literally a documentary. Contrary to popular belief, it is not based on a single hunt. And, to quell another myth, nor did any such hunt end with John shooting the giraffe with a gun, and shooting the film as if the Ju/'hoan had killed the giraffe. In reality, the film was compiled from footage of several different giraffe hunted at different times, with the footage legitimately run together to make one coherent story. It was to influence generations of anthropologists and anthropology students for the better, but, by John's own admission many years later, it did give the mistaken impression that Ju/'hoan territories are based on animal habitats. John was a rarity in anthropology: one who readily admitted his mistakes.

Other famous films include *N!ai, the Story of a !Kung Woman*, shot in the 1950s and released in 1980, and *Bushmen of the Kalahari*, a National Geographic film about John's long-term relationship with the Ju/'hoansi, released in 1974. It was shot in the early 1970s in Botswana at a time when John was not allowed into South West Africa (later Namibia), with additional much earlier footage. Although his father was allowed back and indeed had bought land in the territory, John was, because of his political activism on behalf of the Ju/'hoansi, denied entry for many years. Like a number of other enlightened modernizers, he later tried to encourage cattle herding over other means of subsistence. After Namibia's independence, he argued in lectures that the changes Ju/'hoansi were undergoing should be seen not as a transition from hunting and gathering to farming, but as development from dependency to self-support.

John Marshall supplemented his film-making role with extensive but, as here, often quite controversial work in advocacy. He also held the very noteworthy distinction of the longest experience with San of any ethnographer, having first visited Ju/'hoansi in 1950 and maintaining contact with the same group of people from that time virtually until his death in 2005. While not in general given to print as a means of expression, he co-authored with Claire Ritchie a splendid mono-graph (Marshall and Ritchie 1984) which documents the changes that had over-taken the Ju/'hoansi of Nyae Nyae between his last lengthy period of residence there in 1958 and his and Ritchie's further study of the area in 1981. In 1970, the South West Africa Administration had demarcated what was termed Bushmanland, a long east–west strip cut out of Ju/'hoan territory, with the area to the south declared Hereroland and the area to the north earmarked for a game reserve. The Ju/'hoansi strenuously objected, particularly to the establishment of a game reserve, and in reality Ju/'hoansi were confined just to the eastern half of Bushmanland. The western area was never their traditional territory, and it lacked resources. Eastern Bushmanland simply could not sustain the population forced into it, by hunting and gathering alone.

His advocacy came alive in film through the five-part series appropriately titled 'A Kalahari Family', shown in preliminary versions in the 1990s and released commercially in 2002. The family is meant to be that of Lorna's informants ≠Toma and !U and their descendants, whose lives and relations with the Marshalls, with government authorities and eventually with development organizations are traced from the 1950s to the year 2000. The series, and especially the final film *Death by Myth*, provoked great controversy because of its allegedly one-sided portrayal of the dispute in the 1990s between John and the directors of the Nyae Nyae Development Foundation of Namibia. He had spent his own money and efforts on setting up the organization several years before, but was sidelined by the new-comers among the directorship, and the issues are still not resolved.

Parts of 'A Kalahari Family' depict altercations between Ju/'hoansi and out-siders and arguments among Ju/'hoansi, but those among development workers over the future of Ju/'hoan livelihoods are the most significant. John led the call for modernization, and he had used some of his late father's money in the early 1980s to encourage cattle herding. His opponents, including long-serving devel-opment worker Axel Thoma in the 1990s, preferred attempts to enable Ju/'hoansi to regain a hunting lifestyle, for example to circumvent wildlife legislation by tagging game so that it is 'owned' like livestock but still 'hunted' traditionally. The situation has long been far more complicated that that, of course, but John always liked to display his objection, whether in his own films or to journalists, to putting Bushmen into what he so eloquently called 'a subsidized plastic stone age'. Film was, in part, his means to portray the dangerous ironies of political intervention, especially when that intervention aimed at restoring an inappropriate lost world.

Silberbauer, Lee and the Western Tradition

Interest in Bushmen would grow through the 1950s, thanks to the Marshalls them-selves and also to two others: Phillip Tobias and Laurens van der Post. Tobias was an anatomist, Raymond Dart's successor as Professor of Anatomy at the University of the Witwatersrand, in Johannesburg. In the 1950s he participated in several expeditions to the Kalahari. His influence was significant in South Africa, and in many ways marks a natural transition between earlier times and the modern era exemplified by the Marshalls. He was also important in bringing Bushmen to the attention of a wider anthropological public through articles in general scientific journals like *Nature* and the *South African Journal of Science*, in anthropological journals like *Man* and *Africa*, and in encyclopedias and semi-popular works (e.g. Tobias 1978b).

Sir Laurens van der Post was the face of the Bushman to the worldwide general public, but the interest he attracted rubbed off on anthropology too. There was no love lost between him and the anthropologists who followed, though. He mistrusted 'scientists' with their specialized knowledge and inability to think beyond the confines of their disciplines; and they disliked his mysticism and self-promoting ego, his inability to speak any Bushman language, the short duration of his time in the Kalahari, and his cavalier attitude to differences between Bushman groups (see Barnard 1989; Jones 2001: 211–39). Van der Post wrote a number of books and articles in which Bushman thought or Bushman characters appear, the most famous being his early two-part travelogue *The Lost World of the Kalahari* (van der Post 1958) and *The Heart of the Hunter* (1961). The books were preceded by the six-part BBC series *Lost World of the Kalahari*, aired in Britain in 1956 with viewing figures then second only to the coronation of Queen Elizabeth II three years earlier. Van der Post interspersed his travelogue in the country of Naro, G/wi and Ju/'hoansi with accounts of /Xam mythology collected by 'an old German professor' (Wilhelm Bleek), thereby at least resurrecting in the public mind the richness of Bushman folklore. However, anthropological interest was turning to 'scientists': Phillip Tobias, Lorna Marshall and soon the likes of George Silberbauer and Richard Lee.

George B. Silberbauer

It is hard to know what makes a great ethnography. Bushman studies have been blessed with many, but Silberbauer's (1981) *Hunter and Habitat in the Central Kalahari Desert* remains my own favourite. The book describes an ethnographic present many years before its publication date, when between 1958 and 1964 Silberbauer spent much time at intervals of a few months each visit living with the G/wi. *Hunter and Habitat* is extraordinarily readable, written in a non-technical style but with plenty of detail on habitat and natural resources, hunting and gathering and the use of animal and plant products, band structure and territoriality, and kinship and religion. The original thesis version (Silberbauer 1973) contained a fold-out flow chart with over 200 interconnected boxes, and apparently it illustrated the connection of everything in G/wi society, culture and environment to everything else. (In the late 1970s a senior civil servant in Botswana displayed on the wall of his office a copy of the chart, jokingly labelled 'New Structure: Ministry of …'). The book is more subtle. There is no flow chart, but an attempt to portray in an ecological framework not merely humanity and nature as understood in Western science, but also a G/wi vision of their own ecology. This encompasses such things as good and evil deities, the sky and the underworld, ethno-physiology, the taboos in social behaviour and gender aspects of language.

George Silberbauer had a very unconventional training. Like Lorna Marshall he came into ethnography as an amateur. Like van der Post and John Marshall, he has made films. Yet his introduction to Bushman studies was as a government administrator: Bushman Survey Officer of the Bechuanaland Protectorate and District Commissioner of Ghanzi, the country's most remote district. He served six years in these posts, including three years altogether with the G/wi. His original academic background was in law, but he would spend most of 1958 as a postgraduate student at the University of the Witwatersrand, where he took courses in anthropology and linguistics. After he finished the Bushman Survey he emigrated to Australia, where he taught anthropology at Monash University. He wrote a few articles on the G/wi, but through much of his career his main publication was the *Bushman Survey* report (Silberbauer 1965), a 138–page document consisting mainly of original G/wi ethnography but with recommendations too about the future of what he there called simply the Central Kalahari Reserve (not 'game reserve').

At Silberbauer's instigation, the colonial authorities set up the Central Kalahari Game Reserve (CKGR) in 1961. It was called a 'game reserve' partly for political reasons. Although it is said that Silberbauer had South African Bantustan policy in mind, it would have been quite inappropriate for the British authorities to be instituting a kind of apartheid, particularly in the year in which South Africa left the Commonwealth and became a republic. They could not call it G/wi 'tribal land' because, in Tswana terms the G/wi, G//ana and Kgalagadi who lived in the reserve were not 'tribes'. They had no hereditary chiefs of consequence, and no tribal councils or meeting places. Yet it was Silberbauer's intention that the demarcation of the reserve, which is bigger than Belgium in a country as large as France, should protect human inhabitants as well as wildlife. Botswana became independent in 1966, and the Botswana government would over the coming decades gradually provide resources such as a school and a clinic in the reserve, and then gradually remove such facilities and put pressure on the G/wi and others to move out. In 2004, the now-retired George Silberbauer returned to Botswana as an expert witness, on the G/wi side, in the case of 243 CKGR inhabitants suing their government (successfully) over the rights to their ancestral land.

Richard B. Lee

Richard Lee has a more conventional anthropological background. Born in New York, he studied at Toronto and Berkeley, returning to Toronto in 1972 to take up an Associate Professorship of Anthropology. Perhaps the most eminent of all Canadian anthropologists, he is a Fellow of the Royal Society of Canada and his book *The !Kung San* was named by *American Scientist* as one of the 100 most important works of science of the twentieth century. He began fieldwork among Ju/'hoansi in Botswana in 1963, and has since worked also among First Nations in Canada, on the early state and on topical issues such as AIDS prevention. He is a prolific writer, producing as many as six singly-authored articles per year at some stages in his career. A series of celebratory sessions was held in his honour at a joint meeting of the Canadian Anthropological Society, American Ethnological Society and Society for Cultural Anthropology in Montreal in 2001. A number of papers presented there were published in a special issue of the Canadian journal *Anthropologica* (volume 45, number 1) in 2003.

Most of Lee's !Kung or Ju/'hoan work follows quite directly from his Ph.D. dissertation (Lee 1965), which was based on fieldwork carried out in 1963 and 1964. His most important empirical finding was that Bushmen spend rather less time in subsistence activities than many had thought. Except in times of drought, life for them is not nasty, brutish and short, but actually fairly leisurely. This observation was derived from a work diary he kept for each inhabitant at a Ju/'hoan dry-season camp from 6 July to 2 August 1964. Lee spoke on the issue at the 'Man the Hunter' conference he organized with Harvard primatologist Irven DeVore in 1966 (Lee 1968). His major paper on the subject was published in 1969, with an expanded version included in *The !Kung San* (see Lee 1968, 1969, 1979: 50–80). These papers would eventually come under attack from revisionists like Edwin Wilmsen (e.g. 1986) for underrating the extent to which Ju/'hoansi are dependent on their cattle-herding neighbours for milk and other items, even at Dobe where Lee carried out his research on the topic. Nonetheless, Lee's work became widely respected for its detail on traditional subsistence pursuits and other daily activities, as well as its comprehensive coverage of Ju/'hoan knowledge of plants and animals, the resources available in the Dobe area and, in due course, the changes that affected their society between the time of his early fieldwork and later decades.

The !Kung San is long and painstakingly detailed in these areas. It is aimed mainly at a quite specialist audience. Lee was to follow it with *The Dobe !Kung* (Lee 1984), more readable and designed for undergraduates, even in introductory courses, and covering the whole of Ju/'hoan life rather than just (as the subtitle of the earlier book says) 'men, women and work'. *The Dobe !Kung* is also based not only on his own work but also on the work of many others who have done research with Ju/'hoansi, on topics such as religious belief and spiritual healing. The second edition was retitled *The Dobe Ju/'hoansi* (Lee 1993) and added two new chapters on later developments, especially in Namibia, including the work of John Marshall in economic development. The main text ends on a positive note, seeing 'indigenous peoples' like the Ju/'hoansi as 'repositories of invaluable knowledge ... and as living embodiments of alternative ways of being' (Lee 1993: 176). The most recent edition (Lee 2003) is more pessimistic, with no change in those words but with an additional chapter on ageing and care-giving and with new material on poverty and the challenge of HIV/AIDS.

A Japanese Tradition: the Legacy of Kyoto Primatology

It is interesting for two reasons that Kyoto should be the Japanese university where African hunter-gatherer studies should take root. First, Kyoto University is known for and prides itself on its egalitarian ethos. Ever since the university's beginnings in the nineteenth century, professors there in all fields have been called by surname plus the respectful but less formal *–san* (Mr or Ms) rather than the more formal *–sensei* (teacher), the term still often used in other Japanese universities. Professors reciprocate by calling their students *–san*. The usage is not uncommon today, but Kyoto University was the first to allow, even encourage, it. Secondly, Kyoto is noted for primate studies, and anthropology there grew from that interest.

The first great Kyoto primatologist was Kinji Imanishi, who in the 1940s moved from the study of wild horses to Japanese macaques. The second major figure was Junichiro Itani, who later did field research with Mbuti Pygmies, thereby establishing the Kyoto tradition of doing both primate and human hunter-gatherer research as an aid to comparison. Just as Westerners have used primate studies in the tropics to reflect on what it is to be human, Imanishi, Itani and their school first used Japanese macaques as mirrors of humanity, and as 'nature' living within their own society. Western primatologists (e.g. Asquith 1986; Haraway 1989: 244–58) have pointed out that Japanese do not anthropomorphize primates in the same way as Westerners do. One Japanese primatologist-turned-anthropologist confided in me that he used the same fieldwork techniques among Bushmen that he had among primates. In this context, though, it is possible that this admission would mean something a little different in the West.

Jiro Tanaka

The major figure in San studies in Japan is Jiro Tanaka. Now retired, he taught for decades in the Centre for African Area Studies at Kyoto University, and ended his career as president of the Japan Association for African Studies. His earliest training was in primatology, and he studied primatology with Itani at Kyoto before training in anthropology at Tokyo. He carried out fieldwork with Rendile pastoralists in Kenya, and began work with G/wi and G//ana hunter-gatherers in 1966. In Silberbauer's time, there were few G//ana in the western part of the Central Kalahari Game Reserve, where both Tanaka and Silberbauer stayed, but by the late 1960s members of the two groups there lived in close proximity. He came to call the two together simply the Central Kalahari Bushmen or Central Kalahari San. His 1971 to 1972 research with G//ana was as part of Lee and DeVore's Harvard team, and Tanaka's intention at the time was to compare G//ana with Ju/'hoansi.

Tanaka's major Japanese publication is *Busshuman* (Tanaka 1971), eventually expanded and published in English as *The San, Hunter-gatherers of the Kalahari* (Tanaka 1980). Topics treated include, among others, the natural environment and finding water and food; hunting, gathering and cooking activities; material culture, including detailed descriptions of hunting equipment; sharing and cooperation; kinship and marriage; and fission and fusion of residential groups. Silberbauer's (1982) review of *The San* captured the profound differences between his own findings and Tanaka's: 'We contradict each other on almost every point which is considered to be significant in Western social anthropology and, indeed, on the very question of what *is* of importance' (Silberbauer 1982: 803; see also 1996: 34–6). Silberbauer and Tanaka were both based mainly at ≠Xade pan in the south-western part of the CKGR. Yet Tanaka found highly fluid migration of families, whereas Silberbauer had found clearly defined band territories and migration, aggregation and dispersal within these. Tanaka stressed the detail, whereas Silberbauer's main concern was with the pattern.

In fact, similar disagreements were apparent within the Western tradition too farther north, among the Ju/'hoansi, even before the so-called 'Kalahari debate'. In that area Lorna Marshall (1976 [1960]: 179–200) and to some extent Richard Lee (1976 [1972]) described spatial organization in terms of bands and band territories, whereas ethno-archaeologist John Yellen (1977), working alongside Lee and with Lee's data, analysed the same movements among Ju/'hoansi in terms of individual actions. Yellen's solution stressed different theoretical approaches, whereas Silberbauer's explanation of differences between Tanaka's account and his own stressed changes at ≠Xade pan in the 1960s. Silberbauer speculated that the social structure of the place had been transformed from a more G/wi-type pattern to a more G//ana-type one. In other words, for Silberbauer reality was to be found in forms of social organization attached to sociocultural entities. Tanaka and others in the Japanese tradition were suspicious of reifying such entities well before writers in the West, although Tanka recognized G/wi–G//ana linguistic difference in his vocabulary of the two dialects (Tanaka 1978).

Kazuyoshi Sugawara

A number of Japanese anthropologists followed Tanaka in working with Central Kalahari San. We shall meet some in later chapters. Here I will concentrate on just one, who, like Tanaka, was trained originally in primatology, but whose theoretical position was to differ dramatically. This is Kazuyoshi Sugawara, of Kyoto's Faculty of Integrated Human Sciences. In 2002 I had the good fortune to interview Sugawara, and my student Hiroaki Izumi later followed up my 'fieldwork' in Kyoto with further studies. Unfortunately for those of us from the West, much of Sugawara's work is published only in Japanese; and I draw on Izumi's (2006) occasional paper, based on his M.Sc. dissertation, for my second-hand acquaintance with these and other Japanese writings in San and hunter-gatherer studies. Sugawara (1998a, 2004) has himself traced the history of Japanese San studies eloquently and objectively, although I see at least the work of his that I know as, in a way, a culmination of the tradition of which he is a part. Sugawara's uniqueness derives from the addition of discourse as a focus and from his blend of ecological study (in its broadest sense), linguistic competence and the phenomenology of French philosopher Maurice Merleau-Ponty.

Sugawara's main fieldwork has been with G/wi, with whom he has worked since 1982. He does not see his work as part of 'ecological anthropology', and certainly it is not ecological in the sense of Silberbauer, Lee or Tanaka. Concerned less with the relation between human beings and their habitats, Sugawara is interested more in relations between speech acts and social relations, between apparent egalitarianism and communication theory, between joking and game theory, and between speaking and bodily behaviour. Two of his books (Sugawara 1998b, c), for example, make use of data on G/wi conversation and negotiation to understand how G/wi seek to attain everyday goals. His earlier book on the anthropology of the body (Sugawara 1993) relies less on language, but uses his material on G/wi gestures, sexuality and play fighting. His English publications include various chapters in books and articles in *African Study Monographs*, and some of these cover similar interests but with less detail. There is growing interest within San studies in Japan in relations between language and social structure, as well as a continued dominance of ecological studies in a narrow sense. Some, such as Kazunobu Ikeya and Masakazu Osaki, tend to follow the more ecological interests of Tanaka, often with an emphasis on socio-environmental change, while others, such as Hitomi Ono and Hiroshi Nakagawa, have developed research programmes deeper into linguistics in its narrow sense than Sugawara. The result seems to be the emergence of a set of very diverse but historically and conceptually related approaches to the understanding of San society that are quite different in their theoretical foundations from their Western counterparts.

I have known Tanaka for over thirty years and Sugawara for over twenty years, but my knowledge of their writings remains fragmentary. The divide between the

Japanese and Western traditions may be decreasing (Richard Lee spent a recent sabbatical period at Kyoto), but it is still there. Japanese anthropologists can read everything published in English, but Western anthropologists are reliant on translations into English. Interestingly, the English translation of Tanaka's *Busshuman* only became available after the intervention of Edwin Wilmsen. He paid one of his students to do the translation, and an insurance company subsidized its publication. When eventually more Japanese material does appear in English, San studies in the West will undoubtedly be affected, and I think for the better – not because Japanese studies are superior to Western but because diversity in approach can only improve wider understanding.

Conclusion

My own anthropological writings are probably best described as loosely structuralist, while my writings in the history of anthropology perhaps, as some may see them, border on the postmodern. However, comparisons between Japanese and Western traditions show uncanny parallels and structural oppositions. Lee did not venture into the northern Kalahari alone, but with DeVore and a baboon he picked up along the way (see Kuper 1994: 66). They had spent the period just before, in 1963, studying baboons in Kenya. Both Tanaka and Sugawara began as primatologists, although the kind of anthropology they developed was rather different. Whereas Lee and Tanaka developed conventional approaches to the study of subsistence ecology, albeit with different emphases, Silberbauer and especially Sugawara challenged the bounds of ecological anthropology. Silberbauer remained within the field but came to see ideology as more significant than others did, and Sugawara turned away from cultural ecology in its narrow sense towards the study of language and social interaction. For Sugawara, G/wi not only know their environment well; they communicate it well.

As for the Marshalls, their work, especially Lorna's, marked the new baseline of Bushman studies, and, although not particularly theoretical in itself, its theoretical impact would soon hit home.

–6–

An Original Affluent Society?

The 1960s were times of great change, in Botswana as well as in Europe and North America. George Silberbauer proposed the establishment of the Central Kalahari Game Reserve in 1960, and in 1961 the Bechuanaland Protectorate authorities agreed to it, as a device to protect both the wildlife and the indigenous human inhabitants of the area. Botswana gained its independence in 1966, and the new government took on the great task of formalizing a splendid, and long effective, mix of traditional Tswana democracy and British parliamentarianism, complete with a House of Chiefs modelled on Britain's House of Lords. A near-biblical seven years of drought in most of the country was followed by seven years of abundance. It was not only rainfall and consequent wild foods and pasturage which appeared: diamonds were soon discovered too.

The year 1966 also marks the great 'Man the Hunter' conference, in which Marshall Sahlins first presented his ideas on hunter-gatherers as 'the original affluent society' (Sahlins 1968a). His comments there, and the ethnography presented from various parts of the world, challenged the traditional Hobbesian view of hunter-gatherers as having a difficult struggle for existence. While the ethnographically knowledgeable had known since the nineteenth century that hunting and gathering took less time than herding or cultivation, it took Sahlins, not a hunter-gatherer specialist but a Polynesianist interested in social evolution, to overturn the misconception.

Man the Hunter

Why are hunter-gatherers important? That was the question 'Man the Hunter' was to raise, as between 6 and 9 April 1966 some seventy-five anthropologists from all inhabited continents gathered in Chicago for one of the most important conferences in the history of the discipline. The often-quoted words from the preface to the conference volume explain it well: 'We cannot avoid the suspicion that many of us were led to live and work among the hunters because of a feeling that the human condition was likely to be more clearly drawn here than among other kinds of societies' (Lee and DeVore 1968a: ix).

'Hunters', of course, meant hunter-gatherers: anthropology was yet to wake up to the fact that gathering was not only economically but also conceptually important to women and men who have chosen not to take up the domestication of plants and animals for food. Ironically, Lee's paper did help to turn around that misconception, as it raised ethnographic points relevant to Sahlins's theoretical one: 'The current anthropological view of hunter-gatherer subsistence rests on two questionable assumptions. First is the notion that these peoples are primarily dependent on the hunting of game animals, and the second is the assumption that their way of life is generally a precarious and arduous struggle for existence' (Lee 1968: 30). In his theoretical statements, Lee (e.g. 1968: 43) emphasized the persistence and adaptive capacity of hunting and gathering, as well as the capability of people to make a good living by these means even in a relatively harsh environment such as the northern Kalahari.

Lee's 'Man the Hunter' paper was the only one on Bushmen, although Lorna Marshall also attended the conference. *Man the Hunter* (Lee and DeVore 1968b) became such a classic volume that, it seems, no one wanted to repeat the plan to get the world's specialists together until twelve years later, when from 27 to 30 June 1978 Maurice Godelier called the next generation to Paris. Only one of the planned three volumes from that conference ever appeared, but Lee co-edited that volume too (Leacock and Lee 1982), this time with six papers on Kalahari San. Further hunter-gatherer conferences followed at roughly two- or three-year intervals, later at longer intervals, in Quebec, Bad Homberg, London, Darwin, Fairbanks, Moscow, Osaka and Edinburgh. Increasing numbers of papers on Ju/'hoansi, G/wi, Naro and other San peoples were produced – seventeen at the Edinburgh conference in 2002 – as San increased in their prominence. It is easy to forget that, at least in North America, the hunter-gatherers of the Arctic, the Subarctic and Australia were far better known than those of southern Africa at the time of 'Man the Hunter'.

Man the Hunter remains the baseline in hunter-gatherer studies, partly because it is a virtually complete conference volume. It contains not only the papers, mostly very short, but also edited discussion by participants. Two of the themes within the conference, 'Prehistoric Hunter-gatherers' and 'Hunting and Human Evolution', reflected the underlying evolutionist assumptions of Lee, DeVore and many of the other participants, not least Claude Lévi-Strauss. His points of discussion and his acceptance speech of the Viking Fund Medal given to him at the conference (Lévi-Strauss 1968) hint at a close relation between the modes of thought of living hunter-gatherers and the those of the Palaeolithic ancestors shared by all humankind. The assumption of such a relation would be a driving force in hunter-gatherer studies for some time to come, as the sub-discipline broke ranks with the relativism of much anthropology of the time, in its search for the human condition.

Stone Age Economics

It would be an exaggeration to say that our modern anthropological image of the Bushman is a result of the events of 1968, but it would not be outright nonsense. In anthropology, the link that was to matter was a long essay by Marshall Sahlins that first appeared in abbreviated form, perhaps prophetically, in Paris, 1968, under the French title 'La première société d'abondance' (Sahlins 1968b).

'The original affluent society', as the English version of Sahlins's essay was called, became the lead chapter of his *Stone Age Economics* (Sahlins 1974 [1972]: 1–39). In this, he suggests that there are two routes to 'affluence': producing much, or desiring little. Hunter-gatherers follow the latter route, and sacrifice the accumulation of wealth for the accumulation of free time and the enjoyment of sufficient material plenty to meet their meagre wants. This turned on its head the usual images of hunter-gatherers and their supposed struggle for existence. As he points out, hunter-gatherers often succeed in finding enough food when in bad times others around them are starving. More generally

> The world's most primitive people have few possessions, but they are not poor. Poverty is not a certain small amount of goods, nor is it just a relation between means and ends; above all it is a relation between people. Poverty is a social status. As such it is the invention of civilization. It has grown with civilization, at once as an invidious distinction between classes and more importantly as a tributary relation – that can render agrarian peasants more susceptible to natural catastrophes than any winter camp of Alaskan Eskimo. (Sahlins 1974: 37–8)

Sahlins's notion is based heavily on his reading of Bushman ethnography, notably Lorna Marshall and Richard Lee. He also cites as a key source George Grey (1841) on the abundance of resources, for those who know how to gather them, in north-western Australia. Before moving on to New Zealand and to the Cape Colony, Grey was an explorer on that continent. In retrospect, it is astounding that it had taken until the 1960s for mainstream anthropology to catch up with what many who had observed hunter-gatherers already knew: such groups may struggle in times when resources are poor, but they do not have to work hard when availability is average or better.

The idea of an original affluent society struck a chord not only with hippyish neo-'noble savage' anthropologists, but also with the most materialist of theorists. Marvin Harris (1978: 10–11), citing Lee as his source, comments on how little time Bushmen spend obtaining food and maintaining their protein-rich diet. His emphasis is on the low population density, and his theoretical concern is to compare Bushmen to 'our ancestors', for example in the Upper Palaeolithic. Similarly, Marxist anthropologist Maurice Godelier (1975: 19–20) makes use of Lee's data on subsistence and mobility to explore demographic constraints and ultimately the relation between kinship and modes of production.

Sahlins, however, was not without critics. The most important critique came only many years later when Cambridge-educated Israeli anthropologist Nurit Bird-David (1992) pointed out Sahlins's conflation of two models: one ecological (covering labour time) and the other culturalist (covering needs and wants). Bird-David attacked Sahlins's use of just a small number of examples and his reliance on anecdotal evidence, such as Grey's reports from 1830s Australia, as well as his latent Western materialism in the emphasis he gave to work effort. She pushes instead for a more culturally aware approach that emphasizes hunter-gatherers' own views of their environments – habitats which 'give' or 'share' their resources with those who inhabit them, as opposed to 'natural' forests and deserts to be exploited. Other critics, in turn, found fault with Bird-David for not being radical enough. According to Tim Ingold (1992), for example, what we need 'is not a culture-sensitive account to replace a naturalistic ecology', but, rather, 'a new kind of ecological anthropology that would take as its starting point the active, perceptual engagement of human beings with the constituents of their world'.

Bird-David's culturalist model, which she variously calls 'the giving environment' (1990) and 'the cosmic economy of sharing' (1992), was based in part on her own ethnography of hunter-gatherers in India. It also draws on the idea that most hunter-gatherers have 'immediate-return' economies, which she sees also as a further development of Sahlins's model (Bird-David 1992: 27). In contrast to 'delayed-return' ones, immediate-return systems involve a lack of planning or investment of time in activities whose yield is postponed (cultivating, herding or even any time-consuming making of complex hunting equipment). The idea was that of James Woodburn (e.g. 1982), Bird-David's mentor and premier hunter-gatherer specialist in Britain. Woodburn is a contemporary of Richard Lee. He has worked with the Hadza of Tanzania since the 1960s, and visited Lee among the Ju/'hoansi. Hadza and Ju/'hoansi are among his main examples for this kind of economic system. Thus again, Bushman ethnography served to represent the prototypical economic system of the hunter-gatherer in tune with 'nature'.

Capitalists or Communists?

H.J. Heinz versus Liz Wily

When I met Liz Wily, in 1974, she expressed almost exactly the sentiments of Marshall Sahlins, but she expressed these more in Marxist terms. Bushmen were not poor when they knew only of hunting and gathering; they became poor when pastoralists and ranchers came into contact with them. She had recently been appointed to the new position of Bushman Development Officer in Botswana's Ministry of Local Government and Lands. Her position was soon to be renamed

Basarwa Development Officer, and in 1978 Remote Area Development Officer, each change reflecting the rapidly changing images of those who live in the Kalahari: from denizens of 'the bush', to people who are not Tswana, to those officially designated, with capital letters, Remote Area Dwellers (RADs).

Liz Wily (Liz Alden Wily) is now an independent development consultant specializing in land tenure and community development issues. In the early 1970s, she had been the teacher at a small development scheme known as Bere in the southwestern Kalahari. She had appeared on the scene in 1972 and quickly learned to speak !Xoõ, an incredibly difficult language; and she had formulated a view of Bushman society as one based on communal values and shared access to resources. She seemed to find in Bushman society some of the ideals which she herself espoused. I was just starting my research with Naro then, and she suggested that I alter my plans to focus on social development among !Xoõ and on relations between !Xoõ and Kgalagadi. In retrospect, it would have made an interesting topic, as her vision of what was happening at Bere and other !Xoõ settlements was in such contrast to the emerging ethnography.

Wily's nemesis was H.J. Heinz (known as Doc Heinz), a former parasitologist and the ethnographer of the !Xoõ and later the 'River Bushmen' of the Okavango. Heinz had first ventured to the Kalahari as part of an expedition to the central Kalahari with Phillip Tobias in 1961. He completed an excellent ethnography of !Xoõ social organization as a thesis in 1966, but it remained unpublished until the 1990s (Heinz 1994). In 1969 he introduced livestock to a settlement near Bere, and he moved those who wished to take part in this unfolding social experiment to Bere in 1971 (see Barnard 1992: 73–4). Ultimately, this would lead to the social problems which lay in the disagreement in practical matters between Heinz and Wily, and in the theoretical question of whether the !Xoõ might better be regarded as communists or capitalists. Heinz enlisted the financial support of a number of South African companies and took on volunteers from South Africa, Austria and West Germany. They built a shop, which was run by Heinz's !Xoõ wife N/amkwa, and a school, in which Wily (a New Zealander) was the only teacher. He set up the scheme on expressly capitalist principles, and required each !Xoõ to own at least one (donated) cow. He insisted that individualism, and therefore capitalism, was part of Bushman culture. The idea was to increase the collective herd size, but, with one or two cows each, people stood little chance of utilizing their new wealth in meaningful currency units. A few years on, N/amkwa had acquired more cattle than anyone else, and many others were without livestock or any means to regain the small herds they once had had.

It goes without saying that the inhabitants of Bere had proved themselves neither capitalists nor communists, but what is interesting is that Heinz and Wily each had equated !Xoõ ideology with their own. Wily left, and eventually the government took over the scheme. In a sense both Heinz and Wily were right: individualism and individual ownership are significant elements of Bushman ideology, while collective ownership of land, the sharing of food and the equalization of wealth through various means (giving, lending and so on) are part of Bushman society too.

Enter Margaret Mead

I recall Heinz's excitement the day he said goodbye to Margaret Mead. She had flown into Ghanzi for a few days to visit Bere. Later she wrote the foreword to Heinz's autobiography, and in it she describes her visit:

> I was on a brief lecture tour in South Africa in 1974 as guest of the Johannesburg Marriage Guidance Society, which gave me access to chapters among South Africa's five castes. There is a fixed belief in South Africa that every visiting anthropologist will, of course, have to see Bushmen, and I did not wish to discourage this belief, although I had spent so many hours looking at uncut films on the Bushmen that I thought I knew a lot about them. But there is no substitute in film or book for the experience of standing, feeing like a giant even at my five-feet-two, towering over a tiny Bushman household. (Mead 1978: xi)

She goes on to tell of her meeting with Heinz and N/amkwa (Namkwa) and her stay at Bere. Mead describes Heinz as 'middle-aged', 'educated', 'foreign' (born in eastern Germany, and educated in the United States), using 'sophisticated instrumentation', yet 'only a "boy-child"' (as Heinz had said of himself) in the ways of the !Xoõ. N/amkwa was 'intrepid', 'uncorrupted', as 'determined and resourceful' as Heinz, and her lifestyle 'primitive', with 'extreme simplicity'. Their relationship was 'romantic' and 'poignant'. 'They faced each other over thousands of years of technological change, and she was equal to him, just as their union demonstrated the extraordinary cross-fertility of all human groups, for she had borne him a child' (Mead 1978: xii).

Heinz's autobiography (Heinz and Lee 1978) presents a somewhat unusual view of fieldwork. It is difficult to take it completely seriously, with its hundreds of sentences of remembered dialogue, often on very trivial matters which could not possibly find their way into an anthropologist's notebook. Heinz told me at the time that he had never used a tape recorder, so a notebook it would have been. The text does give a revealing impression of fieldwork, but I suspect too the heavy hand of his co-author, the unlikely-named South African journalist Marshall Lee. The battle between Heinz and Wily is mentioned nowhere in the autobiography proper, though strangely, Marshall Lee tackles it in an eight-page afterword to the book. The Johannesburg *Sunday Times* story of 21 September 1975, headlined 'White Bushman King Exiled', was too good a story not to be included.

Sadly, Doc Heinz, at the age of eighty-three, was brutally murdered at his home in northern Botswana in the southern winter of the year 2000.

Egalitarianism and Leadership

From the time of Thomas's *The Harmless People* (1959) onwards, part of the appeal of Bushman ethnography has been its representation of its subjects as peaceful and free, as sharing and caring individuals, and as sociable and at the same time egalitarian. On the importance of sharing, both material and otherwise, there is much agreement. For example, according to Tanaka (1980: 95), 'The integrating and governing principles of egalitarian San society are the principles of sharing and cooperation. Sharing and cooperation transcend the family unit to include all members of a camp.' Or according to Silberbauer (1994: 130), 'The G/wi repeatedly spoke of harmonious relationships as something toward which to strive, to be desired, and, when experienced, to be celebrated. Good fortune, pleasure, and contentment were referred to in terms of being shared.'

On egalitarianism, opinions are more divided, and it is worthwhile to reflect especially on differences between ethnography before the Marshalls and ethnography since. For example, Dorothea Bleek (1928: 37) tells us: 'There are no class distinctions among Naron and Auen, nor, excepting the medicine men, are there any trades.' However, she also says:

> Both Naron and Auen had chiefs when the old men were young. The middle-aged men just remember them ... It was difficult to find out exactly what a chief's powers were. They seem to have directed the movement of their people from place to place, to have ordered the burning of the veld, and in particular to have led in war. Fights were frequent both between the opposing Bushman tribes, Naron and Auen, and against other natives who were gradually encroaching from all sides. (D.F. Bleek 1928: 36–7)

On the G/wi, Silberbauer says:

> There are no chiefs or headmen and every adult member of the band has rights equal to those of all the other members who reside in the band's territory and to make use of what is found in it in the way of food or materials for tools, weapons, housing, clothing, etc. In the regulation of the band's affairs, none has any more authority than any other by reason of superior status and, except for the obligations within his or her kinship group toward senior kin (children to parents, step-parents, etc.), no man or woman yields to the superior authority of any other member. (Silberbauer 1965: 73)

In later times, such egalitarian values, both in politics and in economics, have been represented to the Western public through Jamie Uys's blockbuster films *The Gods Must Be Crazy* (released in 1980) and its sequel *The Gods Must Be Crazy II* (released in 1989). (There are also at least three unauthorized sequels in Cantonese.) The original depicts a naive Bushman called Xi (played by Namibian Ju/'hoan actor N!xau), who does not know how to get rid of a Coke bottle thrown out of a plane into the desert. The problem is that the Coke bottle causes jealousy, as there is only one of them, so Xi has to get rid of it. To my mind there are certainly moral and possibly quasi-religious overtones in the film: it may not be irrelevant that Uys himself plays 'The Reverend' and filmed the closing scene, of the Coke bottle being thrown off the end of the earth, at a place called God's Window, which is in present-day Mpumalanga, South Africa.

Anthropologists have occasionally picked up on the theme, for example Lee in the title of his paper 'The Gods Must Be Crazy but the State Has a Plan' (Lee 1986). There are also Bushman specialists (or, rather, at least one that I know) who have refused to watch the film on grounds of moral outrage. However, the film can be taken as a lowbrow, visual version of 'The Original Affluent Society'. The film is essentially about the good in such a society above the less egalitarian, more materialistic societies such as modern Botswana and the West. If we can separate politics from economics, the question is whether Xi is a 'chief' or not. I do not think so, but he is a leader of the kind described in numerous ethnographies (e.g. Lee 1979: 343–50). In general, leadership in Bushman societies depends on descent from earlier band-territory 'owners', on age and on personal qualities, including the ability to make good decisions, the ability to persuade and, very importantly, modesty. It is not done to be seen to be wanting to be a leader.

As for the 'harmlessness' of Bushmen, this is a subject of some slight controversy. Dorothea Bleek was echoing earlier writers and no doubt her knowledge of the violent times that much of Bushman country had gone though during the German occupation of the western Kalahari, from 1884 to 1915. Lee (1979: 370–400) discusses conflict and violence within bands at length, but not warfare. His revelations were shocking to some who at the time had become used to Sahlins's image, if not a wish for Uys's more idyllic cinematographic version. Such images as anthropology produces can indeed be recycled, back to anthropology. I once heard, from a civil servant in Botswana, that the Marshall family had once described warfare to the Ju/'hoansi and asked them about whether they knew of it. Then, 'Do your people do these things?' a Ju/'hoan supposedly asked Lorna in return; and Lorna sadly admitted that her people do. 'It sounds like a very silly custom,' said the Ju/'hoan. 'Somebody might get hurt.'

When some years later I asked Lorna about the story, and later still John, they said that they had no recollection. Probably, the interview never occurred, but that makes it all the more apocryphal. It is a myth born of anthropology, and like that borne within anthropology it coincides with the wishful expectations of the liberal public. I still teach from Sahlins's essay at introductory level, because in this spirit Sahlins's story, like the make-believe Marshall one, is a good antidote to the alternative.

Sharing and Giving

Lorna Marshall's famous paper 'Sharing, Talking, and Giving' was first published in *Africa* in 1961 and has been reprinted several times (e.g. Marshall 1976: 287–312). There Marshall described good manners and the style and content of conversation among Ju/'hoansi, and she distinguished two important kinds of exchange: meat-sharing and gift-giving. She also included a section on the absence of theft, and in this she notes that because Ju/'hoansi know each other's possessions and each other's footprints, it is practically impossible for a Ju/'hoan to steal something without being found out. Sahlins's (1974: 185–275) theoretical and comparative paper 'On the Sociology of Primitive Exchange' made use of Marshall's ethnographic observations, and it established the convention among economic anthropologists of seeing exchange in its widest sense as comprising three kinds of 'reciprocity': generalized, balanced and negative. Generalized reciprocity is giving without the expectation of return, and is characterized for example in giving from parent to child. Balanced reciprocity is more what we usually think of as 'reciprocity', exchange of things meant to be of equal value. According to Sahlins it is the norm within communities. Negative reciprocity is aiming to get more than is one's due or something for nothing, for example through haggling, gambling or theft. It is sometimes seen as appropriate outside one's community, for example in warfare.

Discovery of Hxaro and Reinvention of 'Stone Age Economics'

In the 1970s Bushman ethnographers were to put together simple theoretical insights like this one and ethnographic interests like Marshall's (in which, arguably, they were present in any case) in order to come up with a rather deeper understanding of exchange. Polly Wiessner's (1977) thesis was in the forefront of this development. Her great 'discovery' was *hxaro*, defined as 'a regional system for reducing risk' among the Ju/'hoansi. She documented the practice in great detail, and also made contributions to ethno-archaeology (e.g. Wiessner 1984) before moving on to ethnographic research in Melanesia.

Non-Khoisanists often make two mistakes with reference to *hxaro*: first, thinking it is general among San, and, secondly, thinking of it as characteristic only of hunting-and-gathering society. In fact, only two ethnic divisions of San peoples have any such custom: those who speak Ju/'hoan or related dialects, and those who speak Naro or very closely related dialects (specifically Ts'aokhoe). Ju/'hoansi call it *hxaro* (actually *xaro*) as an abstract noun and use //*aī* as the verb. Naro usually describe the custom with the verb //*aī*. No other San group has the custom, or at least no ethnographer of any other group has ever reported it. Once you see it, *hxaro* is everywhere, but it may not be as obvious to ethnographers not looking for it. I discovered it among the Naro only after Wiessner visited my fieldwork site in 1974. She uncovered its mechanisms and its full meaning among the Ju/'hoansi only on her second or third field trip, and only in fieldwork with a deliberate focus on material culture, exchange and reciprocity.

I mention that non-Khoisanists often make the mistake of thinking of *hxaro* as a hunter-gatherer thing. I suspect the same might be true of some San specialists, but the case is interestingly complicated when we imagine historical change. If by *hxaro* we mean simply the giving of non-consumable material possessions in delayed balanced reciprocity, then the custom is also found among Khoisan pastoralists (Barnard 2004b: 12). Damara call it *mā!khunigus* (meaning 'give return each other'). Again, I only found it among Damara because, as in the apocryphal story of Marshall looking for warfare among the Ju/'hoansi, I asked about it. The rule seems to be that as with Ju/'hoan *hxaro* exchange must be delayed, but that consumables are permitted, as long as they are not identical. In an example explained to me, a bag of white sugar could be presented to reciprocate the gift of a bag of brown sugar, but not of another bag of white sugar. So *hxaro*, of a sort, is not just a San custom. Yet the custom described may indeed reflect a time in the past when Damara were more hunters than herders. To add another caveat, in fact, although the abstract noun bearing the reciprocal particle *–gu* (indicating an exchange relationship) is not given in the Khoekhoe dictionary, the transitive verb *mā!khuni* and adjectival form *mā!khunisa* are given. What is more, the example presented there means 'exchange a shirt for a bigger one' (Haacke and Eiseb 2002: 80). One can envisage a social transformation from *hxaro*-like exchange in the past, to a more open form of exchange allowing consumables (among herders), to a modern usage where the word is retained but the custom has changed to reflect the new economy.

Other Studies of Exchange and Giving

What about all the other San, who do not have *hxaro*? In fact, the popularity of *hxaro*, following Wiessner's presentation on it at the Paris hunter-gathererists' conference in 1978 and subsequent publication (Wiessner 1982), seems to have obscured other ethnographic descriptions. This could be partly because Wiessner's account was so well written and because it neatly pulled together balanced reciprocity on the surface and generalized reciprocity to resources as an underlying reason for the custom. Probably no other San people have quite such a neat mechanism. The popularity of *hxaro* to the wider anthropological community may also rest in part on the popularity of the Ju/'hoan or !Kung as 'the Bushman' extraordinaire. Why clutter up ethnographic understanding with half a dozen different forms of exchange in half a dozen different lesser-known San communities, when we have a really good one among 'the !Kung'? The discovery of *hxaro* among the

Ju/'hoansi, as opposed to among any other group who might have something similar, was indeed fortuitous both for popular accounts of Ju/'hoan ethnography (e.g. Lee 2003: 118–23) and for general works in need of familiar examples (e.g. Kelly 1995: 188–9).

Apart from *hxaro* proper, the closest example of such a relation between formal gift-giving and rights to resources is the situation described by Thomas Widlok among the Hai//om. Although not the major focus of his ethnography, he makes use of comparisons of Hai//om gift-giving and *hxaro* three times in his excellent book on this Khoekhoe-speaking northern Kalahari people (Widlok 1999: 81, 86, 142), some of whom live in close proximity to *hxaroing* !Xũ. For me, one of the beauties of Widlok's ethnography is its occasional incorporation of the anthropologist's theorizing and apparent comparative insight on the part of informants. One of his mentions of *hxaro* illustrates this well: 'Although Hai//om maintain that they do not have a hxaro system like the !Kung, they recognize that their long-distance exchange relations are person-bound or, more specifically, "presence-bound"' (Widlok 1999: 142).

Importantly, Widlok has focused not only on exchange within Hai//om communities, but also on exchange with their neighbours. Hai//om live in close association with white ranchers, and also with Ovambo in the far north of Namibia. If Wiessner's great discovery was *hxaro*, Widlok's was 'inverse *mafisa*'. *Mafisa* proper is a Tswana practice whereby poor people (often Basarwa in Botswana) look after livestock for better-off people (usually Tswana) and in return receive milk, and sometimes calves or kids born to the cattle or goats they look after. In the Hai//om practice that Widlok (e.g. 1999: 113–19) calls 'inverse *mafisa*', poor people (Hai//om) who have acquired livestock leave them with well-off Ovambo, who in turn keep the products of the arrangement. Plainly, such a deal is not to the economic advantage of the poor Hai//om. Rather, as it is not good to be seen to have wealth, they in effect pay 'interest' (products of their livestock) to deposit it elsewhere. Widlok (1999: 100–6) also records a practice by which Hai//om sell mangetti or mongongo nuts to Ovambo, and the Ovambo make a strong alcoholic drink from the nuts and sell it to the Hai//om at a profit. Again, Ovambo get wealthier and Hai//om get poorer, with the gain for the latter being the retention of 'original affluence' in the form of more free time.

Widlok's later ethnography among gatherer-herding Nama in the Namib desert and among Australian Aborigines gives much scope for future comparative work, as indeed does his association for many years with the Max-Planck Institute for Social Anthropology at Halle (with its special interest in property relations) and the Max-Planck Institute for Psycho-Linguistics at Nijmegen.

Another major figure in San studies in the last decade was Susan Kent. Her extremely sad, untimely death in 2003 at the age of just fifty leaves a great gap in our field. The relevance of her work here lies in her ethnographic descriptions of Kua of Kutse in southern Botswana. In an important paper published in *Man*, she suggested that social reasons for sharing outweigh economic ones, as in one example where a small squirrel is shared out despite the lack of meat on it (e.g. Kent 1993: 493). Instead of *hxaro*, these Kua have a system of long-term lending and borrowing between kin, which seems to serve some of the same functions (1993: 496–7). Kent's paper established a comparative framework through which to view economic relations. Beyond economics in the narrow sense, she explored gender relations, health and ethnicity, and practised ethnography with a statistical sense far better than that of most Kalahari ethnographers, and she continued the ethno-archaeology she had begun in her youth in the American South-West with similar work late in her life in Lesotho. She also edited some seven volumes, two of which (Kent 1996, 2002b), as we shall see later, had significant implications for the rein-terpretation of relations between Kalahari hunter-gatherers and their neighbours.

Farm Bushmen

Back in the early 1970s, there was a feeling that 'acculturated' Bushmen were being neglected. There had been some studies of Bushman–'Bantu' relations in the 1930s, not least by Schapera (1939). Silberbauer and Kuper (1966) ventured in this direction in the 1960s. But what was missing was work with the large populations of semi-settled 'squatters' living on the vast white-owned cattle farms of Botswana and then South West Africa. Canadian Mathias Guenther stepped into the scene, with field research on a farm and mission station in the Ghanzi district of Botswana.

Guenther's early work on 'farm Bushmen' (e.g. 1973, 1976) moved Bushman studies towards are fuller understanding of the great range of variation that exists. He later came to concentrate more on religion and art among the same people. The interesting fact is that social change came first, traditional religious practice came after – although in one early paper Guenther (1979a) did analyse the intriguing problem of individual variation in religious belief. He argued there that religion in general, not just farm Bushman religion, is 'anti-structure', characterized by idio-syncrasy and a lack of clear function or structure in the sense of traditional Durkheimian or Lévi-Straussian approaches.

The farm Bushmen are not just any Bushmen; they are mainly Naro. It is impor-tant to know what things they do are done because they are Naro, and what ones because they are in closer contact with farmers than are other Bushmen. I have worked to a large extent with Naro as well. Guenther and I can see the ethnic aspects of differences between these people and other Bushmen in female and male initiation, or in rules of kinship classification and behaviour, but it is some-times difficult for us to persuade other anthropologists that Naro differ from Ju/'hoansi in these respects not because of the presence of ranchers, but (to sim-plify slightly) because they are 'Central' rather than 'Northern Bushmen'.

I worked mainly with Naro on the southern edge of the Ghanzi farms, where life was more 'traditional' than in Guenther's north-east area; and Hendrik Steyn worked to the west beyond the farms, where life was more 'traditional' still. My own interests focused on kinship, settlement patterns and other topics amenable to the theoretical position I espoused, known as regional structural comparison (Barnard 1996). The idea, related to Adam Kuper's work on Southern Bantu-speakers, was that we can see more through comparing related cultures than through intensive studies of just one or through wider comparisons. It made a great deal of sense of Khoisan social organization and even topics like religious belief, although it did not catch on among others either inside Khoisan studies or beyond to the degree I had hoped. Steyn was interested in plant utilization and in economic activity generally, and his master's thesis, originally in Afrikaans, was published in English by the South African Museum (Steyn 1971). His career later developed in other directions, but his interest was in those aspects of Bushman society that remained traditional even among those others had prematurely written off as 'acculturated' and therefore not worth serious study as hunter-gatherers.

My focus and Steyn's was on Naro as Naro, and not as 'farm' or 'acculturated' Bushmen. This emphasis increasingly found its way into Guenther's work as well when he turned more to studies of Naro religion and to the Naro as 'a people'. The titles of his two major monographs on the Naro reflect this change, from *The Farm Bushmen of the Ghanzi District, Botswana* (1979b) to *The Nharo Bushmen of Botswana* (1986). In the long run, this change in emphasis may have had some benefit to the Naro themselves, as pride in Naro heritage has grown over the last few decades. There are many reasons for this, and ethnography is no doubt not the only one, or even the major one, but it has at least contributed to the trend through making anthropologists more aware of the Naro as a 'people'. This was, of course, a status accorded them by Dorothea Bleek in the very first ethnographic mono-graph on a Bushman people (Bleek 1928), but it seems to have been overshadowed since the 1950s by the hegemony of '!Kung' studies. Other factors include the development of economic projects and Naro literacy skills, as well as a museum, on the part of the Kuru Development Trust (set up in 1986) at D'Kar at the mission station where Guenther studied, and the political and human rights initiatives by the pressure group First People of the Kalahari (founded in 1991), based in the dis-trict capital Ghanzi.

More recently, James Suzman (e.g. 2000) and Renée Sylvain (e.g. 2003) have worked with farm workers and squatters in the Omaheke region of Namibia. This is the area just south of the Nyae Nyae area, inhabited by Ju/'hoansi, ≠Au//eisi, Naro and others who live alongside white farmers and Herero. Sylvain comments on the first problem of working with such people: the denial of their authenticity or even their existence by many local non-San. 'There are no pure Bushmen left anymore,' one told her. 'They've been intermarrying with other ethnic groups far too long.' Even a Namibian Broadcasting Corporation researcher who had grown up in the region told her that they had disappeared years before. And a missionary on the Botswana side of the border commented, 'Once they get an education they are no longer Bushmen' (quotations from Sylvain 2003: 112).

In those publications and elsewhere, Suzman and Sylvain have consistently argued against slipping into the (for some) easy solution of classifying San as 'indigenous peoples' and seeking special rights for them. Sylvain in particular argues that to emphasize indigeneity (indigenousness) is to gloss over class differences, and further that we do 'farm Bushmen' no favours by portraying them simply as victims of colonialism or global capitalism. There may seem to be logical contradictions in this view, but essentially the argument is that class distinctions become apparent in almost all San/outsider economic relations, and that the emphasis on special relations with land, and so on, tends to make things worse, especially for those such as 'farm Bushmen' who have been deprived of their land (see also Sylvain 2002).

Sylvain and Suzman, incidentally, come from quite different backgrounds themselves and from different anthropological traditions. Sylvain is from Canada and a student of Richard Lee, while Suzman hails from South Africa and did both his degrees in Scotland (an M.A. at St Andrews with a short period of work in Botswana, and a Ph.D. at Edinburgh with extended research in Namibia). Both are quite different in approach from Guenther, whose concerns have long been both with social and cultural change and with the continuity between past and present, or, as Suzman (2000: 7) has put it, with 'the apparent continuity of Bushman cultural forms in spite of, or in response to, the presence of others'. Suzman, especially in his Ph.D. thesis, which is published as *'Things from the Bush'* (Suzman 2000), is concerned with how the Bushmen see themselves and with the way they are understood by their neighbours, especially white farmers. He stresses the Ju/'hoan distinction between present-day life and the ways of 'old-time people' (*ju≠engsi o kxaice*) and sees those Ju/'hoansi associated with the old times, the old stories, and so on, as increasingly marginalized. Sylvain goes further in arguing that it is Ju/'hoan society as a whole which is marginalized by the imagery of past times.

Conclusion

Whether it was actually 'true' or not, the idea of an 'original affluent society' afforded opportunities for anthropology to rethink the very notion of the hunter-gatherer. It also spurred on Kalahari Bushman research in interesting directions. Wiessner's account of *hxaro* is dependent on Sahlins's work, although actually more in respect of his distinctions between generalized, balanced and negative reciprocity than with regard to his theory of original affluence.

If the 'real Bushman' is affluent, then where does that leave the 'farm Bushman'? The contrast was important for a long time. In my view, it was overemphasized. All Bushmen are 'acculturated', and have been for centuries. Farm Bushmen retain kinship ideology, exchange practices, mythology and ritual despite the existence of farmers living just a few kilometres away. Groups like the Ju/'hoansi of Nyae Nyae live not such a different existence, but, as Wily showed in her battle with Heinz, contact with outside economic forces breeds a self-perception, and often a reality, of poverty, as much as it may increase the wealth of some.

−7−

The Return of Myth and Symbol

In the early 1970s, a number of events conspired to create new, more aesthetic visions of 'the Bushman'. Marshall and Lee had documented groups from the north, and Silberbauer and Tanaka those from the central Kalahari. Myth and symbol returned as major interests in Bushman studies, as they had been in the nineteenth century. Two events were critical. One was Megan Biesele's arrival among the !Kung (as anthropologists of the time called them) or Ju/'hoansi (as they are called today). Her interests in folklore and Bushman religion, together with the relative neglect shown these aspects of cultural life by the major ethnographers of the time, made the re-emergence of myth and symbol obvious. When Mathias Guenther came to concentrate more on religion and art and less on contact and social change, the new ethnographic focus developed.

The other event was much less obvious. It was marked by changes in focus within South African archaeology, and most specifically a move away from 'art for art's sake' in rock art studies, towards rigorous statistical analysis. Archaeologists turned from their traditional concerns with pigments and style and with rock art as historical record, towards counting the numbers of animals, people and other images depicted. What they found was that the various species most painted on the rocks did not match their incidence on the ground outside the caves, and especially in the Drakensberg. What is more, the men depicted were not hunters, but San trance dancers, sometimes with animal heads. Often too, the animals were not running away with wounds on their sides; they were bleeding from the nose in the manner of San in trance. In other words, these were not hunting scenes. They were sacred images.

It was not long before archaeologists started using the insights of Biesele, Guenther and other ethnographers to help interpret rock art. They also turned back to the pages of Bleek and Lloyd's *Specimens of Bushman Folklore* (1911) and even to their unpublished notes, and virtually a new field came into being, incorporating archaeology, the history of art, the anthropology of religion, and language and oral literature. The more general archaeology of Later Stone Age South Africa changed too, as other archaeologists also gained expertise and comparative interests through what was happening in the Kalahari. Meanwhile, anthropology outside Bushman studies maintained its distance from studies of Khoisan religion until very late in the twentieth century, when ethnography, rock art studies and theories of symbolic revolution converged.

Studies of Folkore and Religion

Megan Biesele

Marguerite Anne (Megan) Biesele's career has been unusual. She did her Ph.D. at Harvard (Biesele 1975) and has long taught as an adjunct professor at Rice University, but has never held a conventional tenured academic post. In the 1970s she served as Lorna Marshall's secretary, and much of her career since then has been spent in advocacy and development work on behalf of the Ju/'hoansi, as well as in studies of Ju/'hoan folklore and cosmology. In 1973 she helped set up the Kalahari Peoples Fund, and from 1987 to 1992 was director of the Nyae Nyae Development Foundation of Namibia. She is now president of the School of Expressive Culture based at Texas A & M University, and continues to be associated with programmes at Rice as well as the University of Texas at Austin and the University of Nebraska. In this chapter our concern is the folklore part of Biesele's work, but the two strands (folklore and advocacy) are not entirely unrelated. Her efforts in studying indigenous knowledge and communication, co-authoring works on Ju/'hoan culture with Ju/'hoansi, fostering publications on the Ju/'hoan language, and working on education projects both in Namibia (for Ju/'hoansi) and the United States (for Americans to learn about Ju/'hoansi) all bring these together.

Among Biesele's most important works on folklore and religion are two early papers: one based on her thesis (Biesele 1976), the other a paper with David Lewis-Williams on eland-hunting rituals (Biesele and Lewis-Williams 1978). In the former she makes reference to the fact that before her own fieldwork the only substantial collection of oral texts of any San group was Bleek and Lloyd's *Specimens of Bushman Folklore*. She also draws attention to the fact that her paper is not intended as an introduction to San folklore in general: 'Just as the ecological anthropologists cannot answer the question '"What do San hunter-gatherers eat?" without reference to very localized and specific conditions, neither can the student of folklore make many generalizations about their oral traditions' (Biesele 1976: 304–5). However, what she describes – God as a trickster figure, the tale of the moon and the hare (which explains the origin of death), and so on – sound very like those of the /Xam. She also touches on the social context of myth-telling, a theme missing from earlier folklore studies but which would be important in Biesele's later writings. And she draws attention to individual variation in Ju/'hoan myth and the place of creative imagination in myth construction, notions which would become important later in her work, and in that of Mathias Guenther. In Biesele's paper with Lewis-Williams, we learn of the 'striking similarities' between /Xam and Ju/'hoan ritual, specifically the ritual of the first kill of an eland. The data come from Bleek and Lloyd, and from Biesele's then recent fieldwork. Although one relatively obscure earlier study had suggested a pan-Bushman religious system (McCall 1970), here was definitive evidence. It was only from this point that systematic comparisons were to begin, and ultimately the similarities between northern and southern San groups were to guide the interpretation of rock art over the coming decades.

The most important of Biesele's works is probably her ever-popular *Women Like Meat*, published first in Johannesburg (Biesele 1993) and released later the same year by Indiana University Press. In line with her advocacy role, her royalties from the book were donated to the Kalahari Peoples Fund (Botswana) and the Nyae Nyae Development Foundation of Namibia. Yet, in subject matter, the book lies firmly in the traditions of her folklore work, which by 1993 she had expanded to include a complex of things: the relation of folklore to technology and subsistence, the significance of gender in myth and ritual, narrative as communication, memory and the adaptive value of narrative, the role of creativity within tradition, the question of metaphor or the 'special reality' of oral culture, and so on. These are all embedded in her own narrative, which has proved useful as a teaching text in many American and European universities over the past decade and a half.

One other of Biesele's works deserves mention here. This is *Healing Makes our Hearts Happy*, co-authored with clinical psychologist Richard Katz and educational anthropologist Verna St Denis (Katz, Biesele and St Denis 1997). Katz had done fieldwork on trance curing among Ju/'hoansi in 1968 (see, for example, Katz 1982), and had subsequently done similar work on 'community healing systems', as he came to call them, in Fiji, Alaska and Saskatchewan. St Denis, a Cree-Metis from Saskatchewan, is active in community-based or participatory research with 'indigenous' communities. In 1989 Katz made a return journey to the Kalahari, and *Healing Makes our Hearts Happy* is the result. It is part of a growing genre within San studies of part-academic, part-coffee-table books. Its focus is on traditional healing ritual in the context of relations between Ju/'hoansi and their herding neighbours, contact with the Namibian government and with Western medicine, social problems such as alcoholism, and social efforts for their alleviation such as through education. Traditional healing involves, among other things, the use of *n/om* ('medicine' or spiritual energy) in the hands of medicine people, usually men. In what is often called the medicine dance, they go into a state of *!aia* (generally glossed as 'trance') and can use this power to cure illnesses, known and unknown, of everyone present.

Biesele's contribution to the book includes much of the background material, since she is the only one of the authors who speaks Ju/'hoan and who has maintained close contact with the people. Of particular note is the change from the dominance of what is called the giraffe dance, in earlier times, to the drum dance. The former is done mainly by men, dancing in a circle around women, who clap and sing. The latter involves mainly women, dancing to drum music while forming a large horseshoe shape, with a male drummer at the mouth of the horseshoe. The giraffe dance is typical of medicine dances in other parts of southern Africa. The increase in importance of the drum dance through the 1980s and since suggests changes in the relation between the sexes, with a greater number of women in recent times taking up trance curing. Interesting too is the fact that Ju/'hoan healers today have different views of the future. According to ≠Oma !'Homg!ausi, 'Our children will just stand around … they'll just die with no healers.' However, according to ≠Oma Djo, 'N/om is just the same as long ago, even though it keeps on changing … The dance is still here at /Kae/kae. It's doing well, and is still healing the people' (quoted in Katz, Biesele and St Denis 1997: 131). As in this instance, much of Biesele's work stresses agency, the diversity of views among Ju/'hoansi, and the role of informants in framing the ethnography.

Mathias Guenther

The other major figure in the study of San religion is Mathias Guenther. We met him in the last chapter with reference to his work on 'farm Bushmen', but his passion in the last two decades has been the aesthetic in Bushman culture, or more specifically the study of Bushman religious belief, ritual and art, the connections between these, and their relation to modern life. Like Biesele, Guenther has dozens of relevant publications to his name, but let me take four here as exemplary of his interests and approach.

Bushman Folktales (Guenther 1989) includes over a hundred pages of Naro and /Xam narratives plus comments on social and religious context, performance and comparison. It is difficult to number them precisely since a great many are different versions of the same tale. For example, Guenther gives four Naro versions of 'The Moon and the Hare, and the Origin of Death' and two /Xam versions. There are related versions of Naro tales of the differentiation of 'races': 'Bushmen, Bantu and the Cow', 'How People Got their Different Colours', 'God, Bathing in a Water is Laughed at by Bushmen and Bantu', and 'The Tower of Babel'. The last is, of course, of non-Bushman origin, but has been incorporated into the Naro myth cycle. In the version Guenther relates the location of the tower is ambiguous, though I once recorded another Naro version in which Babel is equated with Cape Town (see Barnard 1988a). The beauty of *Bushman Folktales* is that it makes comparison between Naro and /Xam, and between individual versions of myths and stories, so simple: the tales are printed sequentially after brief introductory material.

Guenther classifies the tales into four categories: creation, primal time, tricksters and legends. The last includes one very interesting Naro story called 'How the Servants of the Early Cultivators Turned to Plant Gather and Theft'. It tells of two servants who cultivated fields for 'early people', had an argument with incomers of unspecified origin, witnessed drought, and then left the fields to gather wild foods and steal from their neighbours. Guenther (1989: 158) describes it as possibly 'a specimen of oral history that suggests considerable antiquity for an economic dependency relationship between Bushmen and agro-pastoralists', and 'in tune with the recent findings by archaeologists in the north-central Kalahari'. This is an intriguing comment given Guenther's role, just a few years later, on the traditionalist side in the Kalahari debate (see Chapter 8).

If *Bushman Folktales* is in the Bleekian tradition, *Tricksters and Trancers* (Guenther 1999) is altogether more analytically sophisticated. It is Guenther's masterpiece. He covers a vast literature as well as his own fieldwork material on the relations between social values, religious belief, the trickster figure in Bushman folklore, trance dancing and the place of missionaries in Bushman religion. Guenther himself stayed at a mission station for most of his early fieldwork period in the 1970s, and he blends his own findings with historical material. The book as a whole includes a great deal of comparative analysis of Bushman religion, both through history and in diverse geographical contexts. He calls his approach 'experience-rooted' and refers often to 'ambiguity' in Bushman belief. In a well-argued critique of a semi-structuralist position invoking the idea of religion as an 'inner state', he suggests: 'It is this ineffable, preverbal, non-semantic quality of religion, utterable only through metaphor, which I hold to be the characteristic expressive and conceptual mode of Bushman religion' (Guenther 1999: 236). *Tricksters and Trancers* may not be an easy book to come to grips with conceptually, but it is wonderfully readable and illustrates the complexity of Bushman thought as well as that of the anthropologist. Although derived from five conference papers, parts of which have been published elsewhere, the book has great coherence as an expression of a theory of religion, or at the very least a passionately argued theory of Bushman religion.

In 'Ethno-tourism and the Bushmen', Guenther (2002) turns his attention to a different sort of Bushman 'myth' – the myth of the semi-naked, photogenic, happy inhabitant of a touristic version of the original affluent society. In fact, Guenther presents descriptions of two sorts of tourist venture: this one (exemplified by an upmarket tourist lodge in Namibia) and more realistic community-based schemes (such as those associated with formerly subjugated groups like Naro at D'Kar in western Botswana). Guenther (2002: 59) favours the latter as the way forward, and expresses an optimistic vision of Bushmen 'negotiating a new identity ... that jettisons the static, iconic elements of pristinism of the colonial past and [is] in tune with the economic and politial aspirations of the people today, in their struggle for recognition rights and land'.

In 'Farm Labourer, Trance Dancer, Artist' (Guenther 1998), we find a biographical account of the late Qwaa Mangana, who was a gifted G/wi artist resident in the 1990s near the Kuru Art Centre at D'Kar. Qwaa's paintings were often based on G/wi ritual and mythology, and Guenther knew him well. He was a trance dancer, and had been a hunter in his youth, and later a farm labourer. Guenther explicitly and self-consciously touches on the postmodern, seemingly because Qwaa was already there, painting both 'modern' pictures of animals and traditional life, and 'postmodern' ones of modernity: the reinvention of tradition in the Ghanzi farms. Qwaa's famous *Self-Portrait and Buttons* is a painting of the artist with arms outstretched amidst eight buttons the size of his torso, the point (he explained to Guenther) being that the buttons show what happens when one enters a trance: 'they are round, and [i.e. inside each button] round and round' (quoted in Guenther 1998: 125; Guenther's gloss). *Self-Portrait and Buttons* is not meant to be one of Qwaa's postmodern or 'hybrid' paintings, but it illustrates an inventiveness in tradition, which is altogether characteristic of both Bushman art (especially Qwaa's) and Guenther's theoretical position.

Many of San works of art, such as *Self-Portrait and Buttons*, and also two splendid colour linocuts called *Bicycle and Chameleon* by the younger painter Qhaqhoo (Xgaoc'õ X'are), express both the modern and the traditional. One is shown on the cover of this book. Chameleon is in a sense the old and, at least for me, represents too the ability to shift between old and new. Bicycle symbolizes contradiction. It recalls the disputes in both Namibia and Botswana in the early 1980s. In Namibia, game park officials would not allow San to hunt on horseback (said to be both non-traditional and not sporting, in that animals did not have a chance) but, strangely, did allow chasing game by bicycle.

Art on the Rocks

Changing Fashions: Towards a Symbolic Approach in Rock Art Studies

Since the nineteenth century, rock art has formed a major interest of amateurs associated with Bushman studies, especially in South Africa. Scholars such as G.W. Stow and the Abbé Breuil were interested in rock art for its own sake, of course, but also very much for what it could tell us about prehistory (see Chapter 4). Other important figures were civil engineer and amateur prehistorian Clarence 'Peter' van Riet Lowe (e.g. 1952) and artist Walter Battiss (e.g. 1948). Van Riet Lowe was a close associate of Breuil and of Field Marshall Smuts, and he was also influential on Battiss. Battiss and van Riet Lowe explored rock art in the Drakensberg together, and van Riet Lowe encouraged Battiss in removing rock art panels and also apparently put into his head the idea that South African paintings and engravings alike could be classified as belonging to three periods. The first was 'pre-Bushman', followed by a rather complex period whose artists were unknown, then a 'true Bushman' phase. Battiss hunted with Bushmen in then South West Africa, but he seems not to have held his hosts in high regard intellectually and saw 'true Bushman' art as marking a shift from earlier 'reverence' to mere 'illustration' (Battiss 1948: 96; see also Lewis-Williams 2002: 5–10).

In the 1960s a generation of immigrants to southern Africa brought new ideas (Lewis-Williams 2002: 11–12). They too were mainly amateurs or at least not trained in archaeology proper. From Britain there was quantity surveyor Alex Willcox, businessman Neil Lee and accountant Bert Woodhouse. From Scandinavia, there were Jalmar and Ione Rudner (a town planner and a museum technician) and, from Austria, Harald Pager (a commercial artist). In the end, Pager was the greatest recorder ot rock art for posterity, perhaps precisely because he lacked any pretence of high 'anthropological' insight. Among a number of South Africans, newspaper cartoonist Townley Johnson developed new methods of reproduction that combined photography and drawing, and several in this genera-tion contributed to this difficult task of rendering the art on paper. Because of relief and colour in the natural rock surface, rock paintings and engravings do not lend themselves easily to sympathetic reproduction by simple colour photography. Yet dozens of books appeared, often aimed at a growing public interest in rock art, at least among advantaged sections of South African society. Of all these writers, Willcox is of particular interest in light of the debate that was to follow. In one of his most important papers (Willcox 1978b), he attacked developments in the 1970s and argued instead in favour of an 'art for art's sake' approach. He claimed that Bushmen artists of the Drakensberg had great ability to remember and reproduce exactly what events they had seen or what their mythology had told them, and used art to record what they wished their communities to know.

The breakthrough towards symbolism came from an unlikely source: statistical analysis. The fact is that the incidence of animals in Drakensberg rock art is very different from the incidence of animals on the ground in the Drakensberg. The first such analysis was that of Patricia Vinnicombe, who had grown up on a farm there and noticed the preponderance especially of eland in the art. In the 1960s she began recording precisely twenty attributes of each rock art figure in her study area. These included the subject (human or animal), style (monochrome, bichrome, polychrome, shaded polychrome), scene description (hunting, fighting, dancing, etc.), and so on. Although trained as an occupational therapist, she married an archaeologist and came to devote most of her time to rock art studies. In a crucial paper (Vinnicombe 1972), she dismissed both the 'art for art's sake' view and the 'sympathetic magic' view, and used the relative occurrence of animals in the art and ethnographic comparisons, which showed these to be animals with the most ritual significance, to come to a new understanding of rock art as religious art. Her very rare (low print run) but influential *People of the Eland* (1976) gives the most convincing expression of this hypothesis.

The Symbolic Approach of David Lewis-Williams

The major proponent of the symbolic approach was to be David Lewis-Williams, who studied social anthropology at the University of Cape Town in the 1950s (and once heard Radcliffe-Brown lecture there). He began working on rock art in 1959, and in the 1960s and 1970s he picked up Vinnicombe's interest in statistical analysis and came to develop first structuralist and later semiotic understandings of rock art. His greatest book is *Believing and Seeing* (1981), a semiotic analysis of Drakensberg paintings based on his Natal Ph.D. thesis. Both the foreword by Lorna Marshall and Lewis-Williams's acknowledgement of Megan Biesele's guidance on a trip to the northern Kalahari reflect too the influence of social anthropology and ethnographic analogy in his work.

Believing and Seeing is a wonderfully produced book: very wide format with three columns of text and dozens of images. For Lewis-Williams, the essence of the art is at least in part in the detail of depiction. In this book photography is jettisoned in favour of a form of reproduction used in many, though not all, of his works: detailed but stylized black-and-white tracings of figures. Other essences are brought out through counting the occurrences of pictorial elements, as in Vinnicombe's work, and through ethnographic analogy – especially to /Xam and !Kung (Ju/'hoansi). This allows Lewis-Williams not only to interpret rock art afresh, but also to reinterpret the commentaries of others. For example, a site called Fulton's Rock contains a painting described by Neil Lee and Bert Woodhouse (1970: 103) as possibly 'a burial ceremony with mourners dancing around the dead body'. Lewis-Williams (1981: 43) sees it as far more likely 'a girl's puberty dance'. The eland bull dance is in fact a well-known Kalahari ritual involving one or more men acting as 'eland bulls' (symbolic of male sexuality) and the women they chase in dance step around the outside of the hut in which the female initiate is confined (see, for example, L. Marshall 1999: 195–201). By the postures as well as the elements of the painting, I am quite sure that Lewis-Williams is right (and Lorna Marshall, before me, agreed).

Critics might point out that no such dance is recorded in either the Bleek family material or the historical record of the Drakensberg groups, although the seclusion of individual initiates is. Lewis-Williams (1981: 44–6) provides photos of both Ju/'hoan and Naro eland bull dances, and further suggests circumstantial evidence of an association in /Xam ideology between female puberty ceremonies and eland mating behaviour. The latter (in /Xam thought) rests on the /Xam use of 'respect' terminology for the eland, in other words the avoidance of the 'strong' word *sā* ('eland') in favour of circumlocutions such as *≠koúken-!khwi* (translated by Lloyd, though not very literally, as 'when it lashes its tail'). It also rests on comparative linguistic material from Ju/'hoan. The word 'eland' occurs in the titles of five of the ten chapters, each with a different ritual signification: maiden, hunter, marriage, medicine man and rain. There is no doubt that Lewis-Williams was on the right track, even if some of his stronger comments, on the association of painting and trance (e.g. Lewis-Williams and Dowson 1989), have met with criticism. Lewis-Williams and his associate Thomas Dowson in fact edited one book (Dowson and Lewis-Williams 1994) in which critics argue on points of detail, although there is a broad consensus there on the value of exploring the trance hypothesis.

In the 1980s intense controversy broke out with regard to Lewis-Williams's participation in the World Archaeological Congress (WAC), held in Southampton, England, in September 1986. He was to have co-organized the session on 'Cultural Attitudes to Animals in Art', but for political and financial reasons all South Africa-based scholars were barred from attending. Congress organizer Peter Ucko wrote to Phillip Tobias, another South African he had wanted to participate, that to allow them to attend would have brought the loss of Southampton City Council sponsorship (and with it the loss of at least £100,000 of revenue), as well as a conference boycott from Third World and 'indigenous' representatives (Ucko 1987: 67–9). One problem was that participants were identified as national delegates: the names of countries they 'represented' were listed in conference announcements after each name. In contrast, the organizers of the Fourth International Conference on Hunting and Gathering Societies, held in London the week following the WAC, deliberately avoided designating those who attended by 'their' countries or even institutions; and in London Lewis-Williams was welcomed.

The great irony is that both Tobias and Lewis-Williams were staunch opponents of apartheid. Lewis-Williams used his time in London to appear on British television in debate with the South African ambassador and to argue against South African policies. In 2000 Lewis-Williams was invited by President Thabo Mbeki to create South Africa's new motto, which he duly did – using Dorothea Bleek's dictionary to put it into /Xam. Officially, the motto means 'Diverse people unite', but the /Xam words *!Ke e: /xarra //ke* also carry connotations of talking with one another as well as joining together. In South Africa's new coat of arms, the motto sits beneath a somewhat modified rock art figure of two 'ungendered' people clasping hands. The original of the figure is a man (in the coat of arms, duplicated in mirror image); it was copied by Thomas Dowson from the Linton Stone, a panel full of eland, which is displayed in the South African Museum in Cape Town (see Barnard 2003, 2004c).

Lewis-Williams, now retired, served many years as Professor of Cognitive Archaeoogy at the University of the Witwatersrand (Wits) and was founding director of the Rock Art Research Unit there. He is still active, however, and some of his most recent work delves even more deeply into San spirituality (e.g. Lewis-Williams and Pearce 2004), with ever richer appreciation of relations between ancient rock art and contemporary ethnography, and even between neurology and the mind of the artist. The latter is now all the more significant due to the recent discovery of the world's earliest known material representation of symbolic expression, most famously the engraved pieces of ochre from Blombos cave dated at 77,000 years old.

Dowson has since moved, first to Ucko's old department at Southampton and later to Manchester, but the great tradition of Lewis-Williams's research continues at Wits under the directorship of Ben Smith. Dowson was instrumental in producing many of the tracings of rock paintings for the Wits collection, but has also turned his attention to the more difficult-to-interpret genre of rock engravings, particularly those of Twyfelfontein in northern Namibia (e.g. Dowson 1992). Others have taken up myth, metaphors of space, authorship, gender and comparisons with modern art (all themes in Dowson and Lewis-Williams 1994), and there are now a great many full-time researchers, young and old, working on the meaning of San rock art.

The Integration of Approaches: Recent Developments

It need hardly be said at this point that space precludes a detailed discussion of the richness of contemporary southern African rock art research. That could take a volume or two. Rather, let me comment here on just one very important development: the Living Landscape Project, based at Clanwilliam in the Western Cape.

The Living Landscape Project is the brainchild of John Parkington, Professor of Archaeology at the University of Cape Town. Like many in rock art studies, Parkington immigrated from England and (with decades of archaeological experience in the area) developed a fascination for the landscape in which rock art sits. Unlike most of the others, though, he has in recent years made a very conscious effort to bring to life the paintings in their physical context through the production of books and accompanying CD-ROM guides to rock art in the living landscape. This dimension is added to the symbolic one, and ultimately the anthropological understanding handed down from Bleek and Lloyd.

Let me quote from the cover blurbs of Parkington's first two books in his recent 'Follow the San ...' series:

> In the world view of the San, the eland is the favourite creation of the mantis; in the mind of a young Kalahari hunter it is the key game target ... The eland is a symbol of wife, hunting the euphemism for sexual relations. Rock paintings are essentially depictions of people and game animals. On this journey, following the San, we view the paintings and try to see them through the eyes of the painters. (Parkington 2002: back cover)

> These Cederberg rock paintings are, as Wilhelm Bleek noted in the late 19th century, about the things that 'most deeply moved the Bushman mind' ... Through the dissemination of the written and painted archives, the stories, images and sounds of the /Xam are gradually finding their way back into the minds of Cederberg people. (Parkington 2003: back cover).

Lewis-Williams has brought San religion to a wider reading public interested in rock art, archaeology or, indeed, in the case of some his recent work, spirituality. Parkington, among others, has helped to bring San rock art to a wider community in South Africa. The use of Bleek and Lloyd may be overdone in that country, but wider anthropology has perhaps yet to catch up on the degree of sophistication in local literature on San thought, long established even in populist accounts in rock art studies.

The latest phase in southern African rock art research is marked by some three approaches, all primarily now in the hands of younger scholars. In his introduction to the recent collection *Further Approaches to Southern African Rock Art*, Geoffrey Blundell (2005) identifies these approaches as 'the extension, development and challenging of the so-called shamanistic school's interpretations of particular images', 'rock art that has not received much attention' (that made by Khoekhoe or Bantu-speaking peoples), and 'concern with the role of the art in complex processes of historical interaction' (including the application of 'revisionist' thinking to rock art studies). Examples of the first approach include papers in that volume on snakes, birds, insects and rhebok – extending the depth of symbolism well beyond the proverbial eland of earlier work. Meanwhile, beyond southern Africa the 'shamanistic school' has had great influence, but not without backlash. For example, world rock art expert and archaeological populist Paul Bahn used his Rhind Lectures 'Art on the Rocks', given in Edinburgh in 2006, to question the dominance of shamanism as a worldwide explanation for meaning in rock art.

Bushman Religion in the Wider Anthropology

The Bushman is a pervasive image in anthropology, well beyond Bushman or hunter-gatherer specialists. The central theme in the wider discipline seems to be the split between the material and the mystical. In anthropological thought (as in van der Postian) Bushmen are closely tied both, on the ground, to their limited technology and, above it, to a mystical world of insect gods, misanthropes and ancient rituals.

Clifford Geertz (1966: 42), commenting on the relative degrees of complexity in symbolic elaboration, is typical of one sort of naive reasoning: 'One need only think of the Australians and the Bushmen, the Toradja and the Alorese, the Hopi and the Apache, the Hindus and the Romans, or even the Italians and the Poles, to see that degree of religious articulateness is not a constant even between societies of similar complexity.' Geertz presumes that his readers have all the knowledge necessary to make the comparisons, and that none among them would disagree that Australians and Bushmen have societies of similar complexity but different degrees of religious articulateness. My assumption is that Australian Aborigines, in his view, are intended as the more articulate. We cannot fault him for not knowing the details of ethnography not then written, but I would question whether that kind of statement does justice even to what was available, and equally whether readers of statements like this were even expected to have a comparative knowledge of, say, Bleek and

Lloyd (1911) on the /Xam and Spencer and Gillen (1899) on the Aranda (Arunta) of central Australia.

The notion of Bushmen as mystics had long existed in anthropological literature, and earlier anthropologists interested in this subject sought out appropriate references. We find them, for example, in the works of Sir James Frazer. On homeopathic magic, Frazer notes:

> While many savages thus fear to eat the flesh of slow-footed animals lest they should themselves become slow-footed, the Bushmen of South Africa purposely ate the flesh of such creatures, and the reasons which they gave for doing so exhibits a curious refinement of savage philosophy. They imagined that the game which they pursued would be influenced sympathetically by the food in the body of the hunter … The Bushmen will not give their children a jackal's heart to eat, lest it should make them timid like the jackal; but they give them a leopard's heart to eat to make them brave like a leopard. (Frazer 1949 [1922]: 495)

Both Lucien Lévy-Bruhl and Claude Lévi-Strauss were more concerned that the lack of totemism is found in conjunction with food taboos not unlike those of totemic societies. Lévy-Bruhl (1931: 84), citing Bleek and Lloyd, reports that Bushmen's respect for animals implies sentiments similar to those otherwise found with totemism. Lévi-Strauss (1962: 137–8), citing Fourie, comments on meat distribution and food prohibitions in a system which 'functions on a different plane' (*fonctionne chez eux sur un autre plan*) from totemism.

Perhaps the major emergent theme of the 1990s in the larger field of anthropology (beyond the narrower social anthropology) was the origin of symbolic culture. Here again, San data, and in some cases Khoekhoe data too, have been used to represent survivals of an earlier state of humankind in general. For example, in a paper entitled 'The Origin of Symbolic Culture', archaeologist Ian Watts (1999) cites material by Bleek and Lloyd, Lorna Marshall, Megan Biesele, David Lewis-Williams and others on San cosmology and colour symbolism, and Theophilus Hahn, J.A. Engelbrecht, Heinrich Vedder and many others on similar aspects of Khoekhoe life. Watts's mentor Chris Knight had done much the same in his now classic *Blood Relations* (e.g. Knight 1991: 332–5, 483–8), which argues that symbolic culture, including incest and menstrual taboos, totemism and food taboos, and the representation of sexuality and human–animal relations in ritual and rock art, all began in a revolution instigated by Upper Palaeolithic (equivalent to South African Middle Stone Age) females. According to Knight, females at the time of this revolution collectively refused sex to their respective partners each month as the moon grew larger, which was a period of both synchronous menstruation and bloodshed in hunting, and they feasted and had sex in the period following full moon. The date for this revolution was originally put at about 70,000 years ago, although more recent genetic, archaeological data is pushing the date farther back into prehistory.

Using a Bushman example, evolutionary psychologist Robin Dunbar takes issue with Knight on the emergence of language. At least in Dunbar's reading of Knight, the latter (Knight 1991: 15–18, 75–6) implies that language emerged in order to make ritual possible. Dunbar (1996: 147–8) suggests that language evolved in order to enhance social bonding and later became associated with 'semi-religious' contexts such as the eland bull dance, which may have pre-existed in some primitive form. This is a fairly subtle distinction, but what is interesting is Dunbar's assertion, implied too in the works of Knight and his followers, that eland bull dances are 'very ancient rituals indeed' (1996: 147) and associated with an Upper Palaeolithic revolution giving rise to religious belief and symbolic thought.

Let me give one more example, which I think encapsulates the essence of almost all the imagery of the Bushman as spiritual being. The American Museum of Natural History in New York has a small display of Bushman artefacts and two accompanying information plaques: one on 'The Desert World' and the other on 'The Dream World'. The former mentions the limited technology and limited resources, the seasonal cycle, flexible social organization, skills in hunting and gathering techniques, and sharing practices. It ends: 'The severely limited material life of the Bushmen sharply contrasts with the richness of their dream world.' The latter plaque (as transcribed here in 2006) reads, in part:

> The very severity of their life seems to lead Bushmen to a greater awareness of their debt to the world around them. They see beauty where others would see only ugliness, kindness instead of cruelty. Animals, birds and insects are given spiritual attributes, and the night sky becomes a world of ghostly hunters endlessly chasing unlimited quarry … For the Bushmen, their dream world has a vital reality of its own.

This sort of sentiment is not unique. It permeates much academic and general literature too, as well as popular conceptions and indeed museum displays elsewhere. In the Western mind at least, the Bushman lives two lives: a practical, material one, harsh but adaptive; and a spiritual one which evokes deep understandings of nature.

Conclusion

It is fair to say that Bushman religion did not hold the prominence in twentieth-century anthropology that it held in the nineteenth century. This is a pity, since its richness is obvious and its ethnographers have been both skilled in description and sophisticated in theoretical analysis. If there is one area where sophistication and revolutionary anthropological thinking were strongest, this was in rock art studies. The transformation of that field in South Africa would feed into the wider archaeology of southern Africa, including greater concern with regional diversity and regional similarity: religion is far more uniform throughout Bushman and even Khoisan southern Africa than are material aspects of culture and society. This transformation in turn would feed into the Kalahari debate.

On the one hand, the rich symbolic expression of Bushman thought and especially Bushman painting produced data for those outside Bushman studies, notably anthropologists and others interested in the origins of all language and symbolic culture. On the other hand, concern with the specific, such as the question of Bantu customs like totemism and witchcraft among Bushmen, would end up as footnotes in the works of scholars within Bushman studies, who turned the field towards the relation between Bantu-speaking agro-pastoralist and Bushman hunter and serf. They sought too to turn anthropology into history, and from the 1980s onwards time would never again stand still in an ethnographic present of the kind so useful to ecological anthropologists or folklorists of previous generations.

–8–

Kalahari Revisionism
and Portrayals of Contact

Archaeology has three basic perspectives: traditional, processual and post-processual. Traditional archaeology (especially in Europe) is aligned with historiography, as an approach that tries to understand history through material remains. Processualism came into being with the work of Lewis Binford in North America in the 1960s. It is more aligned with anthropology and especially evolutionism and cultural ecology. It uses ethnographic analogy, and it uses ideas from systems theory and the philosophy of science, supposedly to make informed general statements about past societies. However, general statements are hard to come by, except perhaps hypothetical ones satirized by opponents of the approach, like: 'The size of a Bushman site is directly proportional to the number of houses on it' (quoted in Bahn 1996: 291). Post-processualism, associated especially with the British archaeologist Ian Hodder since the 1980s, seeks to challenge what it regards as the scientistic fallacies of processualism: archaeologists can never recreate a 'real' past. Post-processual archaeologists instead admit a degree of interpretation and subjectivity, and regard archaeology as having political implications. Almost all other perspectives are permutations of these. For example, the New Archaeology is, or was in the 1960s, simply another word for what became known as processualism. Approaches labelled Marxist, feminist, symbolic, cognitive, interpretative, contextualist and so on are essentially permutations of post-processual perspectives.

In the Kalahari, however, there are just two approaches, and they do not fit as neatly into the processual/post-processual distinction as some would like them to. Kalahari traditionalists emphasize the uniqueness of Bushman culture and the relative isolation of Bushman society. Kalahari revisionists emphasize culture contact and the place of Bushmen within a wider political economy of trade, class relations and forced marginalization. The traditionalist/revisionist distinction is not merely archaeological, but is with the same meanings part of discussions in social anthropology and in historiography too. The time depth is considerable, with revisionist thinking pushing relevant periods of contact back some 1,500 years (e.g. Denbow 1984), while traditionalists, perhaps ironically, have often concentrated on the period of their own ethnography. This chapter focuses on the Kalahari debate, its roots in ethnography and archaeology, and some of its wider implications.

What is the Kalahari Debate?

Typically, the Kalahari debate is understood as a battle between the two polarized communities: traditionalists (mainly ethnographers) and revisionists (at first, mainly archaeologists). It came to a head in the late 1980s, with the publication of Edwin Wilmsen's *Land Filled with Flies* (1989), a dense and complex work that argues a case for the Ju/'hoansi as long dominated by their neighbours and by economic structures that covered all of the Kalahari, if not all of southern Africa. The debate had been simmering for some ten years, as critics poked bigger and bigger holes in the classic ethnographies of Lorna Marshall and Richard Lee. Marshall and especially Lee had often mentioned the existence of Herero and other outsiders in the Ju/'hoan areas where they did fieldwork, although anthropology outside Bushman studies seems not to have taken much notice. The problem was that specialists came to be more and more concerned with what the presence of Herero might mean for the 'purity' of their studies. But when does 'traditional' life end and 'social change' begin? The question is not just one of time depth, but also one of degree of social change and one of the implications for the definition of traditional San social life.

Traditionalists do not say there is no social change, but they see it as a recent phenomenon – often as something that took place before their eyes in the 1960s or 1970s. Revisionists argue that it is better to understand Bushmen as an underclass rather than an ethnic group, and that this condition is not recent but a long-standing one. For revisionists, the political economy of the Kalahari or of southern Africa as a whole is the best unit of analysis, rather than an abstract notion of (isolated) Bushman society. For them, the apparent isolation observed by ethnographers, especially in the 1950s and early 1960s, was ultimately a product of the white domination of southern Africa, not only since South Africa's National Party government was elected in 1948, but also, more gradually, since the late nineteenth century. The revisionist view became immediately attractive in the emerging 'new South Africa' of the very early 1990s, although perhaps slightly less so with the new acceptability of ethnicity in liberal circles there after the first democratic elections in 1994.

It is a moot point whether (modern) Kalahari revisionism in its earliest phase, in the early 1970s, was itself a reaction to the invidious excesses of the apartheid regime. That earliest phase was marked not by anthropologists' concerns with what was going on in the Kalahari, but rather by historians' concerns with changes of lifestyle and identity among seventeenth-century Khoisan in the vicinity of the Dutch Cape Colony. Shula Marks (1972), in particular, provided evidence of people shifting back and forth between hunting and herding. It all depended on whether at any one time a group had access to cattle or not. Thus, the 'San' of the Cape were not necessarily a distinct ethnic group from their Khoe neighbours, but rather simply Khoe who had lost their cattle and been forced to hunt and gather or to raid other people's cattle for a living. Among others debating the issue in the 1970s, South African archaeologist Carmel Schrire was most notable. In an important paper written in the 1970s (Schrire 1980; see also 1984), she questions nineteenth-century reports of 'pure' Bushmen who kept apparently stolen livestock, and argues that modern hunter-gatherer studies retain an evolutionist bias. Marks's, Schrire's and Wilmsen's argument was to challenge both established understanding in Bushman ethnography and the 'liberal' tradition in South African historiography.

Archaeology and Anthropology

We met South African archaeology in Chapter 4, and the period of Middle and Later Stone Age research since the one covered there has been splendidly summarized by Peter Mitchell (2002a; see also 2002b: 161–258). My focus here, though, is on archaeology in its interaction with other disciplines. My examples are very few, but indicative of the trends.

John Parkington's work has proved of the greatest significance for Khoisan studies, perhaps especially because of the close alignment of his work on Later Stone Age populations of the Western Cape and that of social anthropologists in the contemporary Kalahari. In both cases, from the 1960s onwards, the focus was on environment, subsistence and seasonal mobility, as well as on shifting identities in the archaeological record (see, for example, Parkington 1980, 1984). Parkington's work on coastal populations both brings a new ethnological dimension to Khoisan studies (because of the paucity of ethnographic material on such populations, except from the earliest times of white settlement at the Cape), and links well with the study of Khoisan history (because of the relatively late, albeit pre-colonial, dates of his sites). Thus, while South African archaeology maintained its distance from the New Archaeology, with its emphasis on ethnographic analogy and archaeology as quasi-anthropology, it nevertheless grew close to the ecological anthropology of the Harvard–Toronto mainstream of Richard Lee and his colleagues. It still provides insights into the transition from hunting to herding and comparative understandings of southern African hunter-gatherer social ecology. Parkington's work is regarded as broadly revisionist, but has touchstones to both positions, as for example when he refers to Western Cape hunter-gatherers as 'a permanent and distinct socio-economic entity, whether in regular contact with pastoralists or as marginal populations on the fringes of the attractive grazing lands' (Parkington 1987: 18).

In addition to the concentration on coastal hunters, since the 1960s there has also been an interest in the archaeology of Khoekhoe herders and their relation to the San hunter-gatherers (see, for example, Robertshaw 1978; A.B. Smith 1986). This interest, together with the movement of some archaeological researchers between Later Stone Age and Iron Age research, and the slowly maturing Kalahari debate, helped to problematize the old categories of 'hunter' and 'herder' and provide for an ever-increasing tendency of writers to link ethnographic, archival and archaeological work in new multidisciplinary historical formulations. Wilmsen's work itself (e.g. 1989) has this tendency. Yet we must not be too quick to see such efforts simply as part of a revisionist tendency, for not even the most hard-line traditionalist would ever deny that southern African groups interacted before and during the colonial period.

Some South African archaeologists have made special efforts to bring gender issues into their discipline, particularly Anne Solomon in rock art studies (e.g. 1992) and Lyn Wadley more broadly (e.g. 1987, 1997). In the monograph based on her Ph.D. thesis, Wadley argues too for the use of Kalahari ethnography in helping to understand southern Transvaal (now Gauteng) Middle and Later Stone Age sites. The effort includes seasonal fluctuations, but also much bolder Ju/'hoan analogies such as the giraffe dance, female and male initiation, left/right symbolism in sign language, and even gender-specific *hxaro* goods. It is no wonder that archaeological and anthropological thought became so intertwined in South African San studies, and this aspect is crucial to the debate, and only partly because of Wilmsen's background in (American) archaeology.

While others pursued interests in analogy between a seemingly timeless northern Kalahari and the ever-changing social landscape of South Africa, Wilmsen and his collaborator Jim Denbow had their main areas of excavation on the Kalahari fringe in eastern Botswana. Denbow is an archaeologist now at the University of Texas at Austin, but who had long been based at the National Museum and Art Gallery in Gaborone. Denbow's position as a revisionist reflects his central concerns with the relations between the Early Iron Age and the hunter-gatherers that came under Iron Age domination (see, for example, Denbow 1990). The major opponent of Kalahari revisionism in archaeology has been Karim Sadr of the University of the Witwatersrand. He has argued against the assumption of the incorporation of all Bushman within the Iron Age economy (Sadr 1997), while recognizing too the evidence of encapsulation of specific groups at specific locations (Sadr 2002).

About the time of South Africa's emergence as a democratic state, Wilmsen took to calling the debate, not simply the 'Kalahari debate', but the 'second Kalahari debate'. To examine the details of the two approaches, traditionalist and revisionist, we need to go back, then, to the 'first' Kalahari debate, in the late nineteenth century, before picking up the roots of the modern debate.

The 'First' Kalahari Debate

The Kalahari debate is a bit like the Anglo-Boer War. Whether you see it as one war or two depends on which side you are on. Just as diehard Afrikaners used to recognize a 'First War of Freedom' (1880 to 1881), which they won, as well as a 'Second' (1899 to 1902), the conventional British dates of the 'Boer War', so too Kalahari revisionists (or at least some of them) see two Kalahari debates. The first Kalahari debate was that between Gustav Fritsch and Siegfried Passarge.

Fritsch was the proto-traditionalist. He saw Bushmen as living in small bands, in relative isolation. He travelled in southern Africa for three years in the 1860s, and published, among other things, an ethnographic and anatomical treatise on peoples of southern Africa (Fritsch 1872), a short attack on the notion of Bushmen as an *Urrasse* (primal race) (1880), and a review of Passarge's key text on Bushmen, with a reply by Passarge himself and a rejoinder to that by Fritsch (Fritsch 1906). Proto-revisionist Passarge spent part of the 1890s in southern Africa, and his publications include a monograph on Kalahari Bushmen (Passarge 1907 [1905]) and a long article on inhabitants of the Okavango delta (Passarge 1905). Both, along with Fritsch's review of the former, are included in English translation in Wilmsen's (1997) *Kalahari Ethnographies of Siegfried Passarge*.

Fritsch's (1880) objection to the idea of Bushmen as a 'primal race' was in response to a conference address given in Berlin shortly before by the great medical reformer and early physical anthropologist Rudolf Virchow. If Bushmen were a 'primal race', then they were relatives of Europeans, and this Fritsch could not have. He also objected to the idea put forward by Karl Richard Lepsius, at the same conference, that Bushmen were related to their black neighbours. In stark contrast, Passarge claimed that Bushmen and Pygmies were 'the original African race ... representing all the original character of humankind' (quoted in Wilmsen 1997: 32).

Passarge's (1907) picture of the Bushmen of his time was very much one of a diversity of peoples, each living in contact with more powerful Bantu-speaking neighbours. He describes some groups, such as the 'Kaukau' (≠Au//eisi, or southern !Kung), as nomadic, with other groups, such as the 'Kqung' (!Xũ, or northern !Kung), as relatively sedentary (Passarge, in Wilmsen 1997: 147–8). Passarge was among the first to name in writing many of the groups now well known through ethnography, like Ju/'hoansi or !Kung, G/wi, Naro and Hai//om, as well as lesser-known groups like Ts'aokhoe (north-eastern Naro), Qabekhoe (a similar group further north) and //Anikhoe (of the Okavango delta). He describes extensively presumed differences between life in the 1890s and life at an unspecified time before then, when there was, he says, more water and more plant food. In those times, he continues, hunting techniques were different, bigger game was more sought after and meat was altogether more plentiful (Passarge, in Wilmsen 1997: 175–9). Importantly, he stresses that even independent and nomadic Bushmen were not the anarchists some would see them as. In the past they had powerful, hereditary headmen. These, he says, were often not noticed by earlier travellers because of those travellers' preconceived notions and because of the lack of any noticeable pomp that Europeans might recognize as characteristic of such leaders in other societies (Passarge, in Wilmsen 1997: 200–2).

From a traditionalist perspective, the exact timing of Passarge's travels in southern Africa may be relevant. He was there from June 1896 to November 1998, during which time a rinderpest epidemic swept from the north through southern Africa killing countless tens of thousands of cattle, and wild animals as well: 'In May 1897, the cattle of the trader, Franz Müller, endured the rinderpest and many Bushmen arrived to feast on the meat of the animals that succumbed ... I estimated [the number of people] at 100 to 200 heads, women and children included' (Passarge, in Wilmsen 1997: 132–3). Thus what he saw may indeed not have been typical of life before then, or after. It may also be relevant, from a revisionist point of view, that Fritsch's travels (unlike Passarge's) were not through the central and northern Kalahari (modern northern Botswana), but rather on the western fringe of the desert through what is now Namibia, and in what is now part of the Republic of South Africa. In short, they could be describing quite different times and places, and indeed this is implied in Passarge's (1907) writings.

The heart of the debate is Fritsch's 1906 review of the preliminary version of *Die Bushmänner der Kalahari*, which had been published in the previous volume. Each makes snide remarks on the extent of the travels, the quality of the data and the general understanding of Bushmen of the other. Let me quote a brief passage from Wilmsen's translation of Fritsch's review to give the flavour. In this passage Fritsch takes issue with Passarge's reconstruction of past times and his choice of a Bushman informant over the great traveller, Fritsch himself:

'Mr Passarge wants to know what it was like among the Bushmen in the 60s. And instead of recovering this from me, *the only surviving traveller of that time and of that region*, he preferred to hear from his old Bushman servant something close to a pack of lies ... No attentive observer can deny the significant role of the Kalahari in the preservation of Bushman freedom and independence; I expressed myself repeatedly about this. (Fritsch, in Wilmsen 1997: 308)

Passarge says in his reply:

Against this, I must fully and completely maintain the assertion that in those regions in which he travelled Mr Fritsch became acquainted with only a few fully dependent and subordinated Bushmen. For those same regions were already then controlled by Bantu and whites and the number of Bushmen that Mr Fritsch could have encountered ran at most to a few hundreds. The true Kalahari, however, he never set foot on, only brushing against its outer edges. Thus, he had to rely on the statements of others. (Passarge, in Wilmsen 1997: 316)

Degree of isolation or dependence, relative population sizes, the availability of natural resources, the location of ethnic groups and even of each other's travels, and indeed the thickness of lines on each other's maps were all issues in the debate. The last two, more specifically the exact routes of early travellers and the thickness of lines on Wilmsen's maps and those of his opponents, were to become issues also in the modern Kalahari debate. Thick lines depicting trade routes (lots of trade?) give a different impression from thin lines (little trade?) (see, for example, Lee and Guenther 1991: 597).

The stigmatization of Bushmen has been common among both neighbouring African pastoralists and European settlers in Africa for over two centuries, and images of Bushman in Europe itself have suffered as a result. The distinction between 'pure' or 'wild' Bushmen, on the one hand, and 'tame' Bushmen, on the other hand, has been common in Western discourse since the late nineteenth century, and indeed was the subject of the debate at that time between Fritsch and Passarge. Like Le Vaillant before him and many anthropologists after, Fritsch romanticized the Bushmen, while Passarge sought to 'correct' the romantic image by emphasizing contact with the outside world, both white and black.

The Kalahari Debate Proper

Traditionalist and Revisionist Portrayals of the San

Let us return to the modern ethnographic era. Typical of the traditionalist stance since the 1960s is the focus on Bushmen (or modern foragers more generally) as models for the reconstruction of human evolution:

> My own view is that the data from hunting and gathering studies have an important role to play in social science. Foraging was a way of life that prevailed during an important period of human history. The modern foragers do offer clues to the nature of this way of life, and by understanding the adaptations of the past we can better understand the present and the basic human material that produced them both. (Lee 1979: 433)

Elsewhere in *The !Kung San* (1979), Lee picks out benefits from this 'past' way of life, e.g. communalism and sharing, but he also picks out problems. The most obvious is the high level of violence within Ju/'hoan society. However, Lee takes foraging for granted, as a basic and adaptive way of life. He also takes for granted the fact that Ju/'hoan society is a relevant unit of analysis, in spite of the presence of members of other groups (Herero and Tswana) within their territories and at their waterholes. The Ju/'hoansi and their cattle-herding neighbours interact but nevertheless seem to occupy different ecological niches.

Traditionalist ethnographies portray San society as relatively unchanging. San society had forms of social organization which were both ancient and adaptive, and outside forces were of minimal influence. Egalitarianism was the prevailing ideology, and sharing was the observed practice. For revisionists, the truth is perceived very differently. Wilmsen (1989) tries to demolish these premises via a simple assumption that the political economy of the Kalahari has been a meaningful construct ever since livestock were first introduced to the fringe areas of the Kalahari more than a thousand years ago. To Wilmsen, San are not even 'traditional' foragers:

> Their appearance as foragers is a function of their relegation to an underclass in the playing out of historical processes that began before the current millennium and culminated in the early decades of this century. The isolation in which they are said to be found is a creation of our view of them, not of their history as they lived it ... A false dichotomy has crept in, a line drawn between those who produce their means of existence and those who supposedly do not, between those who live on nature and those who live in it, between those whose social life is motivated primarily by self-interest and those guided by respect for reciprocal consensus. (Wilmsen 1989: 3)

Wilmsen's approach de-emphasizes ethnicity in favour of class relations and brings to light the great disparity of wealth between producers and foragers. He does not even refer to 'Bushmen' or 'San', but prefers 'San-speaking peoples'. The letter term is more politically correct, especially in Namibia, where liberal sentiment prefers people being spoken of by their language rather than their ethnicity. He accounts for systematic aspects of kinship, land tenure and internal exchange relations in terms of a larger politico-economic structure. Ju/'hoan-speakers form but a part of this.

The Core of the Debate

The core of the Kalahari debate consists of a series of articles and short comments published in the journal *Current Anthropology*. The most significant, in chronological order, are those of Solway and Lee (1990), Wilmsen and Denbow (1990), Lee and Guenther (1991), Wilmsen (1993) and Lee and Guenther (1995). Kalahari debate papers published elsewhere include a perceptive piece by Lee (1991), which warns against both the excesses of revisionism and the over-romanticization of San. There Lee notes that in the 1960s Ju/'hoansi told him that whites had entered their lands in the nineteenth century before blacks, and he suggests that Ju/'hoansi were both surprised and offended at the suggestion that they were being portrayed by anthropologists as having been long-time serfs of black masters. Further debate has been played out in the pages of the journal *History in Africa*, with a long article by Lee and Guenther (1993) and a reply ten years later by Wilmsen (2003). These papers concern mainly the interpretation of nineteenth-century travellers' accounts, including the exact routes taken by travellers as well as their statements on the degree and nature of contact between Ju/'hoansi, on the one hand, and Herero, Tswana and other groups, on the other. 'Interpretation' here sometimes involves literally the translation of nineteenth-century German. There are also a number of commentaries on the debate in the anthropological literature, some of which contribute to it (e.g. Kent 1992; Lee 1991; Shott 1992).

The historical questions which have appeared in the *Current Anthropology* articles test the limits of evidence. The first such piece, by Jacqueline Solway and Richard Lee (1990), was actually an attempt by two traditionalists to bend slightly towards the revisionist line. However, they upheld the cultural integrity of entities such as Ju/'hoan society, and thereby did not go nearly far enough for the revisionists. What is more, in their abstract Solway and Lee accused the revisionists of 'imputing links where none existed and assuming that evidence for trade implies the surrender of autonomy' (1990: 109). The main part of the article concentrates on two areas of Botswana – the western Kweneng (an area of much dependency) and the Dobe area (one of relative autonomy). Their discussion is based largely on the interpretation of late nineteenth-century literature with reference to the significance of agro-pastoralism, the fur trade and clientship, and the degree to which Kalahari groups can be said to be part of a world economy.

To radical revisionists, Solway and Lee's vehement defence of traditional definitions of cultural units was taken as an attack. In their counter-attack, Wilmsen and Denbow argued that '"Bushman" and "San" are invented categories and "Kalahari foragers" an ethnographic reification drawn from one of several subsistence strategies engaged in by all of Botswana's rural poor' (Wilmsen and Denbow 1990: 489). Their evidence too is based mainly on nineteenth-century sources, especially the writings of Passarge. Much also comes from archaeological work which Denbow and Wilmsen have been engaged in for decades (see, for example, Denbow 1984, 1986). More attacks and counter-attacks ensued, with Lee and Guenther (1991, 1993, 1995) dissecting Wilmsen's translations of Passarge and redrawing Wilmsen's maps of early travellers and the trade routes they found from the diaries and published accounts of those travellers. To the amusement of many, they even argued that what one traveller recorded in his diary was the presence of 'onions' rather than 'oxen' in Ju/'hoan country in the 1850s. Apparently, Wilmsen had misread the diary of gentleman adventurer C.J. Andersson and thereby replaced the gathering of wild vegetables with the herding of livestock. Ironically, though, this example showed that detail alone cannot solve even an ethnographic question, for what both sides have been trying to do is to establish time, degree and significance of contact between many groups in what all protagonists agree is a complex system of social and economic relations.

Old and Recent German Work

German ethnology has long had an interest in Khoisan studies. There were extensive studies on language, folklore, magic and culture contact among Kxoe in the

Caprivi Strip by the late Oswin Köhler, who worked with them from 1955 until shortly before his death in 1996. The first volume of his projected five-volume book of texts in Kxoe (with German translation) dealt with culture contact (Köhler 1989). Fellow linguist Rainer Vossen has, since the first volume in 1985, edited a series originally called 'Quellen zur Khoisan-Forschung', also known by the English equivalent 'Research in Khoisan Studies'. This includes a number of books dealing in one way or another with the Kalahari debate (e.g. Wilmsen 1997; Guenther 2005). The first seven volumes were published by Helmut Buske in Hamburg and the rest (the most recent being Volume 18) by Rüdiger Köppe in Cologne, and most are in English. The existence of these specialist publishing houses has enabled dissemination of important linguistic, ethnographic and historical material that might otherwise be commercially less than viable.

The number of German researchers now engaged in San studies is enormous and growing. Several, such as Klaus Keuthmann, Matthias Brenzinger and Christa Kilian-Hatz, specialize in 'River Bushman' areas and specialize in themes related to language and folkore. Others have a direct interest in social change, including some senior researchers such as Michael Bollig, who has previously worked among pastoralists in Kenya and Namibia but has recently turned his attention to detailed comparative analysis of economic activities, development and the effects of government welfare initiatives in western Botswana (Bollig 2003). Bollig's major report of those findings is placed in a volume called *San and the State* (Hohmann 2003b), within a series he edits with Wilhelm Möhlig called 'History, Cultural Traditions and Innovations in Southern Africa'. Contributors to that volume include a number of junior researchers (all pre-Ph.D. at the time of that volume) associated with the University of Cologne, namely Thekla Hohmann (on nature conservancies in Namibia), Suzanne Berzborn (on language policy in South Africa), Gertrud Boden (on the impact of state decisions and armed conflict in Namibia), Ute Dieckmann (on Etosha National Park) and Ina Orth (on the struggle for land in the West Caprivi). It is certain we shall hear more from them in the near future.

Susan Kent and the Latest Twist

One of the key players in the debate was the late Susan Kent. Although her distinction between 'real' and 'ideal' views of hunter-gatherers (Kent 1992) was intended as a compromise between the extremes of revisionism and traditionalism, much of her work through the 1990s came to be seen as essentially traditionalist, with a focus on aspects of social change among the part-time foragers with whom she worked. Like Ed Wilmsen, Sue Kent came into Kalahari studies from the archaeology of the American South-West. Her ethnographic work, on gender, hunting, settlement and other issues, was often highly statistical and reflected the strong empirical tradition from which she had come. She was especially noted as one who could engage others in building towards a consensus view, and this was especially important in her efforts as a conference session organizer and book editor. Two of her edited collections are of special importance here: *Cultural Diversity among Twentieth-century Foragers* (Kent 1996) and *Ethnicity, Hunter-gatherers and the 'Other'* (Kent 2002b). Both volumes bring together papers on southern, eastern and central African peoples.

The first volume was based loosely on a session at the American Anthropological Association meetings in 1993. Let me mention just two of its important papers, those by Silberbauer and by Vierich and Hitchcock. Silberbauer's chapter concerns the great variability found among Kalahari peoples in subsistence, in economic and political autonomy, and in much else. He concludes with the words: 'Wilmsen's hypothesis that the hunting and gathering life was the last resort of a redundant, dispossessed *Lumpenproletariat*, discarded by their pastoralist Bantu-speaking masters, is made improbable by those Basarwa who chose autonomy in their bands, and who returned to their territories despite the hardships' (Silberbauer 1996: 64). Helga Vierich and Bob Hitchcock worked in the 1970s and subsequently in the eastern Kalahari, not far from Kent's research site. They conclude that cultural diversity itself results from responses to disparate social and environmental conditions, and that it can be manipulated by individuals. They stress the different identities individuals assume, some claiming a Tswana identity, others a Kua or Basarwa identity. For Vierich and Hitchcock (1996: 124) past strategies of the mixed economy of livestock production, wage labour and foraging were not enough, and Kua were deliberately diversifying 'culturally' as well as economically.

The second volume brings in historical and archaeological material on encounters between ethnic groups to a much greater extent, with papers, for example, on multidisciplinary aspects of past contact (by ethno-archaeologist Alison Brooks), on nineteenth- and early twentieth-century interaction (by Guenther), on Ju/'hoan memories of colonial times (by Lee), and on relations between prehistoric farmers and hunter-gatherers, and on missionaries and disease (both by Kent). According to Kent (2002a: 182), 'The fact that hunter-gatherers were able to maintain their cultural autonomy in most, although not all, of southern Africa for at least 1,500 years while interacting with Bantu-speaking agropastoralists, but were dominated within 300 to 400 years of contact with Westerners, illustrates the difference in the nature of hunter-gatherers' interactions with Bantus and Europeans.'

The latest twist is that, just as Wilmsen has resurrected the works of Passarge in support of his argument, Guenther (2005) has recently translated and published the writings of six German colonial soldiers and settlers writing on South West African Bushmen in the years from 1908 to 1919. He had about two dozen to choose from, but selected those of farmer J.H. Wilhelm, district commissioner

E. Seydel, and four army officers, namely Leutnant Kaufmann, Oberleutnant
Trenk, Hauptmann Müller and Müller's medical officer Kahle, who wrote part of
the Müller report. All except Kahle were cited by Schapera (1930). Guenther's
purpose is not to undermine proto-revisionist Passarge, and indeed there are passages in the works included in Guenther's volume which tend to support the revisionist cause. However, Kaufmann, who spent time among the ≠Au//eisi a few
years after Passarge, tends towards an environmental determinist view (as, for that
matter, sometimes does Passarge), while Müller in the same period talks of trade
but argues that it does not much affect !Kung (Ju/'hoan) life. Müller comments on
the ability of the !Kung he visited to gain a living easily from their environment
and on the good nutrition of their children. Müller also sees them as a peaceable
people, unlike Kaufmann and Wilhelm, who comment on their warlike nature.
Whether the supposed warlike nature is in the eyes of the oppressors, writing
within a decade of the vicious German–Herero War of 1904–5, is no doubt a
matter for future debate. Be that as it may, what Guenther has done for our time is
to throw in yet another layer of historical complexity, adding new dimensions to
the rather simple level of dispute we might like to think of as the 'Kalahari debate'
or even the 'first and second Kalahari debates'.

Interpreting the Kalahari Debate

As communications towers and wind turbines come to be dotted across the
Scottish hills, landscape artists debate over whether to include them in their paintings or leave them out. What we might call traditionalist painters prefer to leave
them out or look for the pure Scottish scenery; extreme revisionist painters, if such
exist, might look specifically for the largest wind farm they can find as a subject
of their next painting.

The Kalahari debate is sometimes like that, and the notion of purity in 'the
Bushman' is a perennial theme. It is as if a greater degree of purity is expected in
them than in other peoples we might study (see Barnard 1989). Often the same
views are expressed by people of other groups who live in proximity to Bushmen,
though not always. As one Afrikaner rancher told an ethnographer in reference to
itinerant sheep-shearers of the Karoo: 'They have all interbred a bit but actually
they are pure Bushman [*suiwer Boesman*]' (quoted in De Jongh and Steyn 1994:
220). It has been suggested that the revisionist critique 'helped to blur the conceptual boundaries erected by anthropologists and others between "pure" and
"impure" Bushmen' (Suzman 2000: 6), but I see both traditionalists and revisionists searching for 'purity'. Traditionalists want to find it in order to legitimate their
efforts, while revisionists reject Bushman tradition among dominated and marginalized groups as fabricated or imagined. They look for 'purity' in the writings of
their opponents (see Barnard 1988b).

Led by revisionist desires for more accurate representations, the debate has focused on the meaning of bovine fossils, the chance descriptions of trade or foreign artefacts in the reports of explorers, or the aspects of society that have been affected by outside influence. Little is said even by traditionalists of what remains of traditional culture in a post-contact context, and this has misled anthropology as a whole to believe the myth that contact creates cultural 'impurity'. England did not disappear with the Norman Conquest, nor did the Kalahari Bushman way of life with the arrival of Iron Age pastoralists or even Afrikaner ranchers. One might argue that the traditionalists had it coming. Like their counterparts in Highland landscape painting, they concentrated on the most pristine areas for fieldwork. When they sent students to work in other areas, they at first worked on acculturation, social change, relations with outsiders, and so on. The most striking example is Guenther himself.

The Kalahari debate has been beneficial in many respects and for many constituencies: for anthropology and related fields, and for the Bushmen in forcing recognition of their historically weak position in the southern African political economy. Yet it has been damaging as well. One of the most damaging effects has been in its tendency to obscure social and cultural differences between groups. The concentration of effort on contact and change has led directly to this. In terms of kinship structures, for example, G/wi and Ju/'hoansi are very different, with Naro in-between (Barnard 1988c). Naro are in-between because they are a G/wi-like group who have a very long history of contact with Ju/'hoansi; their relatively brief contact period of just over a hundred years (in some areas) with Afrikaners is irrelevant. In similar terms, Naro contact with Kgalagadi and Ju/'hoan contact with Herero are equally irrelevant for the study of kinship, although they may be relevant for other things.

The simple matter is that Ju/'hoansi are not the only Bushmen in the Kalahari. In many respects, they are not even typical of Kalahari Bushmen – although they are the most numerous group (about 30 per cent of the total Bushman population today). It was pure chance that led the Marshall family and then Lee to concentrate on Ju/'hoansi. If in the early 1950s the Marshalls had stayed longer with G/wi before moving on to the Ju/'hoansi, things might have been different. Or, if in the early 1960s Silberbauer had been more open to the idea of Lee working with G/wi, things still might have been different. (Lee's intention had been to work with G/wi, but Silberbauer put him off the idea since, it is said, the G/wi were 'his' people.) For that matter, if in the late 1960s and 1970s Silberbauer had published more on the G/wi than Lee did on the Ju/'hoansi, there might have been yet another chance for G/wi to emerge as the archetype. Japanese research came to dominate G/wi and G//ana studies, but the first publications were in Japanese, and later work has always been less accessible, or at least less accessed, than that of Canadian and American writers.

Just as the Marshall family's fieldwork area became known as Nyae Nyae, Lee's took on the name Dobe. Dobe proper is a waterhole, and to the Ju/'hoansi the term also designates the *n!ore* (band territory) that surrounds it. To anthropologists, Dobe is often taken as a slightly larger area within north-western Botswana. Dobe and Nyae Nyae are not two different Ju/'hoan groups, but the same people who happen to straddle a border. Nevertheless, among anthropologists the designations Nyae Nyae !Kung and Dobe !Kung were convenient, especially in the 1960s and 1970s, as ways to distinguish two bodies of ethnographic writings. With increasing militarization in the 1980s and eventual Namibian independence in 1990, the distinction became, if one can put it this way, more ethnologically meaningful too. The border was no longer easy to cross, and differences due to different kinds of culture contact increased. Later, through the revisionist writings of Wilmsen, through Wilmsen's own fieldwork in Botswana south of Dobe and James Suzman's in Namibia south of Nyae Nyae, the meaningfulness of the distinction between Ju/'hoansi (central !Kung) and ≠Au//eisi (southern !Kung) would be challenged as well. The theoretical premises of both Marshall and Lee depended on anthropologists being able to identify discrete cultural units. Contrary to what revisionists may have thought, traditionalist ethnographers certainly granted them both history and culture contact, but the traditionalists reified boundaries between the 'pure' Bushman and the 'other' Bushman. That San studies should persist in this was not unexpected. Through the last quarter of the twentieth century the field was dominated by an ecological paradigm and was conservative in its adherence to the search for internal social structures. It was also extremely successful: classic '!Kung' ethnography was among the best known in the world. It was also among the best.

Conclusion

There are two key aspects of the Kalahari debate. One concerns the facts of interaction between Bushmen and others at particular points in time. The other concerns the interpretation of these facts in terms of what we understand Bushman society to be. Traditionalists emphasize cultural continuity and the cultural integrity of Bushman groups. They see Bushmen as the inheritors of ancient indigenous environmental knowledge, hunting techniques, kinship practices, religious beliefs, etc. Revisionists de-emphasize these aspects in favour of greater concern with the integration of southern African politico-economic structures taken as a whole.

The imagery behind revisionism is the vision of an integrated framework of social interaction – not an egalitarian framework, but one in which San are placed firmly at the bottom of the social hierarchy. Whereas traditionalists often emphasize egalitarianism within San society, revisionists emphasize the unequal relations between San and others. Neither view is necessarily at all close to a San view of the world.

Through the late 1980s I was working on my *Hunters and Herders of Southern Africa* (Barnard 1992). I intended it in part to offer a third way, neither traditionalist nor revisionist but regional-structural-comparative in the style of Kuper's (1980) Southern Bantu study, *Wives for Cattle*. Still, some, such as the late Sue Kent, saw it as more traditionalist, and others, like Michael Taylor, as an attempt to integrate the best of the revisionist challenge. Perhaps the moral is that there is little point in being too reflexive on such matters; but in my own view it was mainly an attempt to update Schapera's *Khoisan Peoples*, and Schapera himself seemed to see it that way. Nevertheless, in aiming for comprehensive coverage of the literature, I sacrificed the human side of anthropology. In emphasizing cultural diversity, I over-reified 'cultures'. Today, these are not only anachronistic objects of anthropological theory, but also, as the revisionists have taught us, misleading abstractions imposed on both history and contemporary social life. The last third of the book was an attempt to explain the ethnography through a framework based on the notion of an underlying Khoisan sociocultural structure. If I were to do it again, I would leave the model intact in limited spheres such as kinship, settlement patterns and perhaps religious belief, but, beyond those spheres, I would look to the trends of 1990s San studies for both theoretical and literary inspiration. I suspect that the former spheres are resilient and do lend themselves to traditionalist interpretation, while others, to do with political organization for example, may be more susceptible to outside influence.

–9–

Advocacy, Development and Partnership

An Indian anthropologist once told me there were more than thirty hunter-gatherer groups in India, though the Indian government only recognized some of them. He asked how many groups there were in Botswana. I answered that it depends on how they are counted.

There are several points of significance in this very brief tale. It is not just that Indian anthropology follows a positivist paradigm while Western anthropology has a more sceptical tradition. Indian hunter-gatherers differ from those of Botswana in that they tend to be more encapsulated, in forest areas, while those of Botswana live next to other hunter-gatherers as often as they do agro-pastoralists. Self-perceptions are more obvious, and possibly more significant, in the latter case: for example, Naro and Ts'aokhoe (north-eastern Naro) consider themselves members of different ethnic groups, though their language, customs and relations with other peoples are virtually identical. Relations between the state and the foraging populations of India and Botswana are entirely different too. India has a tradition of classifying its ethnic groups; Botswana has scrupulously avoided doing so. In Botswana, all citizens are officially 'indigenous', and Bushmen are classified along with other rural poor as Remote Area Dwellers (RADs) rather than as members of ethnic minorities. Finally, and related to this, relations between the state and anthropology are different too. In Botswana the state is at odds with anthropology's custom of identifying people by culture and ethnicity; in India it is not.

Bushmen, Anthropology and the State

In 1978, Botswana renamed its Basarwa Development Office the Remote Area Development Office, and Basarwa (the Tswana term for Bushmen or San) came to be called RADs. The new name was intended to identify a larger constituency, since non-Basarwa also lived in remote areas. It was also intended quite deliberately to de-ethnicize the category, although in fact the vast majority of those referred to were Basarwa and they came to resent the new designation. Indigenous preferences varied between Basarwa, Bushmen and San, but no one among them to my knowledge ever took to being labelled instead a Remote Area Dweller. As a

Naro informant once told a Tswana researcher: 'If by "tengnyanateng" [remote] it is meant that we are far away from Gaborone, Gaborone is also far away from us. Gaborone is also "tengnyanateng"' (quoted in Mogwe 1992: 1). Cambridge political theorist John Dunn (2005: 53) has recently commented: 'It is not hard to see why the global name for legitimate political authority does not come from the language of the San Bushmen.' His comment, on why we use a Greek word for 'democracy', is more one on the lack of San global power than on Khoisan languages, as his footnote citing two South African historians on what he calls 'a periphery of the periphery' (2005: 200) makes clear.

Botswana was kind to anthropologists in the 1970s. Upon arrival in Botswana, I was called in to see the permanent secretary of what was then the Ministry of Local Government and Lands, who checked my credentials and gave me kindly advice. My application for a research permit under the Anthropology Act was supported by letters from my University College London Ph.D. supervisor and from a former expatriate district commissioner then resident in London. That first research permit was issued seemingly on the basis that I would probably not get lost in the desert, and therefore would not be a burden on police, wildlife personnel or other officials. Later, things did get more difficult, as social anthropologists were first required to do work of perceptible benefit to Basarwa, and later still to gain approval on the basis that they were not likely to be politically troublesome. Archaeologists, covered by the more lenient Scientific Research Act, had less bother. When Liz Wily was appointed Bushman Development Officer in 1974, she urged me to work in areas of most perceived 'need' of research, and she required reports from me and from others then working in the country.

Meanwhile in Namibia, the South African government was in control until 1989, with full independence in 1990. Northern Namibia and southern Angola in the late 1970s and 1980s were experiencing civil war, with San caught in the middle. Many San, both from Namibia and from Angola, took part on the South African side in the Namibian conflict, and those in the liberation struggle were to take against them. John Marshall and Claire Ritchie (1984) documented the situation, and Marshall was then actively involved in encouraging cattle production. His later dispute with development anthropologists, including Megan Biesele, was in part a clash between revisionist and traditionalist tendencies among both anthropologists and Ju/'hoansi themselves. Marshall's side is represented particularly well in his controversial film *Death by Myth*, and he told me in 2004 that he had seen the changes in the Nyae Nyae area, and still saw them, not as a shift from hunting and gathering to farming (cattle herding), but as one from dependency to self-support.

Against this, German expatriate development worker Axel Thoma, Megan Biesele and others, including many Ju/'hoansi, sought to encourage more traditional pursuits. After Namibian independence, Thoma made efforts to document and restore ownership of traditional territories (*n!oresi*), to tag and thereby establish ownership of game so that they would be perceived by the law as 'live-stock', and so on. His booklet *Customary Law and Traditional Authority of the San* (Thoma and Piek 1997) concentrated on the former Western Bushmanland, the area immediately to the west of Nyae Nyae where Ju/'hoansi had been reset-tled in the apartheid era. Some settlements were former South African Defence Force bases. By the middle of the 1990s, most Ju/'hoansi there were involved in farming. Nevertheless, the community workshops Thoma and his team used to elicit opinions stressed the maintenance and recreation of 'traditional' structures of criminal law and authority over land and resources, while many participants argued that stronger local leadership was now required. The findings of that survey may be in accord with the sentiments of many anthropologists. However, the development-studies methodology is strikingly different and weak in compar-ison with more subtle anthropological approaches: 'The workshop facilitators of [three NGOs] were available to share information, prompt questions if necessary, summarize group discussions and encourage the women to participate' (Thoma and Piek 1997: 62). Typically, workshops were held in Afrikaans, with transla-tions as necessary into Ju/'hoan, 'Vasekele' (Angolan !Xũ) or English.

In South Africa, the Bushman had long been perceived as a creature of the past. As Dorothea Bleek put it upon a trip to /Xam country in 1910, 'The folklore was dead, killed by a life of service among strangers and the breaking up of families' (quoted in Skotnes 1996a: 23). Living San, most of whom speak Afrikaans as their first if not their only language, would remain hidden under the category 'Coloured' until the end of apartheid. Their attempts to regain tradition have been the subject of a number of anthropological studies, especially among 'tourist Bushmen' such as those ≠Khomani recruited to move south to Kagga Kamma, not far inland from Cape Town. According to one author whose fieldwork there was in 1991 and 1992, 'Neither a primordial essence nor simply an economically motivated fraud, the "traditional" hunter-gatherer self-representation of the Kagga Kamma Bushmen is a socially significant identity forged in strategic response to a variety of past expe-riences' (White 1995: 51). Hylton White perceptively concludes:

> Revisionist critics have argued that the primordialist discourse represents the distortion and consumption of Bushman culture by the Western metropole. Yet, if the icon of the original forager is at least partially a Western construct ... then ironically it would appear as if it is the Bushmen who are doing the consuming here, in appropriating a Western trope as the organising principle of their own rhetoric of identity. (White 1995: 55)

In the middle of the 1990s, the ≠Khomani area around Kalahari Gemsbok National Park, in the Northern Cape, became a news story. San there sought to regain control over land denied them for most of the twentieth century. However, in 1999 the government accepted the land claim and returned some 50,000 hectares to the ≠Khomani claimants. Anthropologists and sociologists have taken an interest, partly through involvement in social development but partly too in the knowledge that this people, nearly all of whom speak Afrikaans as their first language, have special significance as a test of authenticity and a marker for future concerns with peoples dispossessed not only of land but of 'culture' too (see, for example, Robins 2001). Perhaps strangely here, the ≠Khomani seem to have taken on a renewed romantic aura, not least since the introduction in 2000 of South Africa's motto *!Ke e: /xarra //ke.* The motto is in the /Xam language, and ≠Khomani (N/u) is the closest living language to it, a fact not lost on the advocates of ≠Khomani rights (see Barnard 2003: 243–4).

San Studies Hot Spots

Political hot spots have changed through time. In the 1970s, as indeed in the 1930s (Schapera 1939), the eastern Kalahari could be regarded as the main hot spot, with human rights issues of possible slavery, in the 1930s, or at the very least serfdom, in the 1970s, being focal issues for anthropologists involved. A number of anthropologists have worked there since the 1970s, but the key player has been Bob Hitchcock of the University of Nebraska-Lincoln, first through an influential government report on his socio-economic survey (Hitchcock 1978) and later through a plethora of publications, many bringing together comparative material on San from other parts of Botswana (e.g. Hitchcock 1987; Hitchcock and Brandenburgh 1991; Hitchcock and Holm 1993).

Hitchcock and others working in eastern Botswana have tended to focus on policy and on relations between Basarwa and the state, as much as on relations between Basarwa and their dominant agro-pastoralist neighbours. Among important ethnographic studies has been that of Liz Cashdan of the University of Utah, who also worked in the area in the 1970s. Although much of her work concerns traditional settlement patterns and spatial organization, she has also identified dimensions of trade and reciprocity between hunter-gatherers and agro-pastoralists (the subject of her Ph.D. dissertation) and published significant papers on that subject in the 1980s (e.g. Cashdan 1986, 1987). Curiously, these were never intended as contributions to the emerging Kalahari debate, or as development-oriented works, but they certainly have implications for both.

The three major areas of anthropological concern in recent decades have been the Central Kalahari Game Reserve (CKGR) of Botswana, the former 'homeland' of Eastern Bushmanland in northern Namibia, and Schmidtsdrift in South Africa.

The Central Kalahari Game Reserve, Botswana

Bushman studies have always attracted gifted amateurs. One of the more unique is Carlos Valiente-Noailles, a Buenos Aires lawyer who has spent much of his life working with G//ana or Kua of the CKGR and Himba cattle-herders in northern Namibia. He tests the limits of the notion of 'amateur', as his work touches on Bushman conceptions of law, and in the course of his work he acquired a Ph.D. in anthropology, and he has become president of the Academia Nacional de Ciencias de Buenos Aires. From 1978 to 1990, he made annual expeditions, in the southern summer, and headed teams of some nine to thirteen people (students, driver, cook, photographer, etc.). He did his Ph.D. in Paris on gender relations (Valiente-Noailles 1994), but his major work in English to date is *The Kua* (Valiente-Noailles 1993), an expensive, well-illustrated general ethnography which is an effective cross between a professional monograph and a coffee-table book. The details he presents make clear the still vibrant Bushman traditions during the 1980s, but he also documents intriguing aspects of social change, such as contact with Tswana and Kgalagadi law (*moláo*), which seems to be 'equated' to and yet subtly distinguishable from Kua law (*///née//né*) (Valiente-Noailles 1993: 125–8).

Valiente-Noailles's work has been mainly in the south-eastern part of the Reserve, but in the south-west environmental degradation was on the increase through the 1980s. At ≠Xade (Xade), the population grew from around 200 in the early 1960s to over 1,000 in 1988. Most of the increase was in the late 1980s, when the government began efforts to remove the inhabitants to the settlements. Part of their reasoning was indeed environmental, as the European Union and other governments and non-governmental entities put pressure on Botswana to conserve wildlife (Hitchcock and Brandenburgh 1991: 28–30). The CKGR is, after all, called a 'game reserve', and goat herding, hunting from horseback, and the large population at ≠Xade that pursued such activities, plainly appeared a threat to 'conservation'. Government and negotiators from NGOs held talks between 1997 and 2002, but eventually disputes arose between NGOs, notably Survival International and the Botswana human rights organization Ditshwanelo, and indeed among anthropologists involved as supporters, advisers or negotiators. Basically, Ditshwanelo advocated a soft approach, and Survival a more combative one. In 2002 a special edition of *Pula: Botswana Journal of Social Science* (issue number 27; or volume 16, number 2) came out. The theme was 'Basarwa (Khoe and San) Studies in Botswana', and the editors Onalenna Doo Selolwane and Sidel Saugestad. Especially noteworthy is the paper by S.P. Mphinyane (2002), which tries to tackle the complexities of the issue, though the title suggests its ultimate simplicity: 'Power and Powerlessness: When Support Becomes Overbearing – the Case of Outsider Activism on the Resettlement Issue of the Basarwa of the Central Kalahari Game Reserve'.

Also in 2002, the people of ≠Xade and virtually all the rest of the CKGR were finally evicted. Since then a major court battle has ensued, with 243 G/wi and G//ana suing the government for the return of their land: *moláo* and *//née//né* were indeed in conflict. George Silberbauer was called as an expert witness, on the G/wi and G//ana side, and Norwegian anthropologist Sidsel Saugestad (e.g. 2004a,

2005) has been conducting an ethnographic analysis of the proceedings. The position of many is that diamonds are at the root of the trouble (see Good 2003).

Japanese research continued in the CKGR until the removals, and Sugawara (2004) provides an excellent summary. Among recent work among G/wi and G//ana is that of Akira Takada and Junko Maruyama of Kyoto University. Takada has followed closely in Sugawara's line of interest, examining issues such as perceptions of the environment, language acquisition and care-giver/child interaction among G/wi and G//ana (e.g. Takada 2005). He has also written on development issues, including tension between San groups and agro-pastoralists in northern Namibia (Takada 2002). Maruyama has worked more directly in development concerns, or more precisely in the study of social problems of the former CKGR residents at Kx'oensakene (as G/wi and G//ana call it) or what is known to others as New Xade, and in areas near the settlement. In a style reminiscent of Lee's input–output analysis of the early 1960s, she has found significant variations in economic activity depending on proximity to the settlement, with some households living purely on hunting, gathering and craft production, and others dependent on subsidies or on wage labour (Maruyama 2003). Her work is among the finest of any being done today, and sets new standards for quantitative data collection and analytical insight into the rapidly changing way of life of G/wi and G//ana.

The significance of Japanese research, both on resettled G/wi and G//ana in the last few years and on those of the CKGR before that, cannot be overestimated. Just to take two examples, in a series of articles Kazunobu Ikeya has documented the impact of goat rearing, dry farming, road construction, handicraft production and other activities in the Reserve, as well as the effects of relocation from the Reserve (e.g. Ikeya 1993, 1996a, b, 2001), while Masakazu Osaki (e.g. 1990) has examined the influence of sedentism and changes in hunting technique on sharing practices. Osaki concludes that, while meat-sharing customs differ depending on whether one hunts with dogs or on horseback, sharing ideology is resilient and reflects a deep-seated egalitarian psychology among G/wi and G//ana. But nor is the work of Osaki and Ikeya confined to the gathering of data: Ikeya has criticized Osaki's interpretation for overemphasizing psychology over material factors in G/wi society (see Sugawara 2004: 119). There is no doubt that the axis of both research productivity among living San groups and meaningful debate on their social transformation is gradually shifting from North America to Japan.

Eastern and Western Bushmanland, Namibia

The former Eastern Bushmanland, now part of Otjozondjupa region, is the land known to generations of anthropologists as Nyae Nyae. The administrative centre is at Tsumkwe (or Tjom!kwe), in the centre of the area. It was a major South

African Defence Force (SADF) base during the latter part of the South African occupation, and many of those Bushman soldiers who were sent to Schmidtsdrift upon Namibian independence were based there. This area remains important to anthropology, of course, but it is a crisis area today partly because of the disruption caused by the SADF two decades ago. The army brought in money, which in turn led to over-consumption of alcohol, prostitution and a resulting perception by outsiders of the loss of foraging knowledge and of self-respect.

While there is some truth to this view, nevertheless others have argued that the foraging way of life, both as ideology and in practice, is more common than believed both there and in the environmentally poorer area still known as Western Bushmanland. According to Andy Botelle and Rick Rohde (1995: 121), 'Contrary to popular belief, the !Kung and Hei//om of western Bushmanland rely throughout the year on a variety of veldfoods for their survival. Overall, veldfood is almost equal to food aid in importance, though during the late spring and rainy season it becomes the most important source of food for the majority of HHs [households].' Respondents to their survey, undertaken in 1993, also claimed that, in the future, hunting will be more important (46 per cent) rather than less (29 per cent) (Botelle and Rohde 1995: 89). Certainly, it could be that respondents had a tendency to give their interviewers what they thought the latter wanted to hear, or that their responses were often just wishful thinking. Or it could be that the survey represents a truer picture. Either way, its implications were not neutral and the report has been criticized by others in Namibia with different development agendas. All this reflects a perennial, practical playing-out of the Kalahari debate, with some favouring a return to hunting as what San want (traditionalists) and others a more rapid entry into the modern economy (revisionists). It seems also that here San have been recruited: they too, by the answers they give, line up as traditionalists and revisionists.

In 2002, the American NGO Cultural Survival dedicated an issue of its journal *Cultural Survival Quarterly* to 'The Kalahari San: Self-determination in the Desert', with a number of papers on the former Eastern and Western Bushmanland. Most contributions, of course, were by foreign anthropologists, but some were by Namibian San, including two on this area (Arnold 2002; /Useb 2002). Chief John Arnold, an elected !Xũ leader, describes a tourist venture not far from Tsumkwe called the Omatako Valley Rest Camp. It was set up in 1997 at Arnold's instigation. Joram /Useb is a Hai//om, and assistant to the coordinator of the Working Group of Indigenous Minorities in Southern Africa. His paper is based on an address he gave to the UN Working Group on Indigenous Populations, in Geneva in 2001. His immediate concern is with the threatened relocation, suggested by the Namibian authorities in 2000, of more than 20,000 people from private land to a new settlement scheme near Tsumkwe. The entire population of Tsumkwe district (Bushmanland) is, he notes, only 6,700. Pointedly, he does not mention ethnicity. Those to be resettled are mainly Herero who spent the years since the 1904–5 war in exile in what is now Botswana, and who 'returned' to Namibia in the 1990s. He refers to Ju/'hoansi and !Kung as 'people indigenous to this region', but seemingly avoids the specification of 'indigenous rights'. Instead he calls on the Namibian government 'to assist them in their struggle for development and human rights'.

The return to Namibia of a large Herero-speaking population, with their cattle, and their resettlement in Ju/'hoan areas, is a serious issue. Ju/'hoan country is already squeezed by the encroachment of white-owned farms in the past and by the migration of other San from the north, including from Angola during the more recent conflict. But not only is 'Bushmanland' a hot spot: both the present gradual influx of Herero and plans for large-scale resettlement of more Herero are 'hot potatoes' in need of more intensive anthropological research. Namibia is a country where the idea of 'indigenous' rights for some groups and not others sounds far too much like apartheid, and where even ethnicity is frowned on: hence the linguistic absurdity of references to 'San-speaking people' instead of San.

Schmidtsdrift, South Africa

One noteworthy phenomenon in advocacy was the interest taken in Schmidtsdrift by South African anthropologists, both Afrikaans- and English-speaking. The Schmidtsdrift settlement was an army base eighty kilometres west of Kimberley. It was created in 1990, when in the face of Namibian independence Bushmen who had fought on the South African side in the Namibian war found themselves to be enemies of the state within their own country. The South African Defence Force moved about 4,000 people there, including Bushman soldiers and their families, from northern Namibia. Nearly 3,000 of them were !Xũ, many from Angola as well as northern Namibia, and over 1,000 were Kxoe or Khwe from the Caprivi Strip. They use Afrikaans for much communication, both between the two Bushman communities and to outsiders.

Among Afrikaans-speaking ethnologists, L.P. Vorster (1994) focused on sorcery among Schmidtsdrift !Xũ from Angola, specifically the murder of one alleged sorcerer and the question of the cause of tensions leading to such accusations, and the possible existence of this supposedly un-Bushman phenomenon at Schmidtsdrift. He argued that sorcery occurred because of the traumatic effects of war and migration. H.P. Steyn (1994) looked at the position of elderly people at Schmidtsdrift and argued that they were particularly disadvantaged by the move to South Africa. In contrast to their role in traditional Bushman society, the elders of Schmidtsdrift were marginalized and dependent. Education, for example, had been something in which elders and the young shared, as elders once taught things like food-gathering skills to youngsters. But what were the parents of SADF soldiers to teach their grandchildren at Schmidtsdrift, where there were no wild plant foods to gather and where education was in the hands of strangers? John Sharp (1997), Stuart Douglas (1997; Sharp and Douglas 1996), Linda Waldman (1995) and other anglophone anthropologists have done applied work at Schmidtsdrift too, focusing on issues of identity, gender relations, unemployment and associated social problems.

A number of these studies have used classic Bushman ethnography, such as that of Lee and Marshall, as a baseline. Afrikaans- and English-speaking anthropologists alike shared a sense of the 'traditional' and a functionalist vision, irrespective of their politics. In fact, members of both traditions were already part of the growing political consensus in South Africa, and part of an emerging consensus in anthropology too, which would lead to the merging of the country's two rival anthropological organizations to form Anthropology Southern Africa in 2001. There was an obvious recognition that South African policy had been the cause of the Schmidtsdrift dilemma, and an agreed sense of vocation that declared anthropology to be useful in its solution.

I visited Schmidtsdrift in 1997 and the site of its successor, the nearby farm of Platfontein, not long after the army had agreed to allow people to build their settlements as they wanted to. From the start, !Xũ and Kxoe had asked and been allowed to occupy separate areas in the settlement, but they were required to place their tents in traditional army style, not in Bushman styles. When this policy was changed, they re-formed their canvas shelters. The !Xũ built circular groupings of canvas huts in a layout not unlike a typical !Xũ village, and the Kxoe did much the same but with the addition of large encircling canvas windbreaks, just like the ones made of sticks on the edge of the Okavango. What will have been obvious to any anthropologist who had seen !Xũ and Kxoe settlements in Namibia or Botswana is that they had recreated the 'traditional' in modern materials. I had no part in the transformation, but the army welfare officer reassured me that (to his surprise) the reported drunken behaviour and other social ills of the early days of Schmidtsdrift were suddenly a thing of the past.

Schmidtsdrift was not only a social phenomenon; it is an anthropological one. It is no accident that so many anthropologists, especially South African ones, have taken a professional interest in the place, and now in Platfontein. These are large settlements; the current population of Platfontein, almost all San migrants from Schmidtsdrift, is about 6,500. (There is a plan to 'train' 1,000 of them to use their 'traditional skills' as security guards, tracking stock thieves in the farms of the region.) The sites are easy to get to. Their inhabitants speak Afrikaans, so South African researchers at least require no knowledge of a Bushman language and no interpreters. The previous South African government is responsible for the plight of the inhabitants, and at least some South Africans today feel a responsibility for them. For an anthropologist, it offers a taste of the exotic and an opportunity to use one's understanding for social good and to right wrongs of the recent past.

The problem may be that the accessibility of Schmidtsdrift and Platfontein might easily create a tendency for anthropologists and anthropology students to become short-term fieldworkers. There is a tendency in South African anthropology, along with local anthropology on the African continent more generally, for studies to resemble those of sociology or social work as much as they do Western or Japanese ones. If this has happened at Schmidtsdrift and Platfontein, it may foretell the future for places like Tsumkwe and Ghanzi too. With so many anthropologists concentrated on such a small number of people it is inevitable that there will be much politicking and personalities involved and indeed intellectual inbreeding.

Social Anthropology and Organizational Activity

Anthropologists have not been silent in the struggle for rights for San groups, and the organizational base for anthropological involvement is interesting to reflect upon. Historically, the initial efforts at advocacy and partnership in development have continued, while research moved from being largely a separate endeavour to one governed to a much greater extent by practical, development-related matters.

The Kalahari Peoples Fund

Richard Lee's early work and that of his students were supported by the Harvard Kalahari Research Group, led by Lee and Irven DeVore. In the early 1970s, participants included archaeologist John Yellen, geneticist and demographer Henry Harpending, psychologist Richard Katz, psychological anthropologist Melvin Konner, literature and music student Marjorie Shostak, gender and childhood specialist Patricia Draper, and folklorist Megan Biesele. At that time, Lee and DeVore were finalizing work on *Kalahari Hunter-gatherers* (Lee and DeVore 1976), a collection of papers by all of these researchers and others who had worked with Ju/'hoansi and neighbouring peoples. Biesele was then a graduate student at Harvard, and when she returned from her first fieldwork in the Kalahari in 1972 she put forward the idea of the Harvard researchers giving something back to the community. Lorna Marshall suggested a workshop, and that meeting, in 1973, established the Kalahari Peoples Fund (KPF) as an advocacy and development organization linking the Ju/'hoansi with the researchers. Lorna Marshall provided much of the organization's early funding herself, and the KPF is still run by Biesele from Austin, Texas (Biesele 2003a).

From the beginning, KPF policy emphasized locally initiated development, rather than 'top-down' initiatives. Their first projects were in Botswana, where the KPF is still involved and where it now collaborates with organizations such as the Kuru Development Trust, part of what is now called the Kuru Family of Organizations. Initiatives have included, for example, the provision of water resources in the Dobe area, the mapping of traditional Ju/'hoan territories and genealogical research to establish who has rights to use them. From 1981 KPF work began in earnest on the Namibian side of the border. Today the KPF works closely with a locally based support organization known as the Nyae Nyae Development Foundation of Namibia (formerly Ju/Wa Bushman Development Foundation) and the community-based Nyae Nyae Conservancy (formerly Nyae Nyae Farmers Cooperative). A generation of San, including Hai//om, !Xũ, Ju/'hoan and Naro individuals, has now entered the development scene and several are writing papers either on their own or in collaboration with anthropologists. Most prominent among them are Joram /Useb, a Hai//om from Namibia, and Kxao Moses ≠Oma, a Ju/'hoan from that country. Both of them have addressed sessions of the United Nations Working Group on Indigenous Peoples in Geneva and other conferences on issues such as tourism, education and traditional leadership in a modern context (see, for example, /Useb 2001).

The Kalahari People's Fund is important not least because it was the first major NGO established to aid social and economic development among the San. It is also noteworthy because it was set up and funded by anthropologists. Apart from the Nyae Nyae organizations mentioned above (founded in 1986) and the church-funded Kuru Development Trust (also set up in 1986, in D'Kar, Botswana), all the major NGOs were founded in the 1990s. These include Ditshwanelo, also known as the Botswana Centre for Human Rights (founded in Gaborone, 1992), Kgeikani Kweni or First People of the Kalahari (FPK), set up by the late John Hardbattle, Roy Sesana and other Naro (in Ghanzi, Botswana, 1993), the !Xuu and Khwe Trust (set up in Stellenbosch, also in 1993, to assist displaced San soldiers from the war in Namibia), the South African San Institute or SASI (in Cape Town, 1996), and the Working Group of Indigenous Minorities in Southern Africa (WIMSA), based in Windhoek since 1996, long under the leadership of Axel Thoma, assisted by Joram /Useb (see also Saugestad 2004b).

The Research Tradition in Botswana

Sidsel Saugestad's Tromsø–Botswana link (formally, the University of Botswana and the University of Tromsø Collaborative Programme for San Research and Capacity Building) is certainly one of the most ingenious developments in funding for Basarwa research. Just as the Norwegian Agency for Development Cooperation (NORAD) pulled its main aid programmes from Botswana, because the country was becoming too rich, Saugestad earned a grant from the Norwegian Universities Funding Council (NUFU) to support a five-year project involving her own University of Tromsø and the University of Botswana. Ironically, Norway had funded most of the Remote Area Development Programme in the late 1980s and early 1990s and had supported projects involving Basarwa for much longer (Saugestad 1998a). The NUFU project has run since 1996, and has supported several lecturers at the University of Botswana in obtaining overseas Ph.D.s on San-related, development-oriented topics. Tromsø, still the northernmost university in the world, had been set up in 1972 with a special responsibility towards Norway's Saami population. The link would entail the occasional involvement of Saami, and would bring in mainly ethnic Tswana academics and students, often from privileged backgrounds, from the University of Botswana, together with the disadvantaged Basarwa population they were commandeered to study.

The key involvement on the Norwegian side was anthropological, though Botswana academics included a wider spectrum of social science researchers. For example, the workshop Saugestad organized in a cold Tromsø October (Saugestad 1998b) included among its Botswana contingent two historians, a sociologist, a lawyer, a social worker, an educationist, an environmental scientist and two development anthropologists. Both development anthropologists, interestingly, were from minority backgrounds themselves: Manchester-trained Isaac Mazonde, a Shona-speaking immigrant from Zimbabwe, and Michael Taylor, born in Botswana of British parents and at the time of the conference a postgraduate student at Edinburgh. Taylor's Ph.D. thesis (2000) on Community Based Natural Resource Management (CBNRM) is notable in being a rare study of 'River Bushmen' of the Okavango, and in illustrating in great depth of diversity in Basarwa points of view on poverty, rights, modernization and identity.

There have been a number of conferences bringing together Khoisan (or Khoe and San, as many prefer now) representatives and their advocates and even Khoisan and academics. One example, noteworthy in view of the excellent summary publication that appeared afterwards, was Research for Khoe and San Development, held in Gaborone in 2003. The proceedings (Motshabi and Saugestad 2004) include the background briefing paper, three keynote addresses, academic papers (on education, health, leadership, history, archaeology, land and languages), a summary of discussions on policy issues (education, development and land), and resolutions on policy passed by the conference.

Let me take just one paper to illustrate here the interplay between academic research and policy: Nick Walker's (2004) on the Kalahari debate. Walker, a historian at the University of Botswana, argues that contact between farmers and foragers was more complex than either side in the debate has acknowledged, with relative autonomy and encapsulation simply two extremes, and symbiosis more common. He suggested that foragers controlled their own resources and also contributed to the broader economy while maintaining distinct identities, and further that the Botswana government today ought to take this into account in policy decisions. He emphasizes diversity over time and space, with greater domination by farmers earlier in south-eastern Botswana, very little farmer presence in the southwest, and periods of intense interaction followed by disappearance of the farmers in parts of the north-west. The kind of research required to produce work such as this must, by necessity, be both interdisciplinary and collaborative with the community under study. What is really interesting is that the issues 'resolving the "Bushman problem"' are framed in terms of the Kalahari debate.

The Regional Assessment of the Status of the San

In 1996, the Africa–Caribbean–Pacific European Union (APC–EU) Joint Assembly held its twenty-second session in Windhoek. Noting the 'special difficulties encountered in integrating hunting and gathering peoples in agricultural industrial states', the assembly called for 'a comprehensive study of the San people ... in the light of international conventions' (assembly resolution, quoted in Suzman 2001a: 85). The Working Group of Indigenous Minorities in Southern Africa (WIMSA) prepared a project proposal, and Sidsel Saugestad, at the request of the European Commission, prepared an inception report. The result was a major survey carried out over the next five years under the direction of young Edinburgh-trained South African anthropologist James Suzman.

The results of the regional assessment were published in five volumes: an introduction (Suzman 2001a); an overview of San issues in South Africa, Angola, Zambia and Zimbabwe (Robins, Madzudzo and Brenzinger 2001); an overview of the situation in Botswana (Cassidy, Good, Mazonde and Rives 2001); the same for Namibia (Suzman 2001b); and a gender perspective (Felton and Becker 2001). Not all the authors are anthropologists, and there is as much development-speak as anthropological analysis in the reports. However, they are all very well done. The useful Botswana volume is heavily weighted towards political problems and contains a district-based economic survey by Lin Cassidy, and the introduction contains a fine annotated bibliography by Sidsel Saugestad. Saugestad herself was instrumental in enabling another important annotated bibliography, *The Khoe and San* (Willet, Monageng, Saugestad and Hermans 2001; Willet 2002).

The Indigenous Peoples Debate

James Suzman (2001a: 34) remarks in his recommendations from the Assessment of the Status of the San in Southern Africa: 'given the current political and economic climate in southern Africa, addressing the status of San by way of appealing to rights pursuant to their status as an "indigenous people" is not the wisest strategy at the moment'. He was soon to put it rather more strongly (Suzman 2001c), but also on practical grounds, while Adam Kuper has put forward the theoretical argument that there is no meaningful anthropological category 'indigenous peoples'. According to Kuper (2003: 395), the idea of an 'indigenous people' is based 'on obsolete anthropological notions and on a romantic and false ethnographic vision'. The anti-'indigenous' lobby sees this term as little more than a trendy, politically correct way to say 'primitive peoples' – a concept long rejected by mainstream anthropology.

If we think historically, the 'indigenous peoples' debate seems just the latest manifestation of the 'first' and 'second' Kalahari debates. It is no accident that, independently of the debate, and indeed just preceding it, Wilmsen (2002: 825) has attacked 'potentially dangerous claims to cultural authenticity and the uniqueness of particular cultural visions', and advocated citizenship over ethnicity as a goal for minority groups in Botswana. Indigenous rights activists are in essence traditionalists, who see in San something of the human condition more apparent than in the rest of humanity. Or, at the very least, those on the indigenous side imagine San as more isolated than integrated into mainstream southern African society, and less as disadvantaged minorities within an economic system than as autochthonous peoples still living outside larger economic structures. Those on the other side are revisionists. They regard San not as having special status, or as deserving of special rights, but as impoverished and politically weak and deserving of the same rights as other citizens of Botswana, Namibia, or wherever.

One of the strongest supporters of the 'indigenous peoples' view has been Saugestad, but she notes the complexity of the concept. She suggests four criteria: first-come, non-dominance, cultural difference and self-ascription (Saugestad 2001: 43). She emphasizes the relational nature of the concept. Rather like ethnicity, indigeneity would involve definition in relation to other (non-indigenous) groups. My own view is that, while Kuper is right that 'indigenous peoples' may be an archaic and faulty category for anthropological analysis, we are nevertheless stuck with it. It would be easier for us to jettison the idea of 'indigenous' and to think in terms of 'human rights' instead, but that is not how the world is constructed. 'Indigenous peoples' is a valid legal construct, and has a place in international law, and indeed is no messier than other messy legal concepts, like 'refugee' (Barnard 2006: 6–9). Furthermore, it is the preferred means of battle for San support organizations and San leaders, and is gaining currency among ordinary people as a means of self-identification.

Conclusion

There is today enormous interest in relations between San and outsiders, and especially between San and the state (see Hohmann 2003a). It has only been possible here to scratch the surface, but there is no doubt that social development and advocacy are key areas for research in the present and in the immediate future. It is ironic that senior politicians in both Botswana and Namibia have recently attacked anthropologists, even those opposed to special rights for 'indigenous peoples', for meddling in the touchy field of specifically San development. This is all the more ironic in that, at least in the case of Botswana, it has long been virtually impossible for some highly respected researchers to get permits to do 'pure' as opposed to 'applied' research.

If there is another area of growth at present, it is undoubtedly in the arena of representations of 'the Bushman' and of San culture and society, not least in the political implications of how anthropologists, NGOs, governments and San themselves construct such imagery. The indigenous peoples debate is all about representations, and these have political as well as aesthetic implications.

–10–

Representations and Self-representations

In 1987, historian of anthropology George Stocking noted that, in spite of modern reluctance to describe any populations as 'primitive', the comparative method of the 1870s had still not fallen out of use: 'Thus the Bushmen of the Kalahari, with appropriate antiracialist admonitions, have for thirty years provided evidence on the nature of early hunter/gatherer existence, in a way that Tylor would surely have appreciated – although he might have found the occasionally Rousseauistic rhetoric a bit archaic' (Stocking 1987: 328). The image of the Bushman as both prototype hunter-gatherer and exemplar of early humanity has been recycled at several points in the history of anthropology. Each age gives the image its own gloss: Rousseau's happy and clever *bon sauvage* of 1755 comes back to us in 1955, when Laurens van der Post made his famous expedition and the six-part television series *Lost World of the Kalahari* – a series soon to capture the attention of both the general public and would-be anthropologists of the day (Barnard 2005).

From the 1970s onwards, much of the rest of anthropology has become self-occupied with questions like 'Should we be more reflexive?', 'Is ethnography just a kind of writing?' or 'What comes after metanarratives?' Hunter-gatherer studies in general, and San studies in particular, continued to look to bigger questions – questions in anthropology rather than merely questions about anthropology. Among these were the nature of economics (in the idea of an original affluent society), the definition of a society (in the Kalahari debate), and the meaning of the transition from foraging to food production. Evolutionism, functionalism, structuralism and Marxism remained strong in San studies when others were dispensing with grand theory altogether, or at least pretending to. At the same time, San studies looked to concerns with social development, human rights and the representation of culture.

Interpretation, Incorporation and Reflexivity

At times, ever since Bleek and Lloyd, informants and interpreters have had a place as identifiable individuals in San studies. The names //Kabbo, Dia!kwain and /Han≠kass'o remain powerful in the specialist literature, while recent generations of anthropology students will know of N!ai from John Marshall's acclaimed film

N!ai, the Story of a !Kung Woman, and of another !Kung woman, N/isa, from Marjorie Shostak's popular books *Nisa* (1983 [1981]) and *Return to Nisa* (2000). Informants ≠Toma 'the leader' and his wife !U feature prominently in the writings of Lorna Marshall. Bleek and Lloyd are commonly credited with recording thousands of pages of /Xam folklore and custom. Looked at another way, we could credit //Kabbo with 3,100 pages, Dia!kwain with 2,400 and /Han≠kass'o with 2,800 (estimates by Lewis-Williams 1981: 27–8). It is in the nature of folklore, in contrast to other kinds of ethnographic text, that informants' own words are so ever-present in the record.

Interpreters are less prominent, but perhaps equally important – certainly in the early stages of fieldwork. One of the most long-serving of the Marshall family interpreters was a Hai//om named Ngani. He worked for the Marshalls in South West Africa (SWA) in their expeditions of 1952–3, 1957–8 and 1961 (L. Marshall 1976: xiv). Before that, as a boy growing up between the world wars, Ngani was the servant of SWA Secretary E.P. Courtney-Clarke. Courtney-Clarke was said to have boasted that his servant not only spoke nine languages, but also could mix a good cocktail (Gall 2001: 133). Such linguistic skills (if not bartending ones) are not uncommonly reported, although in more recent decades ethnographers in the Boasian or Malinowskian mould have tended to use interpreters much less and to rely instead on their own language-learning capabilities. Most would agree: what is lost in translation is more than regained in rapport with one's subjects and in a higher level of cultural knowledge.

Some San groups practise naming conventions by which people are named after their grandparents or uncles and aunts, who are classificatory grandparents in some systems (see Barnard 1992: 265–81). Names jump downwards through the generations, from grandparents to grandchildren. Among Ju/'hoansi and Naro, all those who share the same name are believed to be descended from an original namesake ancestor. Namesakes who otherwise do not know one another call each other 'grandrelative', and a grandrelative's sister, for example, is addressed and treated much as if she were one's own sister. This gives these groups (generally speaking, the !Kung or northern groups, and the western Khoe-speaking groups) the ability to treat almost anyone they meet, or at least any members of their own ethnic group they meet, as some kind of kinsman. This is important because they do not have a concept of 'non-kin': everyone is either a 'joking partner' (the informal relationship, which includes grandparents, grandchildren and same-sex siblings) or an 'avoidance partner' (the more formal relationship, which includes parents, children and opposite-sex siblings). When Lorna Marshall began collecting kinship terms, this practice caused her confusion, since the Ju/'hoansi she was with often classified through a namesake equivalence rather than a more distant 'true' genealogical relationship.

Outsiders who live alongside those San who have such a system need San names in order to fit them in. For example, I was friendly early in my fieldwork with two brothers who had a third brother who was absent. Therefore, I was given his name, !A/e. Mathias Guenther, a few years earlier and in a different Naro area, was given the name Kākn//ai, and his wife Patricia the name Di/'kgao, names from the grandchildren's (and grandparents') generation of their chief informants, though not the names of their informants themselves (Smith, Malherbe, Guenther and Berens 2000: 84). Much the same occurred for the Marshall family among the Ju/'hoansi, where ≠Toma gave Lorna his mother's name, Laurence his father's name, Elizabeth his wife's sister's name, and John his own name (Marshall 1976: 204). Even among groups that lack this naming practice, ethnographers are brought into the system of kin classification in an equivalent way. Ethnographers among G/wi and G//ana are classified through friendship links, which function much in the same way as a same-sex sibling link in distinguishing joking and avoidance partners. Thus ethnographers are never merely friends but 'relatives' of their informants. The degree of incorporation is quite different from that of, say, honorary membership of a lineage in a lineage-based system. For the San-incorporated ethnographer, all members of 'his' or 'her' ethnic group are relatives, but of different kinds: some are 'grandparents' the ethnographer can joke with, and others are 'parents' the ethnographer has to treat slightly more circumspectly. The degree to which such rules apply to ethnographers as they do for real San may vary, but the fact of such incorporation undoubtedly places ethnographers in a different category from other kinds of outsider.

The 1970s saw the dawn of a new 'reflexive' spirit in anthropology – but not to any great extent in San studies. Reflexive anthropologists make explicit their own thoughts and actions, at the extreme tending towards autobiography rather than ethnography. Eventually, the reflexive preoccupation with self, or self interacting with 'other', emerged into a greater emphasis on the other. The idea was to give voice to the other, and this has had an impact in San studies. In spite of the positivist inclinations of most San ethnographers, it is not at all odd that one of the very first attempts at 'native voices' ethnography was in fact a Ju/'hoan ethnography. Marjorie Shostak was never a positivist in the narrow sense, but nor was she explicitly reflexivist. Rather, her goal was to present biography. In *Nisa* (Shostak 1983 [1981]), it is N/isa's life which forms the heart of the book, not Shostak's. N/isa discovers sex, has trial marriages, settles down and has children, takes lovers, and so on, and N/isa describes those around her who do the same. Each chapter contains a few pages of general ethnographic background by Shostak, and then N/isa's narrative, her own memories of youth, feelings and descriptions of events surrounding her.

Shostak died in 1996, with the manuscript of *Return to Nisa* still unfinished. Her husband Mel Konner and two friends saw to the extensive editing that needed to be done, and it appeared in 2000. N/isa learned of Shostak's death in 1997 and expressed her sadness with the words: 'The great God took my daughter Hwantla and made me blind. Hwantla was like my eyes, and when God took her away, I became blind. I don't know if I will ever see again, because my daughter has been taken away' (Shostak 2000: 239).

Shostak's ethnography would later find its place as a key source for Mary Louise Pratt (1986) in her contribution to the famous 'Writing Culture' conference of 1984. That conference dictated the pace of postmodernist anthropology in the decades thereafter. Pratt is a literary critic, then at Stanford, and now Professor of Spanish and Portuguese Languages and Literatures at New York University. She uses Bushman material to rather better effect than many anthropologists. She captures well the 'blazing contradiction between a tendency on the one hand to historicize the !Kung as survivor-victims of European imperialism, and a tendency on the other [in the same literature] to naturalize and objectify them as primal beings virtually untouched by history' (1986: 48). It is interesting that she chooses to put it this way. From such a perspective, the Kalahari debate that was to bloom only a few years on was less a debate between two sides and more an ambivalence or tension between two mindsets in the same ethnographer. It is also interesting that she chooses to concentrate on Shostak, most literary of Bushman ethnographers, as an exemplar of this tension. And intriguing too are Pratt's (1986: 46–7) remarks on the longevity of the tension in Bushmanist literature: she finds the same tension in the travelogues of Barrow (1801) and Sparrman (1785). In another paper completed about the same time but for a literary journal, Pratt (1985) remarks at length that Barrow's account is more about traces or 'scratches' of Bushmen on the land than about encounters with living individuals or groups.

Us and Them, Them and Us

Contrasts between ethnographic representations and self-representations can be revealing. Consider these passages from Dorothea Bleek's *The Naron* and from the recent splendid compilation of San self-representations, *Voices of the San* (Le Roux and White 2004). Both refer to Naro male initiation and its comparison with female initiation. According to Bleek:

> When boys have learned to shoot and killed two or three head of big game, they go through an initiation ceremony. Ten or twelve of them are taken into the bush by medicine men and other old men and spend a month of hardship there. Their food consists of a few roots and berries on to which the medicine men sprinkle 'medicine', that is powdered bark. The treatment they receive is very hard, the weaklings die. No woman may come near the camp. Every night they dance. All gather in a circle, clap their hands and sing a weird, solemn tune with the refrain of 'honk a honk'. Then they stamp round in a circle waving their arms to another phase of the melody (no words are used); then they stand still and sing the first part again and so on. I have seen this dance also.
>
> The sound of the tunes used in these two initiation dances leads me to believe that they are the remains of religious ceremonies, of which the meaning is no longer clear

to themselves. The men's function in particular might well have been an assembly for prayer followed by a dance. (D.F. Bleek 1928: 23–4)

The late Chief Willem Ryperd was a Naro leader from Gobabis, not far from Bleek's 1920s fieldwork site. I presume his statement dates from the 1990s, but the time described is indefinite:

> There was also a course for young boys. They attended a course, which was for a teenager on the way to become a man, and he had to attend it. If you worked in the dark, then they had to make a light for you. It was for you when you were on your way. That is what we were taught by the adult males in the veld … For a young man, it is like a young woman who has her first period, and is then taught and treated in a strict manner. We were treated in the same way. (Willem Ryperd, quoted in Le Roux and White 2004: 96)

What is interesting is that both accounts invoke the past. Although apparently Ryperd himself underwent male initiation, that custom (unlike female initiation) is no longer prevalent. It was certainly prevalent in Bleek's time, but in her interpretation the 'meaning' was no longer clear to the Naro and initiation tunes and dances are merely the 'remains' of some now poorly understood ritual. But what is going on here? Was meaning really lost before Bleek arrived on the scene but the customs preserved into Ryperd's time nevertheless?

The ethnographer more than any other responsible for representing a San point of view is Megan Biesele (see Biesele 2003b). Her first major text in this style was a short book called *Shaken Roots*, containing nineteen pages of text by Biesele plus, on unnumbered pages, quotations from Ju/'hoansi and numerous photographs by Paul Weinberg. The imagery is altogether obvious. For example, one Ju/'hoan inhabitant of a Herero cattle-post is pictured stretching a hunting bow. The quotation opposite reads: 'When I pull this bow I feel very happy. It reminds me of the days when we lived well hunting and gathering and life was fine. Then the white man came and took our land. What life is this?' (Ou Jacob ≠Oma, quoted in Biesele and Weinberg 1990). That quotation is perhaps unusual in its fullness of expression, with the inclusion of hunting, memory, a fine life, the arrival of the whites, their theft of the land, and a question on the life that is left. Yet these same sentiments are typical of material quoted from Bushmen and occur time and time again in the work of Biesele and others, and in the ephemeral literature and websites of campaigning organizations as well. The material towards the end of the book, emphasizing possibilities of self-reliance at the time of Namibian independence, look briefly towards a bright future; and the blurb on the back of the book extols the 'documentary portrait of a group of people mythologised and misrepresented by "experts"'.

Biesele, Weinberg and their photographic subjects have done a wonderful job in putting together a new and sympathetic image, but it too is an image, not a matter of pure truth to triumph over the misrepresentations of 'experts'. One wonders who these experts are, and how they have misrepresented the Bushmen. In the texts and quotations, successive governments and non-Bushman ethnic groups come in for criticism, but not anthropologists or scholars of any sort.

Alterity and Recuperation

The 'Living Fossil' Disclaimer

The idea of ethnographic analogy has been important in archaeology, almost since its beginnings. Yet rightly there has almost always been either a resistance to comparisons to material that is too early, or a clear idea that such comparisons must always bear disclaimers concerning the modernity of present-day Bushman peoples. As we shall see, Thabo Mbeki seems to have believed he was safe with Khoisan, because he regarded them as gone. Ethnographic analogy is rife, but almost always accompanied by some disclaimer. A particularly good one is this, from evolutionist sociologist Pierre van den Berghe:

> The !Kung San are prime candidates for the status of living fossils, for they are not only hunters and gatherers, but they also live in a tropical bushland environment close and similar to the presumed cradle of mankind somewhere in the Rift Valley of Eastern Africa. It must be emphasized however, that the San are not fossils; they are our living contemporaries who have continued to evolve for precisely as long as the New York stockbroker or the Parisian metro conductor. (van den Berghe 1979: 133)

So they both are and are not living fossils. Van den Berghe cites their 'living fossil' status as the reason why so many anthropologists have studied this group. And who can deny that they have attracted much ethnographic attention?

Yet they are also very much modern people, and some have access to technology no fossil ancestor could have dreamed of, although this might not normally reach the pages of our ethnographies. I recall once visiting a fellow ethnographer in the field. We heard the unmistakable sounds of medicine dance music in the far distance, then quickly grabbed blankets and a thermos and headed off into the night. When we reached our destination, we found only a San family with a tape recorder playing back the previous month's performance.

Harmless or Belligerent?

The image of the Bushman through the 1960s and 1970s was often one of harmlessness, due largely to the writings of Laurens van der Post, Elizabeth Marshall Thomas and others. Competing against this image was that of adulterers, fighters (over women) and murderers, fostered in part by Richard Lee's (e.g. 1979: 397–8) discovery that the homicide rate among the Dobe Ju/'hoansi was higher than that of the inhabitants of the United States. If Lee's discovery had been left there, that would have been fine. The problem was that, just as the 'flower power' generation took to the image of harmlessness, so too their opponents took Lee's vision to heart and even amplified it. Take, for example, the description of 'The belligerent Bushmen' presented by Carton Coon in *The Hunting Peoples* (1971: 237–9). There Coon describes incidents that had been related by Lee at a colloquium in 1970 (as Coon was writing his book). But what is more interesting is the way in which he invokes the Marshalls: 'In their earlier publications on the Nyae Nyae !Kung Bushmen, Mrs. Lorna Marshall and her daughter Mrs. Elizabeth Marshall Thomas made no mention of fighting, but Mrs. Marshall has stated privately that she had heard of such combats having taken place in former times' (Coon 1971: 239).

Coon was no ordinary commentator. He was an eminent professor, first at Harvard and later at Pennsylvania. In the early 1960s he was president of the American Association of Physical Anthropologists, and he held many honours. In 1981, the year he died, he was appointed US Ambassador to Nepal. He was also notorious for what came to be regarded as racist views on human evolution (Alland 2002: 57–77), and he was a great popularizer of anthropological findings. His view carried weight, and *The Hunting Peoples* was widely read by students and the general public – and probably still is. Of course, it is not enough to envisage simply a right-wing/left-wing split in views of the Bushmen. If Coon was right-wing and Thomas left-wing, then where do the materialists fit? Lee was the source of Coon's material on violence, but he was also a source for Sahlins's vision of 'the original affluent society'. Can the Bushman be at the same time violent to the point of murderous jealousy, and virtuously 'affluent' by virtue of his limited needs?

One of the most shocking of all representations of the Bushman has to be the nineteenth-century exhibit of a stuffed 'Black Man' (a Bushman with spear, shield and leather apron), which was on display in a small natural history museum in the little Spanish town of Banyoles until 1998. Alexander Alland reports on the saga at some length in his book on race (Alland 2002: 189–98). The collection including the body of the 'Black Man' had been that of local veterinarian and taxidermist Francesca Darder. What eventually got the body removed was the effort of a local doctor, of Haitian origin, Alphonse Arcelin, who came across the display not long before the Barcelona Olympics of 1992. He brought the 'Black Man' to the attention of regional and national authorities, who seemed reluctant to interfere in the affairs of the town of Banyoles, especially at that time.

Alterity

A strange twist in representing 'the Bushman' came with his place in psychology and in ethology. These disciplines have a different vision of 'culture' from anthropology. Whereas anthropologists are happy to see technology or environmental adaptation in evolutionist terms, culture in the abstract is for anthropologists always essentially a relativistic construction. Not so for psychologists and ethologists. Among the strangest studies ever conducted have to be those of two psychologists, who visited the Central Kalahari Game Reserve to administer tests to its 'primitive' inhabitants (Reuning and Wortley 1973). These included, for example, musical preference tests in which G/wi were asked to listen to music and indicate which they liked best (G/wi tend to prefer rock music to Mozart). Modern ethnomusicologists (e.g. Olivier 2005) see Bushman music rather differently.

German ethologist Irenäus Eibl-Eibesfeldt, a friend of !Xoõ ethnographer H.J. Heinz, documented social interaction to an extraordinary degree: 40,000 feet of film on the !Xoõ, 45,000 on the G/wi and 6,500 on the Ju/'hoansi. The results confirmed the ethological image of the aggressive and territorial 'Bushman', even in childhood. It is not that Bushmen were different in this regard from other peoples, but that they exhibited patterns of behaviour that belied the image put about by Eibl-Eibesfeldt's opponents:

> Advocates of frustration-free education are fond of referring to the allegedly happy, frustration-free development of children among primitive tribes, no doubt because they have no real knowledge of primitive cultures. The birth of a baby in a Bushman family leads to intense jealousy on the part of an older child. The !Ko [!Xoõ] accept this as an inescapable fact of life. (Eibl-Eibesfeldt 1979: 150)

Far from portraying Bushmen as harmless or sharing people, he emphasizes his observations of disputes and quarrels, of sexual jealousy and violence, and among children of fear of strangers and aggression within play groups (1979: 153–7). He does note, however, that values contradict observed behaviour. They are more peaceable than some other peoples, such as the famous warlike Yanomamö (of the Venezuela–Brazil border area), and socialization includes the intervention by older children to stop aggression among the younger ones and encourage socially appropriate self-awareness (1979: 157).

One of the great controversies of recent years has been over whether to put on display, or not, the famed Bushman diorama in the South African Museum, in Cape Town. The diorama was made in 1959, at the instigation of the museum's ethnologist Margaret Shaw and the then director A.W. 'Fuzz' Compton. It captures in three dimensions a scene painted by Samuel Daniell in the early nineteenth century, using life casts made by the museum between 1908 and 1912. The problem is that some Khoisan groups find the diorama anachronistic and therefore demeaning, and it was removed from display at their request in April 2001. The present head of Iziko, the organization which runs the museum system as a whole, is H.C. Bredekamp. 'Jatti' Bredekamp happens to be a distinguished historian of the Khoisan and early missionization himself, and is the first director of Khoisan descent. The display of Bushmen in past times has been of anthropological concern. Namibian-born anthropologist Rob Gordon (1995) sees in 'our' portrayals of Bushmen roots of some of their problems (see also Gordon, Rasool and Witz 1996).

Recuperation

The ultimate representation of 'the Bushman' is when 'he' is taken over by the state as the symbol of humanity itself. This is precisely what, with the best of intentions, the South African government did in placing Bushman figures in their new coat of arms. In the words of President Mbeki:

> [The new Coat of Arms] pays tribute to our land and our continent as the cradle of humanity, as the place where human life first began ... Those depicted, who were the very first inhabitants of our land, the Khoisan people, speak to our commitment to celebrate humanity and to advance the cause of the fulfilment of all human beings in our country and throughout the world. (Mbeki 2000)

Bushmen or Khoisan are treated as the 'past', and the imagery constructed here by Mbeki's speech and by the South African state makes use of the fact that the /Xam and the rock painters are gone. By selecting redrawn rock art figures for the coat of arms and /Xam words for the motto, no existing ethnic group and none of South Africa's official (and living) languages is privileged (Barnard 2004c). The actual meaning of the motto, incidentally, is itself rich with symbolic undertones. A translation back into English might well yield 'People of different origin are joining together', or 'People who differ in opinion are talking with one another' (Barnard 2003: 249).

According to Keyan Tomaselli (1995: i), Director of the Centre for Cultural and Media Studies at the University of Natal, Durban: 'The "New" South Africa has recuperated a different, affirmative image of the San, in comparison to the negative, prejudiced, representation of "bushmen" previously popularised by pro-apartheid media.' The special issue of the cultural studies journal *Critical Arts* which he edited (volume 9, number 2, 1995) is devoted to 'Recuperating the San'. It captures yet another form of revisionism, stated explicitly so in Tomaselli's introduction and in some of the papers. Anne Solomon (1995), for example, argues in favour of a reflexive awareness of representation that goes beyond a narrow and culture-bound notion of an aesthetic image. Such a representation is both public and political. Even before the end of apartheid, the Khoisan in general and San in particular were hailed as 'the base and fundamental layer of our [South African] unified and multi-complex culture' (Masilela 1987: 58), and Tomaselli, Stuart Douglas (1995) and others have picked up on this point. What is interesting is that in South Africa the San studies scene involves not only anthropologists but media studies people, literary critics, artists and art historians; and many make contributions to anthropological thought that are not widely known beyond specialist circles. Barbara Buntman, for example, teaches art history at the University of the Witwatersrand, but does research into issues such as the politics of identity, or in her own words 'the ways in which visual images [of Bushmen] entrench ideas about stereotyped hunter-gatherer identity' and 'the prospects of self-representation by KhoiSan/Bushmen' (Buntman 2002: 66).

Tomaselli has also edited in the international scene, with a special issue of *Visual Anthropology* (volume 12, numbers 2–3, 1999) to his credit. That issue, called 'Encounters in the Kalahari', is devoted mainly to the films of John Marshall and to tourist representations of Bushmen. The contrast between the two highlights what may best be considered two sorts of San imagery: the local (South African) and global or cosmopolitan. Anthropology is mainly part of the latter. For that tradition, it may be that the books and films of the Marshall family create the imagery, whereas within South Africa the interplay between the variously romantic and horrific Bushman past and the post-apartheid present is what sticks in the mind. That said, the imagery comes in both cases at least partly, and possibly rather a lot, from within. Tourists, filmgoers and anthropologists have their own images of what is authentic and what is not, and therefore define their own 'Bushman' (see Tomaselli 1999).

What to Call Them

Bushman or San?

Neither 'Bushman' nor 'San' nor 'Khoisan' nor 'Basarwa' is an indigenous term. At various points in the history of Khoisan studies there have been debates about what to call them, most importantly in anthropology since around 1970. For the record though, 'Bushman' (in its Dutch form *Bosjesmans*) dates from 1682 and became the most common term by the 1770s. 'San', in the Cape Khoekhoe masculine plural form *Soaqua*, was first written in the journal of Jan van Riebeeck, in 1653. 'Khoisan' (originally spelled *Koïsan*) was invented in 1928 (see Wilson 1986; Barnard 1992: 7–11). 'Basarwa' came into use as a replacement for the traditional Setswana word *Masarwa* (meaning 'Bushmen') in the 1970s, after a schoolchild asked why the word is in the Setswana noun class that normally designates rocks and trees, as opposed to the one for people.

The greatest absurdity in retrospect has to be the collective decision of the nomenclature session of the 1971 conference on 'The Peoples of Southern Africa'. This august conference, sponsored by the Royal Society of South Africa and the South African Institute for Medical Research, decided that San and Khoikhoi were to be the names of biological entities, Bushman and Hottentot were to be 'their' languages, and 'hunters', 'herders', etc., the terms for ways of life (Jenkins and

Tobias 1977). The problem, of course, is that biological San, whatever they are, do not necessarily speak 'Bushman' languages or lead a hunting-and-gathering way of life.

From the 1970s onwards, anthropologists outside South Africa too have anguished over what to call them. 'Bushmen' had long been the agreed generic term, but from around 1972 the seventeenth-century label 'San' had reappeared. It was even claimed, incorrectly, that this was an indigenous term: in fact no hunter-gatherer people, not even the Khoekhoe-speaking Hai//om, employed 'San' or *saan* as a self-designation. The Hai//om had never heard of the word. Through the 1980s, choice vacillated between 'San' and 'Bushman'. In the feminist era of the 1970s and 1980s, many anthropologists shied away from 'Bushman' on grounds that it might be considered sexist, which it would be if the feminine were 'Bushwoman'. Among Khoisan specialists writing in English, the usual feminine plural has always been 'Bushman women' and the masculine 'Bushman men'. In German, neuter *Buschleute* has long been preferred to masculine *Buschmänner*.

Also in the 1970s and 1980s, some anthropologists noted that 'Bushman' had inaccurate connotations of 'living in the bush' (Bushmen do not see themselves as bush-dwellers, but as inhabiting camps). Yet others pointed out that, once 'San' became known to San, they did not like it – and preferred to be called 'Bushmen'. By the 1990s, though, San in some places, especially in newly independent Namibia, had come to prefer 'San'. It had for over a decade been the liberal choice in South Africa, and was certainly the norm among archaeologists, though it was not as strong among social anthropologists or linguists. Historians tended either to use 'San' or to employ period-sensitive terms: 'Sonquas', 'Boschimans', etc., though never in English the current Afrikaans word 'Bosjesmans'.

In a footnote on Lorna Marshall's account of how her family came to work with 'Bushmen', Wilmsen presents a polemic of several hundred words in which he argues against that 'colonial' term. To quote just part:

> [Names] carry the historical burden of their genesis and deployment. The term 'Bushman' when applied to persons must be seen in this light; it represents and re-presents not persons themselves but the entire lexicon of the sordid discourse of dispossession inflicted on persons that not only accompanied but underwrote the process of colonial dispossession itself ... This historicity of nomenclature cannot be erased, certainly neither by academic nor vernacular valorisation of iconic images, no matter whether baptised with either positive or negative locutions. Thus any attempts, scholarly or popular, to retain, or resuscitate, 'Bushman' terminology or imagery must be neo-colonial extensions of colonial ethnographic naming practice. (Wilmsen 1999: 247–8).

Wilmsen adds that he would not intervene in the efforts of some Khoisan 'to recuperate the designation "Bushmen" for themselves', but that he does believe they should 'consider the consequences very carefully' (1999: 248).

True enough, what Wilmsen says: 'Bushman' (*Bosjesman*) was born of eigh-teenth-century colonial writers. But so what? In its earliest usage it was not offen-sive, and it has been in continuous use among sympathetic travellers and ethnographers pretty much since the 1770s. 'Khoisan' (*Koïsan*) was born of early twentieth-century racialist biological nomenclature, and 'San' (*saan*) was some-times racist is usage among nineteenth-century Khoekhoe – a derogatory term for their poor, foraging cousins. If 'Bushman' always conjures images of colonial oppression, then 'San' must be at least as bad. 'Colonialism' has very little to do with Bushmen. It has to do with the subjugation of previously dominant people, in this case Iron Age Bantu-speaking agro-pastoralists.

It is ironic that we call them Bushmen of the Kalahari, because the 'Kalahari' (Kgalagari or Kgalagadi) are a Bantu-speaking people who until very recently kept Bushmen as serfs. The name refers both to the desert and to that ethnic group, who are closely related to Tswana and Sotho. Central Bushmen, including Naro, who are the main group in contact with Kgalagadi, prefer to call themselves N/oakhoe (in modern orthography, Ncoakhoe), which means 'red people'. Naro call blacks 'black people' (the word also means simply dark and also night-time) and they call whites 'white people' (using either the word for 'white' or 'dawn' or a different word meaning 'cloud'). They also have a rude word, which otherwise means 'penis', to refer to blacks, whites or anyone else who is not 'red'. When a Japanese anthropologist visited me in the field, he was referred to as a 'red white-person' in recognition of his supposedly Bushman appearance.

Bushmen of the southern Kalahari were perceived by many in anthropology as too few in number and too 'acculturated' to be bothered with, at least as exemplars of traditional culture. The ≠Khomani of the northern Cape Province of South Africa, for example, were forced to live on handouts and were classified by the government as 'Coloured', so what possible use could they be in understanding traditional Bushman life? It would be another twenty years before the last few ≠Khomani, still speaking the language closest to the extinct /Xam of Bleek and Lloyd fame, would achieve celebrity status in academic circles. Bushmen, since they were in general classified as 'Coloured', were actually better off under apartheid than the majority, black populations of South Africa and Namibia, but they were not well served by anthropology's neglect. Many San call themselves 'red' rather than 'black' or 'white', and the 'neither-this-nor-that' status enabled them to make best use of the tragic circumstances of the subcontinent in that time.

!Kung or Ju/'hoansi?

How do you tell an old Kalahari hand from a novice? Just ask them the ethnic group name for the San (or Bushmen) of Nyae Nyae and Dobe. In Lorna Marshall's ethnography and in much of Richard Lee's work until the 1990s the people were called !Kung. That term, or more accurately !X̰ũ, is a word for person and also the ethnic group name in the dialect spoken in Angola and the far north of Namibia. The people of Marshall's Nyae Nyae and Lee's Dobe areas prefer Ju (pronounced exactly like French *joue*). The latter, sometimes with the spelling Zhu, sometimes in the full form Zhutwasi, Ju/wasi or Ju/'hoansi (meaning 'Real People'), became more common among ethnographers in the 1980s. The orthography of the language was standardized in the early 1990s, and today nearly all Khoisan specialists use the new standard spelling Ju or Ju/'hoan for the people, with or without the suffix –si, which makes it plural. Wilmsen, virtually alone among specialists, still prefers the spelling Zhu, while many anthropologists outside Khoisan studies stick to the very old-fashioned word !Kung. The use of !Kung for Ju/'hoansi now sounds very strange to Khoisan specialists, a vestige of a bygone era – rather like still calling today's city of St Petersburg Leningrad, or modern Zimbabwe Rhodesia. It can also sound inappropriate to a Ju/'hoan, for whom !Kung or !X̰ũ is a term not used to designate themselves, but to designate those who live farther north.

However, for the non-specialist, let me add that one legitimate use of the word !Kung remains, and one may still hear this from the mouth of some old Kalahari hand or from even some recent researcher. !Kung is still sometimes used as a generic term for the Northern Language Group and its speakers, who comprise people calling themselves !X̰ũ (in the far north), Ju/'hoansi (in the areas Marshall and Lee studied) and ≠Au//eisi (south of those areas). The ≠Au//eisi, incidentally, are the people with whom James Suzman and Renée Sylvain have recently worked, and they are sometimes considered southern Ju/'hoansi. These people were known in the early German literature as *Auen* (the same word, without clicks and with a Naro rather than a !Kung suffix), and they are called locally by non-Bushmen Makaukau or Makoko (the same word again, this time with a Bantu prefix rather than a San suffix and with 'k' instead of click).

Those called by the similar-sounding word spelled !Xoõ, !Xóõ, !Xõ, !Ko, Koon, etc., are a different people (those studied by Heinz), also known by more than a dozen other names: Tshashi, /Nu//en, ≠Ãã, ⊙ha, ≠Hoã, etc. As if that were not bad enough, the last term here, ≠Hoã, is used as a self-designation by another group who speak a very different language. It is no wonder that the linguist who specializes in the !Xoõ or (Western) ≠Hoã language joking called his first, preliminary monograph on it *The Compleat Guide to the Koon* (Traill 1974), the archaic spelling of 'complete' intended to hint at the irony.

Conclusion

Who the Bushmen are is a most complex question. To anthropologists they both are and are not, 'living fossils'. To San themselves, the Bushman is both a creature of a lost past and a marginalized member of a larger society. Both traditionalist and revisionist anthropological visions have their counterparts in the self-image of the San.

Old images are being rethought in anthropology more widely. Notions of 'nomadic hunter-gatherers', for example, are so commonplace that they have done harm to land claims, including that of the former residents of the Central Kalahari Game Reserve. Except in times of drought or in specific documented circumstances (e.g. Cashdan 1984), they roamed within defined territories and certainly not randomly. Hugh Brody (2001: 7, 86–90) has suggested more broadly that the structural opposition between 'nomadic hunter-gatherer' and 'settled cultivator' is fallacious, because the grouped terms should be reversed. It is the hunter-gatherer who is settled (on ancestral land in a known territory), and the cultivator who is nomadic. Cultivators migrate, perhaps not every generation but, say, every five generations: much more frequently than a typical hunter-gatherer family. The more overgeneralizations there are about the San, the more anthropologists it takes to overturn these misleading generalizations.

The world's most famous keen amateur anthropologist is Prince Charles, who visited the Kalahari with van der Post in 1987. He also received John Hardbattle at Balmoral Castle in 1996, just a few months before Hardbattle's early death. More recently, Prince Charles has described Bushman society in terms that recall much of the imagery of both professionals and others: 'this gentle civilisation, so in tune with its past, its inner spirituality, and its natural surroundings'. He concludes: 'We all lose if the Bushman disappears' (Charles 2001: xvii).

–11–

Reflections and Conclusions

Anthropological theory is like pop music. It goes through great changes with each generation, but every generation prefers the style of its own youth to what follows. Add to that the fact that practitioners of hunter-gatherer studies are more cautious and at the same time more profound than those in other branches of anthropology; even younger practitioners are drawn to the field by the search for answers to some of anthropology's really big and really old questions. Thus there remain latent structuralists and even Marxists in hunter-gatherer studies today. In the past few decades, trends in the sub-discipline have moved to greater concerns with indigenous voices and towards political action, but only very rarely to any sort of post-modernist rejection of scientific understanding.

With this in mind, it is worthwhile to reflect once more on current political challenges in San studies and on anthropology's impact on them and their challenge to anthropological theory, and finally to the historical interpretation of our discipline.

San as an Indigenous People

It should be no surprise to the initiate in hunter-gatherer studies that the 'Man the Hunter' ethos is still strong. There are some who do not appreciate such theoretical conservatism, but in fact, and in spite of many differences in both method and theory, the quest for 'the hunter' still unites Western and Eastern (Japanese) traditions in the field. This image of 'the hunter' is also what unites these anthropological traditions with non-hunter-gatherer Africa. Not only African anthropology, but African politics and popular culture too contain visions of the 'Bushman' or the 'Pygmy', with either positive or negative stereotypes. Within Western anthropology, such stereotypes have become fuzzier in recent years, and to my mind this is no bad thing. The 'indigenous peoples' debate is no doubt partly responsible for this. Indeed, my own position, while clear in my mind, is intrinsically muddy in practice: I favour Kuper's (2003) side within anthropological theory, but his opponents' side in the practical pursuit of political goals. In other words, 'indigeneity' may be defined relationally (in practical politics), but not in essence (in anthropological theory). In 'Kalahari Revisionism, Vienna, and the "Indigenous Peoples" Debate' (Barnard 2006), I remarked that participants in the Kalahari debate and in the 'indigenous peoples' debate share with early twentieth-century Vienna-based diffusionists a quest for humankind's primal culture. In the case of many in San studies, they think they have found it either in the contemporary San or, more revealingly, in the San of some earlier era – either at the time of one's fieldwork (in the case of traditionalists) or much longer ago (in the case of revisionists). Certainly I had such feelings, on both counts, early in my own fieldwork.

Relational definitions of indigeneity beg the question of whether Bushmen, Pygmies, or whoever, themselves see something in common amongst all such peoples in their relations with outside forces. As individuals from these groups become aware of each other's problems, the potential exists for the phrase 'Indigenous Person' as a truly ethnic label. The Dobe people, the Nyae Nyae people, and so on, are kinds of Ju/'hoansi; and the Ju/'hoansi, the G/wi, and so on, are kinds of San; and (according to such a view) the San, the Pygmies, the Inuit and the Saami would all become kinds of 'Indigenous People'. This great 'people' is quite literally 'subaltern' in its relations with the rest of humanity, and collectively they seem to meet classic definitions of an 'ethnic group'. If they say they are an ethnic group under such conditions, then perhaps they are. This is no question for anthropology to cast judgement on, any more than whether functionalism or structuralism is 'right' is something the average Mosarwa should be quizzed about. Yet neither does it mean that anthropology must abandon its approaches to the study of society or culture.

The Real Bushman?

The 'Bushman' has been used by anthropology throughout the history of the discipline as a figure to be displayed. Whatever the Bushman does, he or indeed she is brought out as an exemplar of something. In recent times, it has been environmental utilization, understanding of animals, native skill and ingenuity, or material impoverishment coupled with spiritual insight. In the nineteenth century, it was often less savoury things.

As Guenther (1980) has suggested, the image and portrayal of Bushmen change along with anthropological theory in every generation. That does not mean, however, that anthropology has got it wrong in the past. There is in fact no 'real', definitive Bushman for anthropology to discover. Rather, our search is more likely to be fruitful if we think in terms of coming close to a description of social life that is either similar to the way San see themselves, or alternatively very accurate in detail on some minute aspect of material culture or social practice, with the imagery left, in so far as it is possible, to the side. Anthropology has not done badly with such ethnographic descriptions. There is very little San ethnography that is just worthless, even though the use of such ethnography by non-specialists has taken its toll.

The main problem with the image of the Bushman is that it can so easily be manipulated to serve the ends of some primitivism or other. Yet, when this happens among specialists, it is usually easy to see how it is being used and to take account accordingly. I have no problem with this, for example in the dispute between Heinz and Wily with its implicit reading of !Xoõ as either capitalists or communists, or that between Wilmsen and Lee on whether or not the presence of outsiders is significant in the degree of 'purity' Ju/'hoansi might retain. These are points of debate involving imagery or analogy.

However, what is more problematic is when anthropologists, usually non-specialists, use the Bushman to exemplify some feature of social typology, such as, in the case of Steward and Service, patrilineal or patrilocal band organization. More often than not, the problem rests on an assumption of a uniformity which is not in fact there. To take this example further, it is true that there were elements of patrilineal social organization among Bushman groups in several different parts of the Kalahari (Barnard 1992: 68, 112, 125–6), although Steward and Service relied on misleading reports from other parts (Barnard 1992: 248). The only comparative demographic study of precise kin links (Steyn 1980) is post-patrilineal model and happens to be published in a fairly obscure South African journal, in Afrikaans, and therefore would be unlikely to be used as a source other than by specialists.

Obviously not everyone can be a specialist. If anything, the problem in San studies is that, while some of the literature is inaccessible except to specialists, non-specialists too often make assertions on San or Bushmen as a whole when the literature refers to just one group. Or, worse, they generalize on the basis of broad knowledge without checking the ethnographic detail. At the same time, experts too often expect that what they are writing about is only of real interest to the specialist, or that serious scholarship must be a boring struggle through minutiae, perhaps with a dictionary by the side, in some difficult alien language. One reviewer (Raum 2000) of Wilmsen's translation of Passarge remarks that any serious student of Khoisan history must be able to read Portuguese, Dutch, Afrikaans and German. There is an implied criticism of Wilmsen and those who might dare to read his rendering of Passarge's words into English. But where would it stop? Even Guenther, who is bilingual in German and English, had to use five German and German–English dictionaries in order to translate 'words or terms which have fallen out of usage' in the ethnographic reports of soldiers and settlers in German South West Africa (Guenther 2005: 5–6). Would one have to be able to read early accounts of Cape Khoekhoe in seventeenth-century Latin, or Tanaka's and Sugawara's work on G//ana and G/wi in Japanese? What about reading the left-hand half of each of Lucy Lloyd's 8,400 notebook pages of transcriptions of /Xam informants' statements? Or will the right-hand half do? (The left side of each page is in /Xam, and the right side in English.) When is one allowed to stop reading? Can it be that comment on an issue must be withheld until one has read a hundred, a thousand or two thousand works on Bushmen? Certainly, there are more works than that of relevance, even in English.

The Answer

The ultimate answer has to be that there is no 'real' Bushman. While there are similarities in language, social structure, and so on, among Bushman peoples, there is by no means uniformity. Where there is great similarity across the region, it still needs to be explained, by specialists, through methods such as regional analysis (regional structural comparison) or through comparative historical studies.

However, the fact that the ethnography is so rich should not put off others. Rather, they should feel free to explore it, either systematically or just by dipping into it, but always in the knowledge that diversities of all kinds exist and that no Bushman is any more real than any other. Diversities exist through time, across ethnic boundaries, between individuals within the same ethnic group, and even within the thoughts and statements of the very same individuals (Barnard 1988a). Such a notion of culture is not quite the kind of thing pioneers of modern anthropology like Franz Boas and Bronislaw Malinowski taught us about.

Where, then, does that leave 'Bushman culture'? For Renée Sylvain (2005), a student of Richard Lee, the problem is bound up both in the problematic nature of 'culture' in general and in the particular use of the notion in 'indigenous peoples' discourse globally and in local contexts. In *Hunters and Herders* (Barnard 1992: 298, 301–2), I expressed a structuralist vision of Khoisan culture, as a hierarchical structure of structures, a cultural system definable at the level of Khoisan as an entity, rather than at the level of Ju/'hoansi, Naro or Nama. Broadly, I would still hold to that vision, but it is important that it defines both San hunters and Khoekhoe herders, and indeed, to use van der Postian terminology, both 'wild' and 'tame' Bushmen. What Sylvain teaches us is that 'Bushman culture', as many actually see it, is now being shaped by class inequalities and identity politics, and by the demands of ethno-tourism. The most extreme aspect of her argument is that the struggle of some San for land (the heterogeneous San population of the Omaheke, in east-central Namibia) is about access of an underclass to resources, not about the restoration of primordial rights:

> The emphasis on 'cultural survival' – with its metaphysical connection between indigenous identity and a unique relationship with the land – also perpetuates the local ideological conditions that keep the incorporated, landless farm San invisible. The only way to make themselves visible, and earn a living off the farms, is to conform to popular stereotypes, which in turn reproduces the very class inequalities that these stereotypes help to sustain. (Sylvain 2002: 1080)

This, it would seem, is a vicious circle, and anthropological images of the 'Bushman' may contribute to its perpetuation. In my view, there is no 'real' Bushman, but there is a Bushman. The Bushman is both the person who sees herself or himself as such, and the abstraction that we have called by many names: Bosjesman, San, Mosarwa, Kua, or even RAD (Remote Area Dweller). There is no point looking for a precise correspondence between the two. As for the 'under-class', that very term may be as problematic as 'Bushman', as has been argued recently by Thomas Widlok (2004: 223–4) with reference to whether it suggests being outside a class system (its original sense) or at the lowest level of one (as implied in the Kalahari debate).

During South Africa's period of transition in the early 1990s, a few itinerant, sheep-shearing *Kaarretjie-mense* (Donkey-cart People), classified as 'Coloured' under apartheid, asked an ethnographer to 'prove' that they were 'really' Bushmen (see also De Jongh and Steyn 1994; De Jongh 2002). In that particular instance I am sympathetic, but in general searching for such essences cannot, to say the least, be anthropology's priority. But let a 'Bushman' have the last word. My copy of *Voices of the San* is inscribed: 'I still honour my culture, pride and dignity, so what about you? Stay tuned.'

References

Alexander, J.E. (1838), *An Expedition of Discovery into the Interior of Africa, through the hitherto Undescribed Countries of the Great Namaquas, Boschmans, and Hill Damaras* (two volumes), London: Henry Colburn.

Alland, Alexander, Jr (2002), *Race in Mind: Race, IQ, and Other Racisms*, New York: Palgrave Macmillan.

Anderson, C. and Benson, T.W. (1993), 'Put Down the Camera and Pick Up the Shovel: an Interview with John Marshall', in J. Ruby (ed.), *The Cinema of John Marshall*, Chur, Switzerland: Harwood Academic Publishers.

Andersson, C.J. (1856), *Lake Ngami, or Explorations and Discoveries during Four Years Wanderings in the Wilds of South Western Africa*, London: Hurst and Blackett.

Arnold, Chief J. (2002), 'A San Development Initiative', *Cultural Survival Quarterly*, 26(1): 41–2.

Asquith, P. (1986), 'Anthropomorphism and the Japanese and Western Traditions in Primatology', in J. Else and P. Lee (eds), *Primate Ontogeny, Cognition and Behavior: Developments in Field and Laboratory Research*, New York: Academic Press.

Bahn, P.G. (ed.) (1996), *Cambridge Illustrated History of Archaeology*, Cambridge: Cambridge University Press.

Bank, A. (2006), *Bushmen in a Victorian World: the Remarkable Story of the Bleek–Lloyd Collection of Bushman Folklore*, Cape Town: Double Story.

Banton, M. (1987), *Racial Theories*, Cambridge: Cambridge University Press.

Barnard, A. (1978), 'Universal Systems of Kin Categorization', *African Studies*, 37: 69–81.

—— (1988a), 'Structure and Fluidity in Khoisan Religious Ideas', *Journal of Religion in Africa*, 18: 216–36.

—— (1988b), 'Cultural Identity, Ethnicity and Marginalization among the Bushmen of Southern Africa', in R. Vossen (ed.), *New Perspectives on Khoisan*, Hamburg: Helmut Buske Verlag.

—— (1988c), 'Kinship, Language and Production: a Conjectural History of Khoisan Social Structure', *Africa*, 58: 29–50.

—— (1989), 'The Lost World of Laurens van der Post?', *Current Anthropology*, 30: 104–14.

—— (1992), *Hunters and Herders of Southern Africa: A Comparative Ethnography of the Khoisan Peoples*, Cambridge: Cambridge University Press.

—— (1994), 'Tarzan and the Lost Races: Parallels between Anthropology and Early Science Fiction', in E.P. Archetti (ed.), *Exploring the Written: Anthropology and the Multiplicity of Writing*, Oslo: Scandinavian University Press.

—— (1996) 'Regional Comparison in Khoisan Ethnography: Theory, Method and Practice', *Zeitschrift für Ethnologie*, 121: 203–20.

—— (2000), *History and Theory in Anthropology*, Cambridge: Cambridge University Press.

—— (2003), '!Ke e: /xarra //ke – Multiple Origins and Multiple Meanings of the Motto', *African Studies*, 62: 243–50.

—— (2004a), 'Hunting-and-gathering Society: an Eighteenth-century Scottish Invention', in A. Barnard (ed.), *Hunter-gatherers in History, Archaeology and Anthropology*, Oxford: Berg.

—— (2004b), 'Mutual Aid and the Foraging Mode of Thought: Re-reading Kropotkin on the Khoisan', *Social Evolution and History*, 3(1): 3–21.

—— (2004c), 'Coat of Arms and the Body Politic: Khoisan Imagery and South African National Identity'. *Ethnos*, 69: 1–18.

—— (2005), 'Un peuple sous le regard occidental. Être Bushman aujourd'hui', in E. Olivier and M. Valentin (eds), *Les Bushmen dans l'histoire*, Paris: CNRS Éditions.

—— (2006), 'Kalahari Revisionism, Vienna and the "Indigenous Peoples" Debate', *Social Anthropology*, 14: 1–16.

Barrow, J. (1801), *An Account of Travels into the Interior of Southern Africa in the Years 1797 and 1798*, Volume I, London: A. Strahan for T. Cadell.

Battiss, W.W. (1948), *The Artists of the Rocks*, Pretoria: Red Fawn Press.

Bertin, G. (1886), 'The Bushmen and Their Language', *Journal of the Royal Asiatic Society of Great Britain and Ireland*, 18(1): 51–81.

Biesele, M. (1975), 'Folklore and Ritual of !Kung Hunter-gatherers', Ph.D. Dissertation, Harvard University.

—— (1976), 'Aspects of !Kung Folklore', in R.B. Lee and I. DeVore (eds), *Kalahari Hunter-Gatherers: Studies of the !Kung San and Their Neighbors*, Cambridge, MA: Harvard University Press.

—— (1993), *Women Like Meat: the Folklore and Foraging Ideology of the Kalahari Ju/'hoan*, Johannesburg: Witwatersrand University Press.

—— (2003a), 'The Kalahari Peoples Fund: Activist Legacy of the Harvard Kalahari Research Group', *Anthropologica*, 45: 79–88.

—— (2003b), 'Benefit of Foresight: Anthropology and Indigenous Voices', *Before Farming*, 2003/1: article 10.

—— and Lewis-Williams, J.D. (1978), 'Eland Hunting Rituals among Northern and Southern San Groups: Striking Similarities', *Africa*, 48: 117–34.

—— and Weinberg, P. (1990) *Shaken Roots: The Bushmen of Namibia*, Marshalltown, South Africa: EDA Publications.

Bird-David, N. (1990), 'The Giving Environment: Another Perspective on the Economic System of Hunter-gatherers', *Current Anthropology*, 31: 183–96.

—— (1992), 'Beyond "The Original Affluent Society": a Culturalist Reformulation', *Current Anthropology*, 33: 25–47.

Bjerre, J. (1960), *Kalahari* (translated by E. Bannister), New York: Hill and Wang.

Bleek, D.F. (1928), *The Naron: a Bushman Tribe of the Central Kalahari*, Cambridge: Cambridge University Press.

—— (1929), *Comparative Vocabularies of Bushman Languages*, Cambridge: Cambridge University Press.

—— (1956), *A Bushman Dictionary*, New Haven: American Oriental Society.

Bleek, W.H.I. (1858), *The Library of His Excellencey Sir George Grey, KCB. Philology Vol. I. South Africa*, London: Trübner & Co.

—— (1874), 'Remarks on Orpen's "Mythology of the Maluti Bushmen"', *Cape Monthly Magazine* (n.s.), 9(49): 10–13.

—— and Lloyd, L.C. (1911), *Specimens of Bushman Folklore*, London: George Allen & Company.

Blundell, G. (2005), 'Introduction: Three Focus Areas of Current Southern African Rock Art Research', in G. Blundell (ed.), *Further Approaches to Southern African Rock Art* (Goodwin Series 9), Vlaeberg: South African Archaeological Society.

Bollig, M. (2003), 'Between Welfare and Bureaucratic Domination: the San of Ghanzi and Kgalagadi Districts', in T. Hohmann (ed.), *San and the State: Contesting Land, Development, Identity and Representation*, Cologne: Rüdiger Köppe Verlag.

Boonzaier, E., Malherbe, C., Berens, P. and Smith, A. (1996), *The Cape Herders: a History of the Khoikhoi of Southern Africa*, Cape Town: David Philip.

Botelle, A. and Rohde, R. (1995), *Those Who Live on the Land: a Socio-economic Baseline Survey for Land Use Planning in the Communal Areas of Eastern Otjozondjupa*, Windhoek: Ministry of Lands, Resettlement and Rehabilitation.

Breuil, Abbé H. (1955), *The White Lady of the Brandberg*, London: The Trianon Press.

Brody, H. (2001), *The Other Side of Eden: Hunter-gatherers, Farmers and the Shaping of the World*, London: Faber and Faber.

Buntman, B. (2002), 'Travels to Otherness: Whose Identity Do We Want to See?', in H. Stewart, A. Barnard and K. Omura (eds), *Self- and Other-images of Hunter-gatherers* (Senri Ethnological Studies 60), Osaka: National Museum of Ethnology.

Cashdan, E.A. (1984), 'The Effects of Food Production on Mobility in the Central Kalahari', in J.D. Clark and S.A. Brandt (eds), *From Hunters to Farmers: the*

Causes and Consequences of Food Production in Africa, Berkeley: University of California Press.

—— (1986), 'Competition between Foragers and Food Producers on the Botletli River, Botswana', *Africa*, 56: 299–318.

—— (1987), 'Trade and its Origins on the Botletli River, Botswana', *Journal of Anthropological Research*, 43: 121–38.

Cassidy, L., Good, K., Mazonde, I. and Rivers, R. (2001), *An Assessment of the Status of the San in Botswana*, Windhoek: Legal Assistance Centre.

Charles, Prince of Wales (2001), 'Foreword', in S. Gall, *The Bushmen of Southern Africa: Slaughter of the Innocent*, London: Chatto & Windus.

Clark, J.D. (1959), *The Prehistory of Southern Africa*, Harmondsworth: Penguin Books.

Cohen, W.B. (1980), *The French Encounter with Africans: White Responses to Blacks, 1530–1880*. Bloomington: Indiana University Press.

Coon, C.S. (1971), *The Hunting Peoples*, Boston: Little, Brown.

Da Gama, V. (1947 [1497]), 'The Route to India, 1497–8' (translated by E.G. Ravenstein), in C.D. Ley (ed.), *Portuguese Voyages, 1498–1663: Tales from the Great Age of Discovery*, London: J.M. Dent & Sons.

Davidson, B. (1994), *The Search for Africa: A History in the Making*, London: James Currey.

Deacon, J. (1990), 'Weaving the Fabric of Stone Age Research in Southern Africa', in P. Robertshaw (ed.), *A History of African Archaeology*, London: James Currey.

—— (1996a), 'A Short Note on Lloyd's !Kung Informants', in J. Deacon and T.A. Dowson (eds), *Voices from the Past: /Xam Bushmen and the Bleek and Lloyd Collection*, Johannesburg: Witwatersrand University Press.

—— (1996b), 'The /Xam Informants', in J. Deacon and T.A. Dowson (eds), *Voices from the Past: /Xam Bushmen and the Bleek and Lloyd Collection*, Johannesburg: Witwatersrand University Press.

—— (1996c), 'A Tale of Two Families: Wilhelm Bleek, Lucy Lloyd and the /Xam San of the Northern Cape', in P. Skotnes (ed.) (1996), *Miscast: Negotiating the Presence of the Bushmen*, Cape Town: UCT Press.

De Jongh, M. (2002), 'No Fixed Abode: the Poorest of the Poor and Elusive Identities in Rural South Africa', *Journal of South African Studies*, 28: 441–60.

—— and Steyn, R. (1994), 'Itinerancy as a Way of Life: the Nomadic Sheep-shearers of the South African Karoo', *Development Southern Africa*, 11: 217–28.

Denbow, J.R. (1984), 'Prehistoric Herders and Foragers of the Kalahari: the Evidence of 1500 Years of Interaction', in C. Schrire (ed.), *Past and Present in Hunter Gatherer Studies*, Orlando, FL: Academic Press.

—— (1986), 'A New Look at the Later Prehistory of the Kalahari', *Journal of African History*, 27: 3–28.

—— (1990), 'Congo to Kalahari: Data and Hypotheses about the Political Economy of the Western Stream of the Early Iron Age', *African Archaeological Review*, 8: 139–75.

Dornan, S.S. (1917), 'The Tati Bushmen (Masarwas) and Their Language', *Journal of the Royal Anthropological Institute*, 47: 37–112.

—— (1925), *Pygmies and Bushmen of the Kalahari*. London: Seeley, Service & Co.

Douglas, S. (1995), 'The Human Isthmus: Dangerous Diluted Sewerage Poison … Recuperating "Bushman" in the "New South Arica"', *Critical Arts*, 9(2): 65–75.

—— (1997), 'Do the Schmidtsdrift "Bushmen" Belong in Reserves? Reflections on a Recent Event and Accompanying Discourse', *Journal of Contemporary African Studies*, 15: 45–66.

Dowson, T. (1992), *Rock Engravings of Southern Africa*, Johannesburg: Witwatersrand University Press.

—— and Lewis-Williams, J.D. (eds) (1994), *Contested Images: Diversity in Southern African Rock Art Research*, Johannesburg: Witwatersrand University Press.

Dubow, S. (1995), *Scientific Racism in Modern South Africa*, Cambridge: Cambridge University Press.

Dunbar, R.I.M. (1996), *Grooming, Gossip and the Evolution of Language*, London: Faber and Faber.

Dunn, J. (2005), *Setting the People Free: the Story of Democracy*, London: Atlantic Books.

Eberhard, E. (1996), 'Wilhelm Bleek and the Founding of Bushman Research', in J. Deacon and T.A. Dowson (eds), *Voices from the Past: /Xam Bushmen and the Bleek and Lloyd Collection*, Johannesburg: Witwatersrand University Press.

Eibl-Eibesfeldt, I. (1979), *The Biology of Peace and War: Men, Animals, and Aggression* (translated by E. Mosbacher), London: Thames and Hudson.

Elphick, R. (1985 [1975]), *Khoikhoi and the Founding of White South Africa*, Johannesburg: Ravan Press.

Farini, G.A. (1886), *Through the Kalahari Desert: a Narrative of a Journey with Gun, Camera, and Note-book to Lake N'gami and Back*, London: Sampson Low & Co.

Fauvelle-Aymar, F.X. (2002), *L'Invention du Hottentot: Histoire du regard occidental sur les Khoisan (XVe–XIXe siècle)*, Paris: Publications de la Sorbonne.

Felton, S. and Becker, H. (2001), *A Gender Perspective on the Status of the San in Southern Africa*, Windhoek: Legal Assistance Centre.

Fourie, L. (1928), 'The Bushmen of South West Africa', in C.H.L. Hahn, H. Vedder and L. Fourie, *The Native Tribes of South West Africa*, Cape Town: Cape Times.

Frazer, J.G. (1949 [1922]), *The Golden Bough: a Study in Magic and Religion* (abridged edition), London: Macmillan & Co.

Fritsch, G. (1872), *Die Eingeborenen Südafrikas: ethnographisch und anatomisch Beschreiben*, Breslau: Ferdinand Hirt.

—— (1880), 'Die afrikanischen Buschmänner als Urrasse', *Zeitschrift für Ethnologie*,12: 289–300.

—— (1906), 'Die Buschmänner der Kalahari von S. Passarge', *Zeitschrift für Ethnologie*, 38: 71–9, 411–15.

Frobenius, L. (1931), *Madsimu Dsangara: südafrikanische Feldsbilderchronik*, Volume II, Berlin: Atlantis-Verlag.

Gall, S. (2001), *The Bushmen of Southern Africa: Slaughter of the Innocent*, London: Chatto & Windus.

Galton, F. (1853), *The Narrative of an Explorer in Tropical South Africa*, London: J. Murray.

Geertz, C. (1966), 'Religion as a Cultural System', in M. Banton (ed.), *Anthropological Approaches to the Study of Religion*, London: Tavistock Publications.

Gluckman, M. (1975), 'Anthropology and Apartheid: the Work of South African Anthropologists', in M. Fortes and S. Patterson (eds), *Studies in African Social Anthropology*, London: Academic Press.

Godby, M. (1996), 'Images of //Kabbo', in P. Skotnes (ed.), *Miscast: Negotiating the Presence of the Bushmen*, Cape Town: UCT Press.

Godelier, M. (1975), 'Modes of Production, Kinship, and Demographic Stuctures' (translated by K. Young and F. Edholm), in M. Bloch (ed.), *Marxist Analyses and Social Anthropology*, London: Malaby Press.

Good, K. (2003), *Bushmen and Diamonds: (Un)Civil Society in Botswana* (Discussion Paper 23), Uppsala: Nordiska Afrikainstitutet.

Goodwin, A.J.H. and van Riet Lowe, C. (1929), 'The Stone Age Cultures of South Africa', *Annals of the South African Museum*, 27(7): 1–289.

Gordon, R.J. (1992), *The Bushman Myth: the Making of a Namibian Underclass*, Boulder, CO: Westview Press.

—— (1995), 'Saving the Last South African Bushman: a Spectacular Failure?', *Critical Arts*, 9(2): 28–48.

—— (1997), *Picturing Bushmen: the Denver African Expedition of 1925*, Athens, OH: Ohio University Press.

——, Rassool, C. and Witz, L. (1996), 'Fashioning the Bushman in Van Riebeeck's Cape Town, 1952 and 1993', in P. Skotnes (ed.), *Miscast: Negotiating the Presence of the Bushmen*, Cape Town: UCT Press.

Grey, G. (1841), *Journals of Two Expeditions of Discovery in North-west and Western Australia, during the Years 1837, 1838, and 1839* (two volumes), London: T. and W. Boone.

Guenther, M.G. (1973), 'Farm Bushmen and Mission Bushmen: Socio-cultural Change in a Setting of Conflict and Pluralism of the San of the Ghanzi District, Republic of Botswana', Ph.D. Thesis, University of Toronto.

—— (1976), 'From Hunters to Squatters: Social and Cultural Change among the Ghanzi Farm Bushmen', in R.B. Lee and I. DeVore (eds), *Kalahari Hunter-gatherers: Studies of the !Kung San and Their Neighbors*, Cambridge, MA: Harvard University Press.

—— (1979a), 'Bushman Religion and the (Non)sense of Anthropological Theory of Religion', *Sociologus*, 29: 102–32.

—— (1979b), *The Farm Bushmen of the Ghanzi District, Botswana*, Stuttgart: Hochschul Verlag.

—— (1980), 'From "Brutal Savages" to "Harmless People": Notes on the Changing Western Image of the Bushmen', *Paideuma*, 26: 123–40.

—— (1986), *The Nharo Bushmen of Botswana: Tradition and Change*, Hamburg: Helmut Buske Verlag.

—— (1989), *Bushman Folktales: Oral Traditions of the Nharo of Botswana and the /Xam of the Cape*, Stuttgart: Franz Steiner Verlag.

—— (1998), 'Farm Labourer, Trance Dancer, Artist: the Life and Works of Qwaa Mangana', in A. Bank (ed.), *The Proceedings of the Khoisan Identities and Cultural Heritage Conference, Held at the South African Museum, Cape Town, 12–16 July 1997*, Cape Town: Institute for Historical Research, University of the Western Cape.

—— (1999), *Tricksters and Trancers: Bushman Religion and Society*, Bloomington: Indiana University Press.

—— (2002), 'Ethno-tourism and the Bushmen', in H. Stewart, A. Barnard and K. Omura (eds), *Self- and Other-images of Hunter-gatherers* (Senri Ethnological Studies 60), Osaka: National Museum of Ethnology.

—— (ed.) (2005), *Kalahari and Namib Bushmen in German South West Africa: Ethnographic Reports by Colonial Soldiers and Settlers*, Cologne: Rüdiger Köppe Verlag.

Gusinde, M. (1966), *Von gelben und schwarzen Buschmännern. Eine untergehende Alkultur im Süden Afrikas*, Graz: Akademische Druck- und Verlagsanstalt.

Haacke, W.H.G. and Eiseb, E. (2002), A *Khoekhoegowab Dictionary, with an English–Khoekhoegowab Index*, Windhoek: Gamsberg Macmillan.

Haggard, H.R. (1885), *King Solomon's Mines*, London: Thomas Nelson & Sons.

—— (1887), *She. a History of Adventure*, London: Longmans, Green, & Co.

Hahn, T. (1881), *Tsuni-//goam: the Supreme Being of the Khoi-khoi*, London: Trubner & Co.

Hammond-Tooke, W.D. (1997), *Imperfect Interpreters: South Africa's Anthropologists, 1920–1990*. Johannesburg: Witwatersrand University Press.

Haraway, D. (1989), *Primate Visions: Gender, Race, and Nature in the World of Modern Science*, New York: Routledge.

Harris, M. (1978), *Cannibals and Kings: the Origins of Cultures*, London: Collins.

'He' [Lang, A. and Pollock, W.H.] (1887), *He, by the Author of 'It', 'King Solomon's Wives', 'Bess', etc.*, London: Longmans, Green, & Co.

Heinz, H.J. (1994), *Social Organization of the !Kõ Bushmen* (edited by K. Keuthmann), Cologne: Rüdiger Köppe Verlag.

—— and Lee, M. (1978) *Namkwa: Life among the Bushmen*, London: Jonathan Cape.

Hiatt, L.R. (1996), *Arguments about Aborigines: Australia and the Evolution of Social Anthropology*, Cambridge: Cambridge University Press.

Hitchcock, R.K. (1978), *Kalahari Cattle Posts: A Regional Study of Hunter-gatherers, Pastoralists, and Agriculturalists in the Western Sandveld Region, Central District, Botswana* (two volumes), Gaborone: Ministry of Local Government and Lands.

—— (1987), 'Socioeconomic Change among the Basarwa in Botswana: an Ethnohistorical Analysis', *Ethnohistory*, 34: 219–55.

—— and Brandenburgh, R.L. (1991), 'Harmless Hunters, Fierce Fighters or Persistent Pastoralists? The Policy Implications of Academic Stereotypes of Kalahari San', *Journal of Asian and African Affairs*, 3: 17–44.

—— and Holm, J.D. (1993), 'Bureaucratic Domnation of Hunter-gatherer Societies: a Study of the San in Botswana', *Development and Change*, 24: 305–38.

Hodgen, M.T. (1964), *Early Anthropology in the Sixteenth and Seventeenth Centuries*, Philadelphia: University of Pennsylvania Press.

Hoernlé, A.W. (1985), *The Social Organization of the Nama and Other Essays* (edited by Peter Carstens), Johannesburg: Witwatersrand University Press.

Hohmann, T. (2003a), 'San and the State: an Introduction', in T. Hohmann (ed.), *San and the State: Contesting Land, Development, Identity and Representation*, Cologne: Rüdiger Köppe Verlag.

—— (ed.) (2003b), *San and the State: Contesting Land, Development, Identity and Representation*, Cologne: Rüdiger Köppe Verlag.

Hollmann, J.C. (ed.) (2004), *Customs and Beliefs of the /Xam Bushmen*, Johannesburg: Wits University Press.

Hudelson, J.E. (1995), 'One Hundred Years among the San: a Social History of San Research', in A.J.G.M. Sanders (ed.), *Speaking for the Bushmen*. Gaborone: The Botswana Society.

Ikeya, K. (1993), 'Goat Raising among the San in the Central Kalahari', *African Study Monographs*, 14(1): 39–52.

—— (1996a), 'Road Construction and Handicraft Production in the Xade Area, Botswana', *African Study Monographs*, Supplementary Issue, 22: 67–84.

—— (1996b), 'Dry Farming among the San in the Central Kalahari', *African Study Monographs*, Supplementary Issue, 22: 85–100.

—— (2001), 'Some Changes among the San under the Influence of Relocation Plan in Botswana', in D.G. Anderson and K. Ikeya (eds), *Parks, Property and*

Power: Managing Hunting Practice and Identity within State Policy Regimes (Senri Ethnological Studies 59), Osaka: National Museum of Ethnology.

Ingold, T. (1992), 'Comments' (on Bird-David, 1992), *Current Anthropology*, 33: 41–2.

Izumi, H. (2006), *Towards the Neo-Kyoto School: History and Development of the Primatological Approach of the Kyoto School in Japanese Primatology and Ecological Anthropology* (CAS Occasional Papers 101), Edinburgh: Centre of African Studies, University of Edinburgh.

Jenkins, T. (1968), 'Genetic Studies on the Khoisan Peoples of Southern Africa', in *Proceedings of the Third Congress of the South African Genetics Society, Pretoria, 1966*, Pretoria: South African Genetics Society.

—— and Tobias, P.V. (1977), 'Nomenclature of Population Groups in Southern Africa', *African Studies*, 36: 49–55.

Jolly, P. (1996), 'Between the Lines: Some Remarks on "Bushman" Ethnicity', in P. Skotnes (ed.), *Miscast: Negotiating the Presence of the Bushmen*, Cape Town: UCT Press.

Jones, J.D.F. (2001), *Storyteller: the Many Lives of Laurens van der Post*, London: John Murray.

Katz, R. (1982), *Boiling Energy: Community Healing among the Kalahari Kung*, Cambridge, MA: Harvard University Press.

——, Biesele, M. and St Denis, V. (1997), *Healing Makes our Hearts Happy: Spirituality and Cultural Transformation among the Kalahari Ju/'hoansi*, Rochester, VT: Inner Traditions.

Kelly, R.L. (1995), *The Foraging Spectrum: Diversity in Hunter-Gatherer Lifeways*, Washington: Smithsonian Institution Press.

Kent, S. (1992), 'The Current Forager Controversy: Real versus Ideal Views of Hunter-gatherers', *Man* (n.s.), 27: 45–70.

—— (1993), 'Sharing in an Egalitarian Kalahari Community', *Man* (n.s.), 28: 479–514.

—— (ed.) (1996), *Cultural Diversity among Twentieth-century Foragers: an African Perspective*, Cambridge: Cambridge University Press.

—— (2002a), 'Dangerous Interactions: the Repercussions of Western Culture, Missionaries, and Disease in Southern Africa', in S. Kent (ed.), *Ethnicity, Hunter-Gatherers, and the 'Other': Association of Assimilation in Africa*, Washington: Smithsonian Institution Press.

—— (ed.) (2002b), *Ethnicity, Hunter-gatherers, and the 'Other': Association of Assimilation in Africa*, Washington: Smithsonian Institution Press.

Knight, C.D. (1991), *Blood Relations: Menstruation and the Origins of Culture*, New Haven: Yale University Press.

Knox, R. (1850), *The Races of Men: a Philosophical Enquiry into the Influence of Race over the Destinies of Nations*, London: Henry Renshaw.

Köhler, O. (1989), *Die Welt de Kxoé-Buschleute im südlichen Afrika*, Volume I:

Die Kxoé-Buschleute und ihre ethnische Umbgebung, Berlin: Dietrich Reimer Verlag.

Kolb, P. (1968 [1719]), *The Present State of the Cape of Good Hope*, Volume I, New York: Johnson Reprint Company.

Kühn, H. (1930), 'The Origin and Distribution of Bushman Art', in H. Obermaier and H. Kühn, *Bushman Art: Rock Paintings of South-West Africa*, London: Humphrey Milford.

Kuper, A. (1980), *Wives for Cattle: Bridewealth and Marriage in Southern Africa*, London: Routledge & Kegan Paul.

—— (1988), *The Invention of Primitive Society: Transformations of an Illusion*, London: Routledge.

—— (1994), *The Chosen Primate: Human Nature and Cultural Diversity*, Cambridge, MA: Harvard University Press.

—— (2003), 'The Return of the Native', *Current Anthropology*, 44: 389–402.

—— (2005a), *The Reinvention of Primitive Society: Transformations of a Myth*, London: Routledge.

—— (2005b), 'Isaac Schapera, 1905–2003', *Proceedings of the British Academy*, 130: 177–202.

Lafitau, J.F. (1724), *Moeurs des sauvanges ameriquains, comparées aux moeurs des premiers temps* (two volumes), Paris: Chez Saugrain l'aîné.

Lang, A. (1913), *Myth, Ritual and Religion* (two volumes), London: Longmans, Green & Co.

Leacock, E. and Lee, R. (1982), *Politics and History in Band Societies*, Cambridge: Cambridge University Press.

Lee, D.N. and Woodhouse, H.C. (1970), *Art on the Rocks of Southern Africa*, Cape Town: Purnell.

Lee, R.B. (1965), 'Subsistence Ecology of !Kung Bushmen', Ph.D. Dissertation, University of California at Berkeley.

—— (1968), 'What Hunters Do for a Living, or, How to Make Out on Scarce Resources', in R.B. Lee and I. DeVore (eds), *Man the Hunter*, Chicago: Aldine.

—— (1969), '!Kung Bushman Subsistence: an Input–Output Analysis', in A.P. Vayda (ed.), *Environment and Cultural Behavior*, New York: Natural History Press.

—— (1976 [1972]), '!Kung Spatial Organization: an Ecological and Historical Perspective', in R.B. Lee and I. DeVore (eds), *Kalahari Hunter-gatherers: Studies of the !Kung San and Their Neighbors*, Cambridge, MA: Harvard University Press.

—— (1979), *The !Kung San: Men, Women, and Work in a Foraging Society*, Cambridge: Cambridge University Press.

—— (1984), *The Dobe !Kung*, New York: Holt, Rinehart and Winston.

—— (1986), 'The Gods Must Be Crazy but the State Has a Plan: Government Policy towards the San in Namibia', *Canadian Journal of African Studies*, 20: 181–90.

—— (1991), 'The !Kung in Question: Evidence and Context in the Kalahari Debate', in P.T. Miracle, L.E. Fisher and J. Brown (eds), *Foragers in Context: Long-Term, Regional and Historical Perspectives in Hunter-gatherer Studies* (Michigan Discussions in Anthropology 10), Ann Arbor: Department of Anthropology, University of Michigan.

—— (1993), *The Dobe Ju/'hoansi* (second edition), Fort Worth, TX: Harcourt Brace College Publishers.

—— (2003), *The Dobe Ju/'hoansi* (third edition), Stamford, CT: Thomson Learning.

—— and DeVore, I. (1968a), 'Preface', in R.B. Lee and I. DeVore (eds), *Man the Hunter*, Chicago: Aldine.

—— and DeVore, I. (eds) (1968b), *Man the Hunter*, Chicago: Aldine.

—— and DeVore, I. (eds) (1976), *Kalahari Hunter-gatherers: Studies of the !Kung San and Their Neighbours*, Cambridge, MA: Harvard University Press.

—— and Guenther, M. (1991), 'Oxen or Onions: the Search for Trade (and Truth) in the Kalahari', *Current Anthropology*, 32: 592–601.

—— and Guenther, M. (1993), 'Problems in Kalahari Historical Ethnography and the Tolerance of Error', *History in Africa*, 20: 185–235.

—— and Guenther, M. (1995), 'Errors Compounded? A Reply to Wilmsen', *Current Anthropology*, 36: 298–305.

Le Roux, W. and White, A. (eds) (2004), *Voices of the San: Living in Southern Africa Today*, Cape Town: Kwela Books.

Le Vaillant, F. (1790), *Voyage de M. Le Vaillant dans l'intérieur de l'Afrique par le Cap de Bonne-Espérance dans les années 1780, 81, 82, 83, 84 & 85* (two volumes), Paris: Chez Leroy.

Lévi-Strauss, C. (1962), *La Pensée sauvage*, Paris: Plon.

—— (1968), 'The Concept of Primitiveness', in R.B. Lee and I. DeVore (eds), *Man the Hunter*, Chicago: Aldine.

Lévy-Bruhl, L. (1931), *Le Surnaturel et la nature dans la mentalité primitive*, Paris: Libraire Félix Alcan.

Lewin, R. (1989), *Bones of Contention: Controversies in the Search for Human Origins*, Harmondsworth: Penguin Books.

Lewin Robinson, A.M. (1954), 'Charles Aken Fairbridge and his Library; I, Biographical Sketch', *Quarterley Bulletin of the South African Library*, 9: 32–49.

Lewis-Williams, J.D. (1981), *Believing and Seeing: Symbolic Meanings in Southern San Rock Paintings*, London: Academic Press.

—— (2000a), 'Introduction', in J.D. Lewis-Williams (ed.), *Stories that Float from Afar: Ancestral Folklore of the San of Southern Africa*, Cape Town: David Philip.

—— (ed.) (2000b), *Stories that Float from Afar: Ancestral Folklore of the San of Southern Africa*, Cape Town: David Philip.

—— (2002), *A Cosmos in Stone: Interpreting Religion and Society through Rock Art*, Walnut Creek, CA: Alta Mira Press.

—— and Dowson (1989), *Images of Power: Understanding Bushman Rock Art*, Johannesburg: Southern Book Publishers.

—— and Pearce, D. (2004), *San Spirituality: Roots, Expressions and Social Consequences*, Cape Town: Double Storey.

Lichtenstein, H. (1928 [1812]), *Travels in Southern Africa, in the Years 1803, 1804, 1805, and 1806*, Volume I (translated by A. Plumptre), Cape Town: The Van Riebeeck Society.

Lindfors, B. (ed.) (1999), *Africans on Stage: Studies in Ethnological Show Business*, Bloomington: Indiana University Press.

Livingstone, D. (1912 [1857]), *Missionary Travels and Researches in South Africa*, London: John Murray.

Lubbock, J. (1870), 'Notes on Some Stone Implements from Africa and Syria', *Proceedings of the Ethnological Society of London*, 1870: 92–97.

—— (1874), *The Origin of Civilisation and the Primitive Condition of Man: Mental and Social Conditions of Savages*, New York: D. Appleton and Company.

McCall, D.F. (1970), *Wolf Courts Girl: the Equivalence of Hunting and Mating in Bushman Thought*, Athens, OH: Center for International Studies, Ohio University.

Maingard, L.F. (1963), 'A Comparative Study of Naron, Hietshware and Korana', *African Studies*, 22: 97–108.

Malinowski, B. (1944), *A Scientific Theory of Culture and Other Essays*, Chapel Hill: University of North Carolina Press.

Marks, S. (1972), 'Khoisan Resistance to the Dutch in the Seventeenth and Eighteen Centuries', *Journal of African History* 13: 55–80.

Marshall, J. (1993), 'Filming and Learning', in J. Ruby (ed.), *The Cinema of John Marshall*, Chur, Switzerland: Harwood Academic Publishers.

—— and Ritchie, C. (1984), *Where are the Ju/wasi of Nyae Nyae? Changes in a Bushman society: 1958–1981* (CAS Communications 9), Cape Town: Centre for African Studies, University of Cape Town.

Marshall, L. (1976), *The !Kung of Nyae Nyae*, Cambridge, MA: Harvard University Press.

—— (1999), *Nyae Nyae !Kung Beliefs and Rites*, Cambridge, MA: Peabody Museum of Archaeology and Ethnology.

Maruyama, J. (2003), 'The Impacts of Resettlement on Livelihood and Social Relationships among the Central Kalahari San', *African Study Monographs*, 24(4): 223–45.

Masilela, N. (1987), 'The White South African Writer in Our National Situation', *Matatu*, 3/4: 48–64.

Mbeki, T. (2000), 'Address by President Thabo Mbeke at the Unveiling of the Coat of Arms, Kwaggafontein, 27 April 2000', www.gov.za/speeches/.

Mead, M. (1978), 'Foreword', in H.J. Heinz and M. Lee, *Namkwa: Life among the Bushmen*, London: Jonathan Cape.

Metzger, F. (1993 [1950]), *Naro and His Clan: the Lost World of the Bushmen* (translated by P. Reiner), Windhoek: Kuiseb-Verlag.

—— (1995 [1952]), *The Hyena's Laughter: Bushman Fables* (translated by P. Reiner), Windhoek: Kuiseb-Verlag.

Millar, J. (1806), *The Origin and Distinction of Ranks: or, an Inquiry into the Circumstances which Give Rise to Influence and Authority, in the Different Members of Society* (fourth edition). Edinburgh: William Blackwood.

Mitchell, P. (2002a), 'Hunter-gatherer Archaeology in Southern Africa: Recent Research, Future Trends', *Before Farming*, 2002/1: article 3.

—— (2002b), *The Archaeology of Southern Africa*, Cambridge: Cambridge University Press.

Mogwe, A. (1992), *Who Was (T)here First? An Assessment of the Human Rights Situation of Basarwa in Selected Communities in the Gantsi District, Botswana*, Gaborone: Botswana Christian Council.

Motshabi, K. and Saugestad, S. (eds) (2004), *Research for Khoe and San Development International Conference, University of Botswana, 10–12 September 2003*, Gaborone: University of Botswana; Tromsø: University of Tromsø.

Mphinyane, S.P. (2002), 'Power and Powerlessness: When Support Becomes Overbearing — the Case of Outsider Activism on the Resettlement Issue of the Basarwa of the Central Kalahari Game Reserve', *Pula: Botswana Journal of Social Science*, 16: 75–85.

Newton-King, S. (1999), *Masters and Servants on the Cape Eastern Frontier, 1760–1803*, Cambridge: Cambridge University Press.

Olivier, E. (2005), 'La musique ju/'hoan: de la création à la consumation', in E. Olivier and M. Valentin (eds), *Les Bushmen dans l'histoire*, Paris: CNRS Éditions.

Orpen, J.M. (1874), 'Mythology of the Maluti Bushmen', *Cape Monthly Magazine* (n.s.), 9(49): 1–13.

Osaki, M. (1990), 'The Influence of Sedentism on Sharing among the Central Kalahari Hunter-gatherers', *African Study Monographs*, Supplementary Issue, 12: 59–87.

Parkington, J.E. (1980), 'Time and Place: Some Observations on Spatial and Temporal Patterning in the Later Stone Age Sequence in Southern Africa', *South African Archaeological Bulletin*, 35: 75–83.

—— (1984), 'Soaqua and Bushmen: Hunters and Robbers', in C. Schrire (ed.), *Past and Present in Hunter-gatherer Studies*, Orlando, FL: Academic Press.

—— (1987), 'Changing Views of Prehistoric Settlement in the Western Cape', in J. Parkington and M. Hall (eds), *Papers in the Prehistory of the Western Cape,*

South Africa (BAR International Reports 332, Part I), Oxford: British Archaeological Reports.

—— (2002), *The Mantis, the Eland and the Hunter*, Cape Town: Krakadouw Trust.

—— (2003), *Cederberg Rock Paintings*, Cape Town: Krakadouw Trust.

Passarge, S. (1905), 'Das Okavangosumpfland und seine Bewohner', *Zeitschrift für Ethnologie*, 37: 649–716.

—— (1907), *Die Buschmänner der Kalahari*, Berlin: Dietrich Reimer.

Péringuey, L. (1911), 'The Stone Ages of South Africa as Represented in the Collection of the South African Museum', *Annals of the South African Museum*, 8: 1–218.

Pratt, M.L. (1985), 'Scratches on the Face of the Country, or What Mr. Barrow Saw in the Land of the Bushmen', *Critical Inquiry*, 12: 119–43.

—— (1986), 'Fieldwork in Common Places', in J. Clifford and G.E. Marcus (eds), *Writing Culture: the Poetics and Politics of Ethnography*, Berkeley: University of California Press.

Prichard, J.C. (1813), *Researches into the Physical History of Man*, London: John and Arthur Arch.

—— (1851), *Researches into the Physical History of Mankind*, Volume I (fifth edition), London: Sherwood, Gilbert & Piper.

Radcliffe-Brown, A.R. (1952), *Structure and Function in Primitive Society: Essays and Adresses*, London: Cohen & West.

Ratzel, F. (1897), *The History of Mankind* (translated by A.J. Butler), Volume II, London: Macmillan & Co.

Raum, J. (2000), 'Review of *The Kalahari Ethnographies (1896–1898) of Siegfried Passarge* (edited by E.N. Wilmsen)', *American Anthropologist*, 102: 668.

Reuning, H. and Wortley, W. (1973), *Psychological Studies of the Bushmen*, Johannesburg: National Institute for Personnel Research.

Robertshaw, P.T. (1978) 'The Origin of Pastoralism in the Cape', *South African Historical Journal*, 10: 117–33.

Robins, S. (2001), 'Whose "Culture", Whose "Survival"? The ≠Khomani San Land Claim and the Cultural Politics of "Community" and "Development" in the Kalahari', in A. Barnard and J. Kenrick (eds), *Africa's Indigenous Peoples: 'First Peoples' or 'Marginalized Minorities'?*, Edinburgh: Centre of African Studies, University of Edinburgh.

——, Madzudzo, E. and Brenzinger, M. (2001), *An Assessment of the Status of the San in South Africa, Angola, Zambia and Zimbabwe*, Windhoek: Legal Assistance Centre.

Rousseau, J.J. (1971 [1755]), 'Discours sur l'origine et les fondements de l'inégalité parmi les hommes', in *Discours sur les sciences et les arts. Discours sur l'origine et les fondements de l'inégalité parmi les hommes*, Paris: G.F. Flammarion.

Sadr, K. (1997), 'Kalahari Archaeology and the Bushman Debate', *Current Anthropology*, 38: 104–12.

—— (2002), 'Encapsulated Bushmen in the Archaeology of Thamaga', in S. Kent (ed.), *Ethnicity, Hunter-gatherers, and the 'Other': Association of Assimilation in Africa*, Washington: Smithsonian Institution Press.

Sahlins, M. (1968a), 'Notes on the Original Affluent Society', in R.B. Lee and I. DeVore (eds), *Man the Hunter*, Chicago: Aldine.

—— (1968b), 'La première société d'abondance', *Les Temps modernes*, 268: 641–80.

—— (1974). *Stone Age Economics*, London: Tavistock Publications.

Saugestad, S. (1998a), 'The Rise and Fall of Norwegian Support to Remote Area Dwellers in Botswana', in S. Saugestad (ed.), *Indigenous Peoples in Modern Nation-states: Proceedings from an International Workshop, University of Tromsø, October 13–16, 1997*, Tromsø: University of Tromsø.

—— (ed.) (1998b), *Indigenous Peoples in Modern Nation-states: Proceedings from an International Workshop, University of Tromsø, October 13–16, 1997*, Tromsø: University of Tromsø.

—— (2001), *The Inconvenient Indigenous: Remote Area Development in Botswana, Donor Assistance, and the First People of the Kalahari*. Uppsala: Nordiska Afrikainstitutet.

—— (2004a), 'The Central Kalahari Game Reserve (CKGR) Court Case: a Slow Progress Indeed', *N≠oahn/Newsletter* [of the University of Botswana and the University of Tromsø Collaborative Programme for San Research and Capacity Building], 7(1), 5–6.

—— (2004b), 'The Indigenous Peoples of Southern Africa: an Overview', in R. Ritchcock and D. Vinding (eds), *Indigenous Peoples' Rights in Southern Africa*, Copenhagen: IWGIA.

—— (2005), '"Improving Their Lives." State Policies and San Resistance in Botswana', *Before Farming*, 2005/4: article 1.

Schapera, I. (1929), 'The Tribal System in South Africa: a Study of the Bushmen and the Hottentots' (two volumes), Ph.D. Thesis, University of London.

—— (1930), *The Khoisan Peoples of South Africa: Bushmen and Hottentots*, London: George Routledge & Sons.

—— (1939), 'A Survey of the Bushman Question', *Race Relations*, 6(2): 68–83.

Schmidt, S. (1996), 'Lucy Catherine Lloyd, 1834–1914', in J. Deacon and T.A. Dowson (eds), *Voices from the Past: /Xam Bushmen and the Bleek and Lloyd Collection*, Johannesburg: Witwatersrand University Press.

Schmidt, W. (1933), *Der Ursprung der Gottesidee: Eine historishc-kritishce und positive Studie*, Volume IV: *Die Religionen der Urvölker Afrikas*, Münster: Aschendorffsche Verlagsbuchhandlung.

Schoeman, P.J. (1957), *Hunters of the Desert Land*, Cape Town: Howard Timmins.

Schrire, C. (1980), 'An Inquiry into the Evolutionary Status and Apparent Identity of San Hunter-gatherers', *Human Ecology*, 18: 9–32.

—— (1984), 'Wild Surmises on Savage Thoughts', in C. Schrire (ed.), *Past and Present in Hunter Gatherer Studies*, Orlando, FL: Academic Press.

Schultze, L. (1907), *Aus Namaland und Kalahari*. Jena: Gustav Fischer.

—— (1928), 'Zur Kenntnis des Korpers der Hottentotten und Buschmanner', *Zoologische und anthropologische Ergebnisse einer Forschungsreise im westlichen und zentralen Sudafrika*, 5(3): 147–227.

Service, E.R. (1962), *Primitive Social Organization: an Evolutionary Perspective*, New York: Random House.

Sharp, J. (1997), 'Otherness Imposed, Otherness Redeemed: the Politics of being Bushman at Schmidtsdrift', in J. Mouton and J. Muller (eds), *Knowledge, Method and the Public Good*, Pretoria: Human Sciences Research Council.

—— and Douglas, S. (1996), 'Prisoners of Their Reputation? The Veterans of the "Bushman" Battalions in South Africa', in P. Skotnes (ed.) (1996), *Miscast: Negotiating the Presence of the Bushmen*, Cape Town: UCT Press.

Shaw, M. (1973), 'Hottentots, Bushmen and Bantu', in *François Le Vaillant: Traveller in South Africa, and His Collection of 165 Water-colour Paintings, 1781–1784* (two volumes), Cape Town: Library of Parliament.

Shostak, M. (1983 [1981]), *Nisa: The Life and Works of a !Kung Woman*, Harmondsworth: Penguin.

—— (2000), *Return to Nisa*, Cambridge, MA: Harvard University Press.

Shott, M.J. (1992), 'On Recent Trends in the Anthropology of Foragers: Kalahari Revisionism and Its Archaeological Implications', *Man* (n.s.), 27: 843–71.

Shrubsall, F.C. (1898), 'The Crania of African Bush Races', *Journal of the Anthropological Institute*, 27: 263–90.

Silberbauer, G.B. (1965), *Report to the Government of Bechuanaland on the Bushman Survey*, Gaberones: Bechuanaland Government.

—— (1973), 'Socio-ecology of the G/wi Bushmen', Ph.D. Thesis, Monash University.

—— (1981), *Hunter and Habitat in the Central Kalahari Desert*, Cambridge: Cambridge University Press.

—— (1982), 'Review of Jiro Tanaka, *The San, Hunter-gatherers of the Kalahari*', *Man* (n.s.), 17: 803–4.

—— (1994), 'A Sense of Place', in E.S. Burch, Jr and L.J. Ellanna (eds), *Key Issues in Hunter-gatherer Research*, Oxford: Berg.

—— (1996), 'Neither are Your Ways My Ways', in S. Kent (ed.), *Cultural Diversity among Twentieth-century Foragers: an African Perspective*, Cambridge: Cambridge University Press.

—— and Kuper, A.J. (1966), 'Kgalagari Masters and Bushman Serfs: Some Observations', *African Studies*, 25: 171–79.

Skotnes, P. (ed.) (1996a), 'Introduction', in P. Skotnes (ed.), *Miscast: Negotiating the Presence of the Bushmen*, Cape Town: UCT Press.

—— (1996b), *Miscast: Negotiating the Presence of the Bushmen*, Cape Town: UCT Press.

Slotkin, J.S. (ed.) (1965), *Readings in Early Anthropology*, Chicago: Aldine.

Smith, A. (2003 [1776]), *The Wealth of Nations*, New York: Bantam Books.

Smith, A.B. (1986), 'Competition, Conflict and Clientship: Khoi and San Relationships in the Western Cape', in M. Hall and A.B. Smith (eds), *Prehistoric Pastoralism in Southern Africa* (Goodwin Series 5), Claremont: South African Archaeological Society.

—— and Pheiffer, R.H. (1993), *The Khoikhoi at the Cape of Good Hope: Seventeenth-century Drawings in the South African Library*, Cape Town: South African Library.

——, Malherbe, C., Guenther, M. and Berens, P. (2000), *The Bushmen of Southern Africa: A Foraging Society in Transition*, Cape Town: David Philip.

Smith, W. (1972), *The Sunbird*, London: William Heinemann.

Solomon, A.C. (1992), 'Gender, Representation, and Power in San Ethnography and Rock Art', *Journal of Anthropological Archaeology*, 11: 291–329.

—— (1995), 'Representation and the Aesthetic in San Art', *Critical Arts*, 9(2): 49–64.

Solway, J.S. and Lee, R.B. (1990), 'Foragers, Genuine or Spurious? Situating the Kalahari San in History', *Current Anthropology*, 31: 109–46.

Sparrman, A. (1785), *A Voyage to the Cape of Good Hope, towards the Antarctic Polar Circle and Round the World, but chiefly into the Country of the Hottentots and Caffres, from the Year 1772 to 1776* (two volumes), London: G.G.J. and J. Robinson.

Spencer, B. and Gillen, F. (1899), *The Native Tribes of Central Australia*, London: Macmillan.

Spohr, O. (1962), *Wilhelm Heinrich Immanuel Bleek: a Bio-bibliographical sketch*, Cape Town: University of Cape Town Libraries.

Steward, J.H. (1955), *Theory of Culture Change: the Methodology of Multilinear Evolution*, Urbana: University of Illinois Press.

Steyn, H.P. (1971), 'Aspects of the Economic Life of Some Nomadic Nharo Bushman Groups', *Annals of the South African Museum*, 56: 275–322.

—— (1980), 'Die San versus die Patrilineêre Bende', *Ethnologie*, 3: 9–17.

—— (1990), *Vanished Lifestyles: the Early Cape Khoi and San*, Pretoria: Unibook.

—— (1994), 'Role and Position of Elderly !Xũ in the Schmidtsdrift Bushman Community', *South African Journal of Ethnology*, 17: 31–7.

Stocking, G.W., Jr (1968), *Race, Culture, and Evolution: Essays in the History of Anthropology*, New York: The Free Press.

—— (1987), *Victorian Anthropology*, New York: The Free Press

Stow, G.W. (1905), *The Native Races of South Africa: A History of the Intrusion of the Hottentots and Bantu into the Hunting Grounds of the Bushmen, the Aborigines of the Country*. London: Swan Sonnenschein.

—— and Bleek, D.F. (1930), *Rock Paintings in South Africa from Parts of the Eastern Province and Orange Free State*, London: Methuen & Co.

Street, B. (1975), *The Savage in Literature: Representations of 'Primitive' Society in English Fiction, 1858–1920*, London: Routledge & Kegan Paul.

Sugawara, K. (1993), *Shintai no Jinruigaku* (Anthropology of the Body), Tokyo: Kawadeshobo-shinsha.

—— (1998a), 'Ecology and Communication in Egalitarian Societies: Japanese Studies of the Cultural Anthropology of Southern Africa', *Japanese Review of Cultural Anthropology*, 1: 97–129.

—— (1998b), *Kataru Shintai no Minzokushi* (Ethnography of Speaking Body), Kyoto: Kyoto University Academic Press.

—— (1998c), *Kaiwa no Jinruigaku* (Anthropology of Conversation), Kyoto: Kyoto University Academic Press.

—— (2004), 'The Modern History of Japanese Studies on the San Hunter-Gatherers', in A. Barnard (ed.), *Hunter-gatherers in History, Archaeology and Anthropology*, Oxford: Berg.

Suzman, J. (2000) *'Things from the Bush': A Contemporary History of the Omaheke Bushmen*, Basle: P. Schlettwein Publishing.

—— (2001a), *An Introduction to the Regional Assessment of the Status of the San in Southern Africa*, Windhoek: Legal Assistance Centre.

—— (2001b), *An Assessment of the Status of the San in Namibia*, Windhoek: Legal Assistance Centre.

—— (2001c), 'Indigenous Wrongs and Human Rights: National Policy, International Resolutions and the Status of the San of Southern Africa', in A. Barnard and J. Kenrick (eds), *Africa's Indigenous Peoples: 'First Peoples' or 'Marginalized Minorities'?*, Edinburgh: Centre of African Studies, University of Edinburgh.

Sylvain, R. (2002), '"Land, Water, and Truth": San Identity and Global Indigenism', *American Anthropologist* 104: 1074–85.

—— (2003), 'Class, Culture and Recognition: San Farm Workers and Indigenous Identities', *Anthropologica*, 45: 111–19.

—— (2005), 'Disorderly Development: Globalization and the Idea of "Culture" in the Kalahari', *American Ethnologist*, 32: 354–70.

Szalay, M. (1995), *The San and the Colonization of the Cape, 1770–1879: Conflict, Incorporation, Acculturation*, Cologne: Rüdiger Köppe Verlag.

Tabler, E.C. (1973), *Pioneers of South West Africa and Ngamiland, 1738–1880*, Cape Town: A.A. Balkema.

Takada, A. (2002), 'The !Xu San: Poverty and Tension', *Cultural Survival Quarterly*, 26(1): 18–19.

—— (2005), 'Early Vocal Communication and Social Institution: Appellation and Infant Verse Addressing among Central Kalahari San', *Crossroads of Language, Interaction, and Culture*, 6: 80–108.

Tanaka, J. (1971), *Busshuman: Seitai jinruigakuteki kenkyu* (The Bushmen: a Study in Ecological Anthropology), Tokyo: Shisaku-sha.

—— (1978), *A San Vocabulary of the Central Kalahari: G//ana and G/wi Dialects*, Tokyo: Institute for the Study of Languages and Cultures of Asia and Africa.

—— (1980), *The San, Hunter-gatherers of the Kalahari: A Study in Ecological Anthropology*, Tokyo: University of Tokyo Press.

Taylor, M. (2000), 'Life, Land and Power: Contesting Development in Northern Botswana', Ph.D. Thesis, University of Edinburgh.

Theal, G.M. (1902), *The Beginning of South African History*, London: T. Fisher Unwin.

Thoma, A. and Piek, J. (1997), *Customary Law and Traditional Authority of the San* (CASS Paper No. 36), Windhoek: Centre for Applied Social Sciences.

Thomas, E.M. (1959), *The Harmless People*, London: Secker and Warburg.

—— (1994), 'Management of Violence among the Ju/wasi of Nyae Nyae: the Old Way and a New Way', in S.P. Reyna and R.E. Downs (eds), *Studying War: Anthropological Perspectives*, Philadelphia: Gordon and Breach Scientific Publishers.

Tobias, P.V. (1978a), 'The San: an Evolutionary Perspective', in P.V. Tobias (ed.), *The Bushmen: San Hunters and Herders of Southern Africa*, Cape Town: Human & Rousseau.

—— (ed.) (1978b), *The Bushmen: San Hunters and Herders of Southern Africa*, Cape Town: Human & Rousseau.

Tomaselli, K.G. (1995), 'Introduction: Media Recuperations of the San', *Critical Arts*, 9(2): I–xxi.

—— (1999), 'Psychospiritual Ecoscience: the Ju/'hoansi and Cultural Tourism', *Visual Anthropology*, 12: 185–95.

Traill, A. (1974), *The Compleat Guide to the Koon* (ASI Communication No. 1), Johannesburg: African Studies Institute.

—— (1994), *A !Xóõ Dictionary*, Cologne: Rüdiger Köppe Verlag.

Tylor, E.B. (1871), *Primitive Culture: Researches into the Development of Mythology, Philosophy, Religion, Art, and Culture* (two volumes), London: John Murray.

—— (1881), *Anthropology: an Introduction to the Study of Man and Civilization*, London: Macmillan & Co.

Ucko, P. (1987), *Academic Freedom and Apartheid: the Story of the World Archaeological Congress*, London: Duckworth.

/Useb, J. (2001), '"One Chief is Enough!" Understanding San Traditional Authorities in the Namibian Context', in A. Barnard and J. Kenrick (eds), *Africa's Indigenous Peoples: 'First Peoples' or 'Marginalized Minorities'?*, Edinburgh: Centre of African Studies, University of Edinburgh.

—— (2002), 'Land Crisis: a San Perspective', *Cultural Survival Quarterly*, 26(1): 32.

Valentyn, F. (1973 [1726]), *Description of the Cape of Good Hope with Matters Concerning It, Amsterdam 1726, Part II* (edited by E.H. Raidt, translated by R. Raven-Hart), Cape Town: The Van Riebeeck Society.

Valiente-Noailles, C. (1993), *The Kua: Life and Soul of the Central Kalahari Bushmen*, Rotterdam: A.A. Balkema.

—— (1994), 'Les sexes chez les Kúa (Bochiman) du centre, du sud et de l'est de la Réserve Centrale du Kalahari, au Botswana: relations, différences et complémentarités dans les roles et les symboles' (two volumes), Doctoral Thesis, École des Hautes Études en Sciences Sociales, Paris.

van den Berghe, P.L. (1979), *Human Family Systems: An Evolutionary View*, Westport, CT: Greenwood Press.

van der Post, L. (1958), *The Lost World of the Kalahari*, London: The Hogarth Press.

—— (1961), *The Heart of the Hunter*, London: The Hogarth Press.

van der Riet, J., van der Riet, M. and Bleek, D.F. (1940), *More Rock-paintings in South Africa from the Coastal Belt between Albany and Piquetberg*, London: Methuen & Co.

van Riet Lowe, C. (1952), *The Distribution of Prehistoric Rock Engravings and Paintings in South Africa* (Archaeological Series V), Pretoria: Archaeological Survey.

Vermeulen, H.F. (1995), 'Origins and Institutionalization of Ethnography and Ethnology in Europe and the USA, 1771–1845', in H.F. Vermelen (ed.), *Fieldwork and Footnotes: Studies in the History of European Anthropology*, London: Routledge.

Vierich, H. and Hitchcock, R. (1996), 'Kūa: Farmer/Foragers of the Eastern Kalahari, Botswana', in S. Kent (ed.), *Cultural Diversity among Twentieth-century Foragers: an African Perspective*, Cambridge: Cambridge University Press.

Vinnicombe, P. (1972), 'Myth, Motive and Selection in Southern African Rock Art', *Africa*, 42: 192–204.

—— (1976), *People of the Eland: Rock Paintings of the Drakensberg Bushmen as a Reflection of Their Life and Thought*, Pietermaritzburg: Natal University Press.

Visser, H. (2001), *Naro Dictionary: Naro–English, English–Naro*, D'Kar, Botswana: Naro Language Project/SIL International.

Vorster, L.P. (1994), 'Towery by die !Xũ van Schmidtsdrift: 'n Verklaring', *South African Journal of Ethnology*, 17: 69–82.

Wadley, L. (1987), *Later Stone Age Hunters and Gatherers of the Southern Transvaal: Social and Ecological Interpretation* (BAR International Series 380), Oxford: British Archaeological Reports.

—— (ed.) (1997), *Our Gendered Past: Archaeological Studies of Gender in Southern Africa*, Johannesburg: Witwatersrand University Press.

Waitz, T. (1859–72),*Anthropologie der Naturvölker* (six volumes). Leipzig: G. Gerland.

—— (1863), *Introduction to Anthropology* (edited by J.F. Collingwood), Volume I, London: Longman, Green, Longman, and Roberts.

Waldman, L. (1995), 'Women and the Army: "Bushmen" Women at Schmidtsdrift Military Camp', Paper Presented at the Pan African Association of Anthropologists Annual Conference, University of Nairobi, October 1995.

Walker, N. (2004), 'The Relevance of the So-called Kalahari Debate in Resolving the "Bushman problem" in Botswana', in K. Motshabi and S. Saugestad (eds), *Research for Khoe and San Development International Conference, University of Botswana, 10–12 September 2003*, Gaborone: University of Botswana; Tromsø: University of Tromsø.

Watts, I. (1999), 'The Origin of Symbolic Culture', in R. Dunbar, C. Knight and C. Power (eds), *The Evolution of Culture: an Interdisciplinary View*, Edinburgh: Edinburgh University Press.

White, H. (1995), *In the Tradition of the Forefathers: Bushman Traditionality at Kagga Kamma*, Cape Town: UCT Press.

Widlok, T. (1999), *Living on Mangetti: 'Bushman' Autonomy and Namibian Independence*. Oxford: Oxford University Press.

—— (2004), '(Re-)current Doubts on Hunter-gatherer Studies as Contemporary History', in A. Barnard (ed.), *Hunter-gatherers in History, Archaeology and Anthropology*, Oxford: Berg.

Wiessner, P.W. (1977), 'Hxaro: a Regional System of Reciprocity for Reducing Risk among the !Kung San' (2 volumes), Ph.D. Dissertation, University of Michigan, Ann Arbor.

—— (1982), 'Risk, Reciprocity, and Social Influence on !Kung San Economics', in E. Leacock and R. Lee (eds), *Politics and History in Band Societies*, Cambridge: Cambridge University Press.

—— (1984), 'Reconsidering the Behavioral Basis of Style: a Case Study among the Kalahari San', *Journal of Anthropological Archaeology*, 3: 190–234.

Wikar, H.J. (1935 [1779]), 'Berigt aan den Weleedelen Gestrengen Heer Mr. Joachim van Plettenbergh (Report to His Excellency Joachim na Plettenergh), with Translation by A.W. van der Horst', in E.E. Mossop (ed.), *The Journals of Wikar, Coetsé and van Reenen*, Cape Town: The Van Riebeeck Society.

Willcox, A.R. (1978a), 'The Bushman in History', in P.V. Tobias (ed.), *The Bushmen: San Hunters and Herders of Southern Africa*, Cape Town: Human & Rousseau.

—— (1978b), 'An Analysis of the Function of Rock Art', *South African Journal of Science*, 74: 59–64.

Willet, S. (2002), *The Khoe and San: an Annotated Bibliography*, Volume II, Gaborone: Lightbooks.

—— Monageng, S., Saugestad, S. and Hermans, J. (2001), *The Khoe and San: an*

Annotated Bibliography, Volume I, Gaborone: Lightbooks.

Wilmsen, E.N. (1986), 'Historical Process in the Political Economy of San', *Sprache und Geschichte in Afrika*, 7(2): 413–32.

—— (1989), *Land Filled with Flies: a Political Economy of the Kalahari*, Chicago: University of Chicago Press.

—— (1993), 'On the Search for (Truth) and Authority: a Reply to Lee and Guenther', *Current Anthropology*, 34: 715–21.

—— (ed.) (1997), *The Kalahari Ethnographies (1896–1898) of Siegfried Passarge: Nineteenth Century Khoisan- and Bantu-speaking Peoples*, Cologne: Rüdiger Köppe Verlag.

—— (1999), 'Knowledge as the Source of Progress: the Marshall Family Testament to the "Bushmen"', *Visual Anthropology*, 12: 213–65.

—— (2002), 'Mutable Identities: Moving beyond Ethnicity in Botswana', *Journal of Southern African Studies*, 28: 825–41.

—— (2003), 'Further Lessons in Kalahari Ethnography and History', *History in Africa*, 30: 327–420.

—— and Denbow, J.R. (1990), 'Paradigmatic History of San-speaking Peoples and Current Attempts at Revision', *Current Anthropology*, 31: 489–24.

Wilson, M.L. (1986), 'Notes on the Nomenclature of the Khoisan', *Annals of the South African Museum*, 97(8): 251–66.

—— (1993), 'The "Strandloper" Concept and Its Relevance to the Study of the Past Inhabitants of the Southern African Coastal Region', *Annals of the South African Museum* 103(6): 293–382.

Woodburn, J. (1982), 'Egalitarian Societies', *Man* (n.s.), 17: 431–51.

Yellen, J.E. (1977), *Archaeological Approaches to the Present: Models for Reconstructing the Past*, New York: Academic Press.

Index